FOUR VIEWS

GOD & TIME

Edited with Introduction

BY GREGORY E. GANSSLE

IVP Academic

An imprint of InterVarsity Press
Downers Grove, Illinois

InterVarsity Press
P.O. Box 1400, Downers Grove, IL 60515-1426
World Wide Web: www.ivpress.com
E-mail: email@ivpress.com

InterVarsity Press® is the book-publishing division of InterVarsity Christian Fellowship/USA®, a movement of students and faculty active on campus at hundreds of universities, colleges and schools of nursing in the United States of America, and a member movement of the International Fellowship of Evangelical Students. For information about local and regional activities, write Public Relations Dept., InterVarsity Christian Fellowship/USA, 6400 Schroeder Rd., P.O. Box 7895, Madison, WI 53707-7895, or visit the IVCF website at <www.intervarsity.org>.

Scripture quotations, unless otherwise noted, are from the New Revised Standard Version of the Bible, copyright 1989 by the Division of Christian Education of the National Council of the Churches of Christ in the USA. Used by permission. All rights reserved.

Cover photograph: Brian Peters/Masterfile

ISBN 978-0-8308-1551-7

Printed in the United States of America ∞

 InterVarsity Press is committed to protecting the environment and to the responsible use of natural resources. As a member of the Green Press Initiative we use recycled paper whenever possible. To learn more about the Green Press Initiative, visit <www.greenpressinitiative.org>.

Library of Congress Cataloging-in-Publication Data

God & time : four views / edited by Gregory E. Ganssle ; contributors, William Lane Craig . . . [et al.].
     p. cm.
   Includes bibliographical references (p.) and indexes.
   ISBN 0-8308-1551-1 (paper : alk paper)
     1. God—Immutability. 2. Time—Religious aspects—Christianity. I. Title: God and time.
   II. Ganssle, Gregory E., 1956-III. Craig, William Lane.
   BT153.I47 G63 2001
   231.7—dc21

                                                                                2001026462

P   26   25   24   23   22   21   20   19   18   17   16   15   14   13   12   11   10   9

Y   25   24   23   22   21   20   19   18   17   16   15   14   13   12   11

for Jeanie

CONTENTS

1

INTRODUCTION
Thinking About God & Time

GREGORY E. GANSSLE

*O*ne day when my son David was five, he asked me, "Is all of God
in this room, or only part of God?" At the time I was only beginning to
work on my doctoral dissertation on God's relation to time, so I did
what many parents do. I deflected the question. I told him that I might
know the answer when I finished my dissertation.

David's question is no less perplexing for an adult than it is for a five-
year-old child. We hold that God is everywhere, but it is not always clear
what we mean by such a claim. In what sense is God in the room? We
do not think he is spread out in space the way I am spread out when I
lie down for a nap on the couch. It is not that part of God is here at the
foot of the couch and a different part of God is at the head of the couch.
Do we want to say that all of God is here and all of God is there? Is God
wholly in two places at once?

These options do not exhaust the possibilities. God is not a physical
being the way I am. When we think that God is everywhere, perhaps
we are thinking that there is no place where his love, power and knowledge cannot reach. God is not limited by space. Every point in space is

directly accessible to him. One philosopher, Richard Swinburne, has expressed God's omnipresence in the following way:

> God is supposed to be able to move any part of the universe directly; he does not need to use one part of the universe to make another part move. He can make any part move as a basic action. . . . The claim that God controls *all* things directly and knows about *all* things without the information coming to him through some causal chain, e.g., without light rays from a distance needing to stimulate his eyes, has often been expressed as the doctrine of God's omnipresence.[1]

It is God's direct access to every point in space that constitutes his omnipresence. If we do not think of God as existing literally somewhere (that is, at some location in space) it is easier to think of him as standing outside space and creating it, and acting within it. Some of the reason that it is easy to think in this way is that we often think of space as a container—sort of like a box—in which all of the events of the universe happen. God created the box and stands outside it watching. He also interacts with the things in the box.

Where was God when he created the box? If God "stands outside" the box, he does not do so in any literal way. There is no place outside of space. If all of space is in the box and came into being when God created the box, then God was not in any place when he created space. If God stands outside the box, then he does not stand at any place as he stands there. Where can we go from his presence? Nowhere! Everywhere we go, he is there. He is there in that he has direct knowledge and access to every place we could go. We do not mean that God is contained in every place in the universe. When we say that God is everywhere, perhaps we do not mean either that God is spread out throughout the physical universe or that God is wholly located at every point in the universe. Instead maybe we mean that God is not contained in space and that he has direct access to every point in space.

Did God create time in the same way he created space? If so, is he standing outside time? What of God's relation to time? God is, the psalmists affirm, "from everlasting to everlasting." He is not limited by time. He did not have a beginning in time, nor will his existence end in time. But is he in time the way we are? Is there any sense in which he can be

---

[1]Richard Swinburne, *The Coherence of Theism* (Oxford: Clarendon, 1977), pp. 103-4.

said to stand outside time as he stands outside space? What is the best way to think about God's relation to time? This is the question taken up by the writers of this volume.

Methodology: Faith Seeking Understanding

How do we go about thinking about God's relation to time? To be sure, we want our thinking to be rooted in the Scriptures. It is not clear that any particular theory of divine eternity can claim scriptural authority. After all, the Bible does not make many purely metaphysical claims. We might not want to think that we can read our view of God's relation to time directly from the few texts that seem to have relevant implications. What the Bible will do for us, however, is provide the parameters for any adequate understanding of God's relation to time. On the one hand, we read that God is the Creator of all and he did not begin in time. Anything that has come into being was brought into being by his agency. As a result, God is Lord over creation. He is the rightful ruler, and he is subject to nothing outside of himself. The fact that God is the Creator of all implies that God is sovereign over everything, including time. If God brought time into being, then he existed without time. If he existed without time, even if he is temporal now, he was timeless.

Now I have to admit that it is strange to say that God *was* timeless. It sounds as if I am claiming that there was a point in time at which he was timeless. What I mean to stress here is it is possible for God to exist without time. If past time is finite, and if God brought time into being, he is independent of time in this way.

On the other hand, the Scriptures uniformly portray God as loving and as interacting with created beings. He upholds the creation, he gives life, he redeems and forgives sinful people. He answers our prayers and knows what we need even before we ask. No theory of God's relation to time will be adequate if it does not allow for genuine interaction between God and his people.

These parameters allow for a plurality of positions about how God is related to time. Determining which position is most adequate takes us beyond the particular data of the Scriptures. We will have to think philosophically while remaining within the parameters of Scripture. That is, we must think both Christianly and philosophically about the issue.

Christian philosophers have traditionally sought to think Christianly by thinking in the mode of *faith seeking understanding.* This mode was introduced as early as Augustine (354-430) and has been articulated throughout the history of the church. What it means to operate in this mode is that Christian philosophers recognize that they know some things by faith in a reliable authority. For example, they know some things simply because they see them in the Scriptures. As God's written revelation, the Scriptures are reliable indicators of what is true. Philosophers begin with this knowledge (we could call it faith-knowledge) and try to reach another kind of knowledge (understanding-knowledge). Understanding-knowledge is knowledge gained through the application of one's own reason.

Faith seeking understanding is not an approach for turning mere beliefs into knowledge. Rather, it is a mode for turning one kind of knowledge into another kind. It turns faith-knowledge into understanding-knowledge. We begin with God's revelation in the Scriptures, recognizing that we know certain things based on it. We then apply our reasoning to these things to see if we can also grasp the same things by our reason. Grasping some issue by our reason often involves a process of unfolding what is only suggested or hinted at in the Scriptures. Thus philosophers may differ from each other in what they claim to have grasped.

The great Christian thinkers of the early and high Middle Ages applied the method of faith seeking understanding and came to the conclusion that God is eternal in the sense of being *atemporal* or outside time.[2] If God is atemporal, he is not in time at all. Usually there are two aspects to such a claim. First, God exists but does not exist *at* any time. Second, God does not experience things in succession. God does not experience the birth of Caesar before he experiences the making of a Caesar salad at the Yorkside Restaurant in New Haven. Both of these events are experienced by God in the "eternal now." This position is similar to the one discussed about God's relation to space. God is not located at any point in time, and his relation to each

---

[2]The word *eternal* was used by writers such as Augustine, Boethius, Anselm and Aquinas to mean "outside time." Now *eternal* is used to assert the limitless nature of God's life. As such, it can mean either temporally everlasting or atemporal. When I want to describe God as being outside time, I use *atemporal.* When I wish to describe God as inside time, I use *everlasting.*

point in time is the same as his relation to any other.

Most philosophers today disagree. While agreeing that God is eternal, they understand his eternality as his being temporally everlasting. He exists at all times and through all times.[3] God never began to exist, and he will never go out of existence, but he is in time. God experiences temporal succession. God experiences the birth of Caesar before he experiences the making of the Caesar salad. God, on this view, exists *at* all times. He exists at the present moment, he has existed at each past moment, and he will exist at each future moment.

One approach to figuring out which of these positions is stronger is to try to fit what we think about other aspects of God's nature together with a theory about God's relation to time. What we want to say about God's power or knowledge or omnipresence will have some bearing on our understanding of how it is that God is eternal. In addition, we will try to fit our theories together with other issues besides what God himself is like. Some of the most obvious issues include the nature of time, the nature of change and the creation of the universe.

There are a number of concerns that can arise when we try to fit our thinking about these issues together. First, it may be that some of the things we hold about the nature of God or of time or the universe contradict what we want to say about his relation to time. Such a contradiction would be reason enough to change our view of God's attributes or our view of how he is related to time. Second, it may be that some of what we think is true about God or the world is *better explained* either by the view that God is in time or by the view that he is outside time.

Five Important Issues

Let's briefly consider five important issues that are relevant to thinking about God and time. They are the nature of time, the creation of the universe, God's knowledge of the future, God's interaction with his people and the fullness of God's life.

The nature of time. There are many issues concerning the nature of

---

[3]It is interesting that as recently as 1975 it was thought that the majority view was that God is not in time. See Nicholas Wolterstorff, "God Everlasting," in *God and the Good: Essays in Honor of Henry Stob,* ed. Clifton J. Orlebeke and Lewis B. Smedes (Grand Rapids, Mich.: Eerdmans, 1975), reprinted in *Contemporary Philosophy of Religion,* ed. Steven M. Cahn and David Shatz (New York: Oxford University Press, 1982), pp. 77-98, esp. p. 77.

time that are both relevant to our topic and interesting in their own right. The one on which I shall focus has to do with whether "the Now" exists independently of our experience. There are two basic answers to this question. Not surprisingly, they are yes and no. Those who answer yes hold the A-theory of time (also known as the *process* or *tensed* theory). Those who answer no, "the Now" is merely a feature of our experience of the world, hold what is called the B-theory of time (also called the *stasis* theory or the *tenseless* theory). The labels "A-theory" and "B-theory" were introduced by the Cambridge philosopher J. M. E. McTaggart in the early years of the twentieth century.[4] Although they are not very descriptive, they have become fairly standard ways of distinguishing theories of time.

The B-theory holds that the most important thing about locating events in time is their relation to other events. So something happens before, after or at the same time as something else. The A-theory does not deny that events stand in these relations, but it holds that the more important thing about events is that some are in the past, some are in the future and some are happening now. The B-theorist thinks that the relations of past, present and future can be explained in terms of the relations *before, simultaneous with* and *after.* The A-theorist denies that these explanations are adequate. They are not adequate, it is argued, because they leave out the reality of the Now.

What is the Now? The A-theorist says that the Now exists in a way that the past and the future do not. The Now is a privileged temporal location. The B-theorist holds that the Now is dependent on the psychological states of knowing minds. In other words, it is part of how we are conscious of the world. If there were no minds, there would be no Now. It is part of our subjective take on the world. Each moment of time, according to the B-theory, is as real as any other moment.

Take some particular event, such as the event of a particular elephant taking a drink of water 141 years ago. Most A-theorists will hold that this event does not exist. It is not real. It did exist (141 years ago), but it no

---

[4]J. M. E. McTaggart, *The Nature of Existence,* vol. 2 (Cambridge: Cambridge University Press, 1927), chap. 33. The argument in this chapter appeared in an earlier version in the journal *Mind* (17 [1908]: 457-74). The chapter is reprinted in *The Philosophy of Time,* ed. Robin Le Poidevin and Murray MacBeath (Oxford: Oxford University Press, 1993), pp. 23-34.

longer does.[5] The B-theorist will believe that the event in question is real. It does exist. It exists now even if it is not occurring now. It occurred 141 years ago.

These theories are important to our topic because many philosophers think that if the A-theory of time is true, then God must be a temporal being. God can be atemporal only if the B-theory is true. Not every philosopher thinks there is this connection between the atemporality of God and the B-theory, but many, including some of our authors, do. Why do some philosophers make this connection? There are two reasons. First, they believe that, if the A-theory is true, God must change (and therefore he must be temporal). Second, they also think that if the A-theory is true, an atemporal God could not be omniscient. The claim that God knows everything that can be known is a claim with strong scriptural support.

God must change, it is held, because he stands in relation to a changing reality. For example, if God sustains a changing world in existence, he sustains Caesar's existence before he sustains the existence of the Caesar salad. On the A-theory, the existence of Caesar is most fundamentally past. So God no longer sustains Caesar's existence. Now he is sustaining the existence of the Caesar salad. God is doing different things at different times. He is changing.

If the A-theory is true, there is an irreducible fact about what is happening now. The fact is irreducible in that it cannot be fully explained in terms of its relation to other events. Suppose my wife, Jeanie, is eating a Caesar salad at Yorkside right now. That this fact is happening now cannot be fully explained by saying things like "Jeanie eats the salad at the same time that Greg types this sentence (or at the same time that you read this sentence)." It is true that Jeanie eats the salad at the same time that I type or that you read. What is not the case is that this sentence explains fully what we mean by "Jeanie is now eating the Caesar salad at Yorkside." We can learn about all of the events that happen at the same time that Jeanie eats the salad and still not know that it happens now.

If God is atemporal, his relation to each event is the same. He knows them all in his eternal Now. How does he know which of them occurs

---

[5]Garry DeWeese has reminded me that some A-theorists, such as Michael Tooley and himself, think that both the past and the present are real but the future is not.

now and which has already occurred? Since every event is "present" to him, he cannot know which is actually present. Some atemporalists will embrace this difficulty and hold to the B-theory. There is no Now independent of our temporal location. Since God is not temporally located, there is no objective Now. By knowing that Jeanie eats the salad at the same time that you read this sentence (and at the same time as a whole lot of other events), God knows everything there is to know about when Jeanie eats lunch.

These, then, are two of the reasons that some believe that if the A-theory is true, God must be temporal. Whether they are correct is, I think, still an open question.

God and creation. Another parameter for our thinking that is given to us in the Scriptures, besides the fact that God is omniscient, is that God created the universe. The Bible is not too clear about exactly how he did this, and there are exegetical controversies over *when* he did it, but the fact remains that the universe is a created thing. The fact that the universe is a created thing raises several important questions for our study. I shall discuss two of them here. First, can the universe be infinitely old? Second, even if the universe had a beginning, must time have a beginning?

Can the universe—a created universe—be infinitely old? Most of us think of creation as creation *ex nihilo,* out of nothing. That God created the universe out of nothing is usually thought to imply that the universe is not infinitely old. It had a beginning. Christian thinkers such as Aquinas, however, thought that the universe could have been infinitely old and still have been created out of nothing by God. God's creative action would not be the act of *bringing* the universe into existence. Rather, it would be the act of *sustaining* the universe in existence. If God did not hold the universe in existence, even for a moment, it would fall out of existence into nothingness. God, then, holds it out of nothing rather than brings it out of nothing.

Considerations such as Aquinas's are important for thinking through God's relation to time. If the idea that the universe has an infinite past is consistent with the doctrine of creation, then it is also possible that time never began. If time never began, then it is possible that God has been in time for the complete extent of his existence. The Scriptures say that he is "from everlasting to everlasting." If time is infinite and God is in time, then this passage can be taken at face value. God is in time and he never began to be in time and he will never cease being in time. God has existed throughout the infinite past and will exist throughout an infinite future.

It might be the case, therefore, that the biblical doctrine of creation allows room for an infinitely old universe. Whether this is the best view on the topic is another matter. Most of us think that God did bring the universe into existence. If this is the case, there is still the open question of whether God brought time into existence as well. Time may have had an infinite past but the universe only a finite one. If this is the case, then at some moment in time God created the universe. He existed throughout an infinite amount of time and then brought the universe into existence.

There are, it turns out, some good reasons to think that this story is not the way it happened. Whether these reasons should be persuasive remains to be seen. First, there is the nagging question of why God created the universe exactly when he did. It nagged Augustine until he began to think of God as atemporal. It seems as though any point in the infinite past is as good as any other, since there is nothing that makes them different from each other. Did God arbitrarily pick out some point and decide "Now I will do it," as on a whim? Or did God have some reason to prefer one moment to all of the others? Either way of answering this question seems a bit strange. Whether the strangeness is enough to send us looking for a different answer or not is an open question.

The second reason it may not be the case that time has an infinite past is that there is a strong argument that such a thing is not possible. I call it a strong argument because I find it persuasive and am not impressed by any of the objections I have seen. I must admit, though, that many philosophers do not think it is very strong. It is called the Kalam cosmological argument.[6] The basic idea is that it is impossible for the past to be infinite because *it is impossible to complete any infinite*

---

[6]For more on the Kalam cosmological argument, see William Lane Craig, *Reasonable Faith* (Wheaton, Ill.: Crossway, 1994), chap. 3, and J. P. Moreland, *Scaling the Secular City* (Grand Rapids, Mich.: Baker, 1987), chap. 1. For more technical discussions of the argument, see William Lane Craig, *The Kalam Cosmological Argument* (London: Macmillan, 1979), and William Lane Craig and Quentin Smith, *Theism, Atheism and Big Bang Cosmology* (Oxford: Clarendon, 1993), sec. 1.

series by successive addition. I can explain what I mean by using an example. Think about this question. Why is it impossible to count to infinity? The reason is not that we will die before we reach the end. It is that no matter how many numbers we count (even if we count by tens) we will always be at some finite number and will always have an infinitely many more numbers to go. An infinite series cannot be completed one at a time. The past is a complete series. Furthermore, it was completed by successive addition. Each moment was added to the past one at a time. If no infinite series can be completed in this way, then the past must be finite.

Some philosophers have objected to this argument by pointing out that when you count *to* infinity, you begin at a particular number, the number one. The whole point of thinking that the past may be infinite is that there is no starting point. Thus they conclude that the analogy with counting to infinity is not very strong. I think there are two replies that can be made to this concern. First, we can run the counting analogy in the other direction and ask whether it is possible to count backward from infinity to zero (or frontward, from negative infinity to zero.) This case is more analogous to the claim that the past is infinite. It is apparent to me that completing an infinite series by successive addition is shown to be impossible whichever direction we count. The second reply is to recall that each past moment in time was, at one time, present. If the past is infinite, then an infinite number of moments were present one at a time. The only way an infinite number of moments can have been present one at a time is if it is possible that an infinite series of moments can elapse one at a time. The counting to infinity analogy appears, in light of this, to be strong after all.

The question of why God created the universe when he did and the Kalam argument give us good reason to think that time came into existence. To be sure, there are objections to both of these points, and some of our authors will discuss some of these objections, but for now I want to point out that the position that both the universe and time came into existence has some reason behind it. If time came into existence but God did not, then God existed without time. God *was* atemporal. It may be the case that God *became* temporal as he created time, or he could be atemporal even with the existence of time.

God's knowledge of the future. The most prominent issue in many people's thinking about God's relation to time is God's foreknowledge of free actions. It has long been held that the Scriptures portray God as knowing everything. He knows the secrets of our hearts, he knows every event that is now occurring, and he knows everything about the past and the future. There is no problem with God's knowledge of the future if future things are fixed in some way. For example, given the way the world is and the laws of physics, it is true that the earth will be in a certain position relative to the planet Jupiter exactly one year from now. This kind of future truth is not problematic. Consider another kind of future truth. Suppose that tomorrow morning I shall choose, as my boys David and Nick often do, between Lucky Charms and Fruity Pebbles for breakfast (my daughter prefers macaroni and cheese). Suppose also that my choice will be a free choice. Can God know which cereal I shall choose ahead of time? It seems as though there is the following problem. If God knows today that I shall choose Pebbles, then when I get up tomorrow, it is already true that I shall choose Pebbles. If it is true that I shall choose Pebbles, am I really able to choose Lucky Charms? The only way I can choose Lucky Charms is if I can make it the case that God had different beliefs from those he had. Since God knew before the foundation of the world that I would choose Pebbles, I can choose Lucky Charms only if I can act on the past. But I cannot act on the past. I cannot make it the case that God believed something other than what he did believe. So I cannot choose Lucky Charms after all. The choice that I thought was free turns out not to be free after all.[7]

Many thinkers have noticed that the argument I discussed works only if God is in time. It works only if God's knowing things is something that happens *at* times. As a result, if God is not in time, he does not know things at times, and his knowledge of my breakfast choice does not occur before my choice at all.

In fact the position that God is not in time but is outside time is often cited as the best solution to the problem of reconciling God's knowledge of the future and human freedom. Boethius, Anselm, Aquinas and many others have appealed to God's atemporality to solve this problem.

---

[7]The literature on God's knowledge of future free actions is enormous, and I have left out lots of details here. For a good discussion of the problem of divine foreknowledge and human freedom see James Beilby and Paul Eddy, eds., *Divine Foreknowledge: Four Views* (Downers Grove, Ill.: InterVarsity Press, 2001).

If God is atemporal, after all, he does not *fore*know anything. His knowledge of any event is not something that happens at some time. It is eternal. If it is not temporally located, it is not located *before* the free choice in question.

While the atemporalist's solution seems to offer a good strategy, at least one significant problem remains. This problem is prophecy. Suppose God tells Noah, among other things, that I shall eat Fruity Pebbles for breakfast tomorrow. Now we have a different situation entirely. While God's knowledge that I shall eat Fruity Pebbles is not in the past, Noah's knowledge that I shall eat Pebbles *is* in the past. Furthermore, since the information came from God, Noah cannot be mistaken about the future event. By the time I was born in 1956, it was already true that I shall eat Fruity Pebbles in the year 2000. The only way I can pick Lucky Charms, then, is if I can act on the past.

Prophecy is a problem, some will argue, only if God actually tells Noah (or anyone else) what I shall do. God, it seems, does not tell much to Noah or any other prophet. After all, why should God tell Noah? Noah certainly does not care about my breakfast! Since prophecy of this sort is pretty rare, we can be confident that God's knowledge does not rule out our freedom. Some have argued, however, that if it is even *possible* for God to tell Noah (or anyone else for that matter) what I shall do, then we have a version of the same problem we would have if we held that God is in time and foreknows my choice of breakfast. We could call this version the "possible prophet" problem. If the possible prophet problem is serious enough to show that God's atemporal knowledge of future acts (future, that is, from our present vantage point) makes it the case that those acts are not free, then holding God to be atemporal does not solve the problem of foreknowledge.

Even if prophecy of this kind is rare, Scripture includes cases of very specific prophecies. Jesus, for example, told Peter that he would deny him three times before the cock crowed. Yet it seems that Peter's denial was a free action. Examples such as this one are important reminders that Christian philosophy must deal faithfully with the Scriptures. It will not do for us to be dismissive of these cases.

Issues about God's knowledge of future free acts, then, may not give as strong a reason to think of God as atemporal as many have thought. Attempting to answer the possible prophet problem is beyond the scope of this introduction. It is enough to point out that there is still much work to be done on God's knowledge of the future.[8]

God's interaction with his people. Various reasons have been put forward for thinking that God must change. God, for example, intervenes in the world. He spoke to Jesus at his baptism, and later he raised him from the dead. Later still, he spoke through the apostles in the writing of the New Testament. If God spoke to Jesus *before* he raised him from the dead, then God's actions occur at different times. If his actions take place *at* different times, it looks as though he is temporal.

It may be, though, that the *effects* of God's actions occur at different times but his *acting* does not. In one eternal act he wills the speaking to Jesus at one time and the raising from the dead at another. The fact that the effects of God's eternal will occur sequentially does not imply that God's acts themselves take place in sequence and are therefore temporal.

Apart from God's acting in the world in such dramatic fashion, the Scriptures indicate that God interacts with ordinary human beings. He answers our prayers and forgives our sin. He also comes to our aid and comforts and strengthens us. He is "a very present help in time of trouble." If God is not in time, can he interact in these ways? It all depends, of course, on what is necessary for genuine interaction to occur. If it is not possible to answer a prayer request unless the answer is given *after* the request, then the fact that God answers prayer will guarantee that he is temporal. Some thinkers have argued that although answers to requests normally come after the request, it is not necessary that they do so. In order to count as an answer to a request, an action must happen *because of* the request. These thinkers recognize, however, that not any "because of" relation will do. The answer must be given in order to

---

[8]I should point out that some theologians and philosophers have argued that God does not know future free actions. These thinkers hold that God knows all that can be known and therefore is omniscient. The position they put forward is that there are fewer things that can be known than we have traditionally thought. These thinkers believe that this view is more consistent with how the Scriptures portray God's nature and interaction with people than the traditional view. Three books on this theme are worth mentioning: Clark Pinnock et al., *The Openness of God: A Biblical Challenge to the Traditional Understanding of God* (Downers Grove, Ill.: InterVarsity Press, 1994); David Basinger, *The Case for Freewill Theism: A Philosophical Assessment* (Downers Grove, Ill.: InterVarsity Press, 1996); and John Sanders, *The God Who Risks: A Theology of Providence* (Downers Grove, Ill.: InterVarsity Press, 1998).

respond to the request. The relation that is relevant to answering a request has to do with intention or purpose. If I make my daughter, Elizabeth, a bowl of macaroni and cheese for breakfast in answer to her request, I make it, at least in part, in order to do what she asked me to do. I make the macaroni and cheese because she asked for it—in response to her request. My action counts as an answer to her request because of my intention to fulfill her request.

Now when I make breakfast for Elizabeth, the request comes before I make the macaroni. But if I knew ahead of time what she was going to ask for, I could make it ahead of time. My action would still count as an answer to her request. I would perform the action because of and in order to fulfill the request. Notice that the request does not have to come before the answer. If the relation between a request and an answer does not have to be a temporally sequential one, then it is possible that an atemporal God could answer prayer. It may be that he hears all our prayers in his one eternal Now and in that same eternal Now he wills the answers to our various requests.

The fullness of God's being. In thinking about God's nature, we notice that whatever God is, he is to the greatest degree possible. He knows everything that it is possible to know. He can do anything that it is possible to do. He is maximally merciful. This "maximal property idea" can be applied as well to the nature of God's life. God is a living being. He is not an abstract object like a number. He is not inanimate like a magnetic force. He is alive. If whatever is true of him is true of him to the greatest degree possible, then his life is the fullest life possible. Whatever God's life is like, he surely has it to the fullest degree.

Some philosophers have argued that this fact about God's life requires that he be atemporal. No being that experiences its life sequentially can have the fullest life possible. Temporal beings experience their lives one moment at a time. The past is gone and the future is not yet. The past part of my life is gone forever. I can remember it, but I cannot experience it directly. The future part of my life is not yet here. I can anticipate it and worry about it, but I cannot yet experience it. I only experience a brief slice of my life at any one time. My life, then, is spread out and diffuse.

It is this transient nature of our experience that gives rise to much of the wistfulness and regret we may feel about our lives. This feeling of regret lends credibility to the idea that a sequential life is a life that is less than maximally full. Older people sometimes wish for earlier days, while younger people long to mature. We grieve for the people we love who are now gone. We grieve also for the events and times that no longer persist.

When we think about the life of God, it is strange to think of God longing for the past or for the future. The idea that God might long for some earlier time or regret the passing of some age seems like an attribution of weakness or inadequacy to God. God in his self-sufficiency cannot in any way be inadequate. If it is the experience of the passage of time that grounds these longings, there is good reason not to attribute any experience of time to God. Therefore God is atemporal. He experiences all of his life at once in the eternal present. Nothing of his life is past, and nothing of it is future. God possesses his life "all at once." Boethius's famous definition of eternity captures this idea. "Eternity, then, is the whole, simultaneous and perfect possession of boundless life."[9]

Those who think that God is in some way temporal do not want to attribute weakness or inadequacy to God. Nor do they hold that God's life is less than maximally full. They will deny, rather, that God cannot experience a maximally full life if he is temporal. These philosophers will point out that many of our regrets about the passage of time are closely tied to our finitude. It is our finitude that grounds our inadequacy, not our temporality. We regret the loss of the past both because our lives are short and because our memories are dim and inaccurate. God's life, temporal though it may be, is not finite, and his memory is perfectly vivid. He does not lose anything with the passage of time. Nor does his life draw closer to an end.

If our regrets about the passage of time are a function more of our finitude than of our temporality, much of the force of these considerations is removed. Furthermore, if the tensed theory of time is correct, it may be that fullness of God's life will require his temporality. The discussion about whether an atemporal God can know facts or proposi-

---

[9]"Aeternitas igitur est interminabilis vitae tota simul et perfecta posessio," *Consolation of Philosophy* V prose VI, in Boethius, *Tractates and The Consolation of Philosophy*, trans. H. F. Stewart, E. K. Rand and S. J. Tester, Loeb Classical Library (Cambridge, Mass.: Harvard University Press, 1918), pp. 422-23.

tions about the present concerns the fullness of his life. As we have pointed out, some philosophers hold that God's knowledge, and therefore his life, will be impoverished considerably if he is eternal, since there will be propositions or facts about the present time that he will not know.

One important issue that this argument concerning the fullness of God's life ought to put to rest is the idea that those who hold God to be atemporal hold that God is something inert like a number or a property. Whether or not they are correct, the eternalist holds that it is the *fullness* of God's life (rather than its impoverishment) that determines his relation to time.

The Essays, the Authors

I have briefly introduced five of the issues that are relevant to understanding God's relation to time. My goal has been to set some direction and to whet your appetite for the discussion that follows. Our authors are some of the leading thinkers in the area of God and time. They have published many technical books and articles on this and related topics. There are no better people to bring to you four views of God and time. Each author will present an essay in which he argues for his view of the relation between God and time. Each essay is followed by a brief response from each other author. Finally, each author will have a chance to respond to the criticisms of his view that his three coauthors raise. The format of this book allows for a substantial interaction between philosophers holding various positions. All that is left for me to do is introduce our authors.

Paul Helm is the J. I. Packer Professor of Theology and Philosophy at Regent College in Vancouver, B.C. Previously he taught as professor of the history and philosophy of religion at King's College at the University of London from 1993 to 2000, and he has published numerous books and articles, including *Eternal God: A Study of God Without Time* (Clarendon, 1988) and *Faith and Understanding* (Eerdmans, 1997). In his chapter, "Divine Timeless Eternity," he defends the traditional view that God is absolutely timeless. Helm adds the qualifier *absolutely* to emphasize that God's timelessness is not affected by his creation of the temporal universe. God is timeless without the universe (if the universe is not everlasting), and God is timeless with the universe (now that the universe exists). God's timelessness is completely independent of the existence and nature of the universe.

The doctrine of timelessness is defended against both philosophical and biblical objections, and several reasons are given in support of this view. The most salient reasons, Helm claims, rest on "the idea of divine fullness or self-sufficiency." It is the fullness of God's life that makes timelessness the more appropriate mode of his being. God's experience of his own life and being is too full to be contained in any time or to be experienced part by part or moment by moment. Thinking of God as temporal, then, is thinking of his life as somewhat impoverished. Because God is atemporal, Helm argues, God experiences the full extent of his own life and being in one atemporal experience.

Alan G. Padgett is professor of systematic theology at Luther Seminary in St. Paul, Minnesota. He has written *God, Eternity and the Nature of Time* (1992; reprint, Wipf & Stock, 2000) and has coauthored *Christianity and Western Thought*, vol. 2, *Faith and Reason in the Nineteenth Century* (InterVarsity Press, 2000) as well as several papers on God's relation to time. He argues, in "Eternity as Relative Timelessness," that both the traditional atemporalist position and the view that God is temporally everlasting are inadequate. The picture of God as everlasting is inadequate because our doctrine of creation implies that God will transcend time in some way. Time, at least if modern physics is near the truth, is a created thing. Therefore it depends on God. God brought it into being, yet he himself was not brought into being. God's life, then, transcends time.

Padgett argues that the atemporalist position is also inadequate. The inadequacy here is philosophical. God can be atemporal, Padgett reasons, only if the stasis theory (or B-theory) of time is true. If the process theory (A-theory) is true, then God must be temporal in some sense. Padgett argues that this conclusion follows from God's sustaining the changing world in its existence. Padgett's third view is that God is relatively timeless. He is timeless relative to physical time, but he is temporal relative to metaphysical time. Metaphysical time is a pure duration that can flow without any changes. It is not dependent on the physical universe and is not created. God, then, is not constrained by any created thing. God's being is ontologically prior to the metaphysically temporal aspect of his life. God is not limited by metaphysical time. He is the ground of it. God is timeless relative to our physical time, but God exists in his own time.

William Lane Craig is research professor of philosophy at Talbot School of Theology. He has published many articles and books about time and God's relation to time, including *The Tensed Theory of Time: A Critical Examination* and *The Tenseless Theory of Time: A Critical Examination* (both Kluwer Academic, 2000) and *Theism, Atheism, and Big Bang Cosmology,* coauthored with Quentin Smith (Oxford University Press, 1993). In "Timelessness and Omnitemporality" he argues that since the creation of the universe God has been temporal. Independent of creating the universe ("before" creation) God is best thought of as being timeless. There are two reasons God must be temporal if a temporal world exists. First, God has real relation to any created world, and a real relation to a temporal world cannot be had by a timeless being. Second, God must be temporal if he is omniscient. If there is a temporal world, there are tensed facts God must know. Attempts to eliminate tensed facts fail, Craig argues, and any revision to the concept of omniscience that does not require God to know tensed facts seems ad hoc.

Craig thinks that if there were no temporal creation, God would be timeless. Any appeal to some kind of amorphous time that has no metric prior to creation will not make it possible that God has existed everlastingly. Craig rejects this alternative because even given an amorphous, nonmetrical time, God would have to endure "a beginningless series of longer and longer intervals," which is impossible. Such an infinite series of longer intervals is as impossible to complete as an infinite series of temporal intervals of some equal metric in duration. So God is timeless without the temporal creation, and he has become temporal since creating a world in which time is real.

Nicholas Wolterstorff is Noah Porter Professor of Philosophy at the Yale Divinity School. He has published many books and articles, including *Locke and the Ethics of Belief* (Cambridge University Press, 1996) and *Divine Discourse: Philosophical Reflections on the Claim That God Speaks* (Cambridge University Press, 1995) as well as the seminal paper "God Everlasting." In "Unqualified Divine Temporality," he points out that Christian philosophers ought to take the language of Scripture literally unless there are good reasons not to do so. Given the way that God is portrayed as having a history, those who hold that God is atemporal bear a heavy burden of proof. Wolterstorff's arguments that God is in time are not meant to be independent of the scriptural testimony. Rather, he is providing additional reasons for taking those claims as literal.

Wolterstorff brings two considerations to support his contention. First, he argues that the A-theory of time is true. If the A-theory is true, then God must be temporal. He must be temporal because he must know what is happening now. Wolterstorff defends his position against attempts to eliminate the A-series. Our usage of temporal indexical terms, he argues, is not strictly parallel to our usage of spatial indexicals. As a result, temporal indexicals cannot be eliminated the way spatial indexicals can be.

Wolterstorff's second major consideration is that the language of Scripture describes God as unfolding his plan to redeem the world in history. The historic nature of God's unfolding his plan implies that God performs certain actions before he performs others. Wolterstorff holds that this history cannot be interpreted as God timelessly bringing it about that, for example, Moses *is spoken to* before Jesus *is spoken to*. He insists that the sequence is of *God speaking* first to Moses and then later to Jesus. This interpretation is required because the Scriptures affirm that God responds to his people's crying out to him. He can respond to our cries only when it is the case that we are crying out. He must, then, be in time.

The Christian church has always believed that God himself invites us to explore his nature. These brief descriptions of the essays in this book highlight the varied considerations that are important in thinking out God's relation to time. There is no better place to start this investigation than with the following essays.

2

DIVINE TIMELESS ETERNITY

PAUL HELM

*I*n this chapter I shall endeavor to set out and defend what may reasonably be regarded as the classical Christian view of God's relation to time, the view that God exists timelessly eternally. On this view God does not exist in time, he exists "outside" time. Though this view (let us call it "eternalism") has an impressive pedigree in the history of Western theism—it is the "mainstream" view represented by Augustine, Anselm, Aquinas, Calvin and hosts of others—there is reason to think that it is very much the minority view among contemporary theologians and philosophers of religion. Nowadays most theologians and philosophers of religion think that God is in time (we'll call this "temporalism"). Why this is—why there is at present such a large-scale repudiation of the classical position—is an interesting question, which in turn raises further interesting issues, but to take up any of these would be to distract us from our main task, which is exposition and defense.

But we can be sure of one thing, that the God who is timelessly eternal is a God who is much less anthropomorphic than the God of much contemporary theology and philosophy of religion. For to affirm that

God is timeless is to deny to him an entire category of powers and relations that human beings have, and so to make it impossible to say that in these respects he is as we are. Conversely if people, for whatever reason, favor a humanlike conception of divinity, then they are more likely to favor, other things being equal of course, the idea of God "in" time than that of a God "outside" time. I shall begin the exposition by sketching the basic rationale for the idea that God is outside time.

Timeless Eternity: Its Rationale

What are the theological attractions of timelessness as applied to God? There are a number, but they all may be said to rest, as many of our most basic claims rest, on an intuition that has had an enormous appeal to many thinkers and still has to some. It is the idea of the divine fullness or self-sufficiency.

Consider, for a moment, the obvious alternative (though not, of course, the only alternative; there are at least four ways of thinking of God and time!). Suppose that God is in time, in a similar sort of way to the way you and I are in time. One of the striking facts about being in time, of having an existence that continues through time, is that each of us has a past, a present and a future. Whatever detailed philosophical story we tell about our past, present and future, it is clear that our pasts and futures are very different from our presents. The past is what has been, the present is what is, while the future is what is to be. We may make ourselves a cup of coffee in the present, and we may have made ourselves a cup of coffee in the past week, but we cannot now enjoy the past week's cup of coffee as we enjoy the present cup. We can remember our enjoyment of last week's coffee and so (in a sense) continue to enjoy it, but we cannot presently enjoy it any longer. On a reasonable assumption about the directionality of time we cannot go back in time now to sip and savor last week's coffee as we savor today's. And even if we could go back in time, our experience of the past that we would return to (even if such a return were intelligible) would have a different character from the past when we first experienced it as the present. Similarly with the future.

Now suppose that God is in time in the sort of way that we are in time. It follows that he has a past, a present and a future. Perhaps (making the reasonable supposition that he has always existed) he has a past that is backwardly everlasting. There never was a time when God was not. It follows that there are segments of his life—those segments that existed before the present moment—which together constitute a part of God's life that is over and done with. And the eternalist will say that such an idea is incompatible with God's fullness and self-sufficiency.

The eternalist's objection need not be to the idea that God has parts, even though some would object to this very idea on the grounds that God is simple (so if an eternalist bases her defense of the idea of divine timeless eternity on the idea of divine simplicity, she would proceed differently at this point). Further, even if we suppose that God is in time, this would not mean that each day God is getting older, as we are getting older. If God is everlasting, then however long he has existed he has just as long to exist. Nor, finally, does it mean that God is subject to the imperfections of memory as we are. For us, part of the poignancy of having part of our lives over and done with is that we cannot recall them in their original vividness and immediacy. But we may suppose that a temporalist God is omniscient and hence can perfectly recall those backwardly everlasting phases of his life which are now over and done with.

However, these are not the main things that the eternalist objects to about the idea of God's being in time. Let us grant that a God in time may perfectly recall every detail of his past, as (we may suppose) we on occasion recall details of our pasts. Let us suppose that God's recall is sharp and vivid and total—beyond anything that we experience in our rememberings. The main thing is that though God may infallibly and vividly remember his past, those bits of his life that he remembers are over. One cannot, by definition, remember what is not past; and what is past is not present. God may "relive" them through memory, but he cannot, literally, live them again. Nor would a divine analogue of time travel be of any more help, for the reasons already given. The uniqueness of the present moment is forever lost when that moment becomes past.

Despite the eternalist's basic objection to divine temporality, such a view of God, a God who exists at all times, seems perfectly intelligible. God's relation to time could be like that just sketched. But, eternalists claim, this view, even if intelligible, flouts the basic theistic intuition that God's fullness is such that he possesses the whole of his life *together*. To many, the idea that God is subject to the vicissitudes of temporal passage, with more and more of his life irretrievably over and done with, is incompatible with divine sovereignty, with divine perfection and with that fullness of being that is essential to God. The temporalist view may be intelligible, but it does not do justice to the nature of God's being.

But perhaps there is a problem of a different kind for the eternalist. I have said that those who defend the idea of divine timeless eternity appeal to an intuition about the divine fullness and self-sufficiency. But a Christian may say. "That is all very well, but is the intuition in accordance with the data of the Christian revelation, Holy Scripture? For after all, all our thoughts, including our intuitions, ought to be made subject to the teaching of Scripture."

A number of things are important here. First, in my view God's timeless eternity is consistent with the teaching of Scripture. That teaching is, with respect to our particular question, somewhat underdetermined; that is, the language of Scripture about God and time is not sufficiently precise so as to provide a definitive resolution of the issue one way or the other. So it would be unwise for the eternalist to claim that divine timeless eternity is *entailed* by the language of Scripture. But a lack of entailment need not alarm us, because such situations quite commonly arise in connection with the careful, reflective construction of Christian doctrines. Let us take a moment to look at these points in a little more detail.

Here are some representative scriptural statements about God and his relation to time. God is the "lofty one who inhabits eternity" (Is 57:15); though his creation will grow old, he remains the same, his years never end (Heb 1:10-12); before the mountains were brought forth God is from everlasting to everlasting. (Ps 90:2; see also 1 Cor 2:7; 2 Tim 1:9 and other verses that refer to God existing "before the foundation of the world.") These verses are consistent with eternalism in that they can fairly be interpreted in an eternalist way. Whether the authors intended by their words to teach eternalism is a more difficult question, for the statements can equally well be interpreted in a temporalist way. And it is equally difficult to decide if by their words the writers intended to affirm temporalism.

The reason for this is indeterminacy is clear. It seems that the issues of temporalism and eternalism as we have sketched them were not before the minds of the writers as they wrote—or at least there is no real evidence that they were. One possible reason for this is that the issues were not part of a controversial question for the writers—in the way, say, that whether justification is by faith or by works was a controverted issue in the New Testament. For this reason I say that the data of Scripture *underdetermine* the issues raised by later controversies about God and time. The data are compatible with eternalism but do not require it.

Someone may think that because certain ideas were not before the minds of the biblical writers they should not be before our minds and that therefore we should remain resolutely agnostic on the question of God's relation to time—be agnostic, that is, as a matter of principle. But I think that this would be too extreme a position to take, quite apart from the question of whether it is psychologically possible. For once important questions have been raised it is extremely difficult, if not impossible, to live as if they had never been raised. The point may be illustrated in the following way.

Orthodox Christians believe the New Testament teaches that there is a sense in which God is one and a different sense in which he is three. One popular and influential way of expressing this has been to say that God exists as one substance (or essence) in three Persons. But when Christians recite such a formula, while believing that this formula is faithful to the New Testament, they do not usually claim that when, say, the apostle Paul uttered trinitarian sentiments (as in 2 Cor 13:14) he had in mind the concepts of *person, essence* or *substance* as these came to be used in the worked-out trinitarian formulas of the church. Such terms are used in an effort to summarize carefully the New Testament data. No one who is willing to use such terminology about the triunity of God could consistently have a principled objection to divine eternalism on the grounds that the idea takes us beyond the very words of the Bible.

It may be that the conceptual apparatus of eternalism owes much to the language of Neo-Platonism; it is undoubtedly true that the classical formulas of orthodox trinitarianism owe much to the language of Greek metaphysics. But though perhaps Neo-Platonism influenced the way eternalism is formulated and expressed, it would be hasty to suppose that the use of such language signals a takeover of biblical ideas by pagan ideas. The relevant question is, does the use of such ideas help us to summarize and epitomize the thought of the canonical writers in ways that, because of their situation, they were not able to do them-

selves? And do such formulas help us to rule out certain types of inferences about God that are unscriptural? It is the claim of the many
eternalists that eternalism is a better approach to the relevant scriptural
data than any of its rivals and that it prevents us from making certain
types of false inferences about God.

Someone may say that citing biblical verses as I did a few para-
graphs ago is terribly one-sided. Granted that there are such data,
and that they may be interpreted in eternalist fashion, ought they not
to be supplemented by the pervasive biblical language about God
which cannot be interpreted in eternalist fashion but which seems to
entail that God is in time—language about God's learning and forget-
ting, say, or about his changing his mind? This is certainly an important question, and I shall return to it later. In saying that I think the
biblical data are consistent with eternalism I do not wish to deny that
there is a prima facie case for another view in the case of some of
that data.

Not only do eternalists believe that this position is consistent with the
biblical data about God and time, but they hold that by employing the
idea of timelessness it is possible to articulate the distinction between
the Creator and the creature, and to make clear that divine creation is a
unique metaphysical action, the bringing into being of the whole temporal order, not a creation of the universe by One who is already subject to
time. God creates every individual thing distinct from himself. Finally,
for Christians, the affirmation of God's timeless eternity appears to be
necessary in order to avoid difficulties in affirming the eternal begetting
of the Son by the Father; for if God is in time then the begetting of the
Son looks like an event in time. But examining these further ideas would
take us beyond our present purpose.

Let us look at some representative statements of eternality and at the
way the connection is made between divine eternity and divine fullness.
Augustine of Hippo (354-430) links eternality with divine fullness and
self-sufficiency:

> In you it is not one thing to be and another to live: the supreme degree of
> being and the supreme degree of life are one and the same thing. You are
> being in a supreme degree and are immutable. In you the present day has
> no ending, and yet in you it has its end: "all these things have their being
> in you" (Romans 11:36). They would have no way of passing away unless

you set a limit to them. Because "your years do not fail" (Psalm 102:27), your years are one Today.[1]

And Anselm (c. 1033-1109):

> On the other hand, if this Nature [i.e., the divine nature] were to exist as a whole distinctly and successively at different times (as a man exists as a whole yesterday, today and tomorrow), then this Nature would properly be said to have existed, to exist, and to be going to exist. Therefore, its lifetime—which is nothing other than its eternity—would not exist as a whole at once but would be extended by parts throughout the parts of time. Now, its eternity is nothing other than itself. Hence, the Supreme Being would be divided into parts according to the divisions of time.[2]

And, most famous perhaps, Boethius (c. 480-524):

> It is the common judgement, then, of all creatures that live by reason that God is eternal. So let us consider the nature of eternity, for this will make clear to us both the nature of God and his manner of knowing. Eternity, then, is the complete, simultaneous and perfect possession of everlasting life; this will be clear from a comparison with creatures that exist in time.[3]

So eternality has two main sources: the data of Scripture coupled with a priori reflection on the ideas of the divine fullness and aseity and on the Creator-creature distinction. A possible third source may be found in the conclusions of what were taken to be valid cosmological arguments for God's existence. Arguments from the fact of change to the existence of a Changeless One imply that it is impossible for the Changeless One to change. In what is sometimes referred to as Perfect Being theology,[4] eternality implies and is implied by divine simplicity (the view that though we are able to think of distinctions in the Godhead it is actually uncompounded, without parts, including temporal parts). Whether or not an eternalist believes in divine simplicity (the two ideas seem to be contingently connected), eternality implies immutability in a very strong

---

[1]Augustine *Confessions,* trans. Henry Chadwick (Oxford: World's Classics, 1992), p. 8. He cites the Septuagint.

[2]Anselm *Monologion* 21, in *Anselm of Canterbury,* trans. J. Hopkins and H. W. Richardson (London: SCM Press, 1974), 1:34.

[3]Boethius *The Consolation of Philosophy,* trans. V. E. Watts (Harmondsworth, U.K.: Penguin, 1969), 5.6.

[4]For discussion of this phrase see T. V. Morris, *Anselmian Explorations* (Notre Dame, Ind.: University of Notre Dame Press, 1987).

sense. It is not that God is immutable because he is unwilling to change, but because his perfect nature is such that he need not and cannot change.

Is Divine Timeless Eternity Incoherent?

It has been argued that the eternalist view is straightforwardly incoherent: if God's timeless life is simultaneous both with, say, the inauguration of President Wilson and the inauguration of President Kennedy, then these events must occur at the same time, since simultaneity is a transitive and symmetrical relation. Whatever is simultaneous with another event E is also simultaneous with whatever else is simultaneous with E. And since it is absurd to suppose that the inauguration of President Wilson is simultaneous with the inauguration of President Kennedy, the idea of divine timelessness is absurd. Thus Richard Swinburne argues:

> The inner incoherence can be seen as follows. God's timelessness is said to consist in his existing at all moments of human time—simultaneously. Thus he is said to be simultaneously present at (and a witness of) what I did yesterday, what I am doing today, and what I will do tomorrow. But if t1 is simultaneous with t2 and t2 with t3, then t1 is simultaneous with t3. So if the instant at which God knows these things were simultaneous with both yesterday, today and tomorrow, then these days would be simultaneous with each other. So yesterday would be the same day as today and as tomorrow—which is clearly nonsense.[5]

And Sir Anthony Kenny: "On St. Thomas' view, my typing of this paper is simultaneous with the whole of eternity. Again, on this view, the great fire of Rome is simultaneous with the whole of eternity. Therefore, while I type these very words, Nero fiddles heartlessly on."[6]

Whatever else we may think we know about time and eternity, we know that if one event is later than another then they cannot occur at the same time. But timelessness is incoherent in this sense only if it is supposed that timeless eternity is a kind of time that could be simultaneous with some truly temporal time. And there is no compelling reason to think that timeless eternity is a kind of time, as we shall see.

Boethius's definition of God's timeless eternity as "the complete,

---

[5]Richard Swinburne, *The Coherence of Theism* (Oxford: Clarendon, 1977), pp. 220-21.
[6]Anthony Kenny, *The God of the Philosophers* (Oxford: Clarendon, 1979), pp. 38-39.

simultaneous and perfect possession of everlasting life" may seem to encourage the Swinburne-Kenny riposte. But of course the simultaneity to which Boethius is referring is simultaneity within the Godhead, expressing the thought that God possesses everlasting life all at once. As Boethius elsewhere puts it, God's knowledge of all time is "knowledge of a never-passing instant."[7]

Attempts have been made to explain and refine the idea of eternality by claiming, for example, that though timeless eternity is not a kind of time, it has some of the features of temporal duration. For example, in an important article that has done much to stimulate fresh discussion of divine eternity, Eleonore Stump and Norman Kretzmann articulate the timelessness view in terms of presentness that is in some sense simultaneous with the events of the creation.[8]

> What really interests us among the species of simultaneity . . . [is] a simultaneity relationship between two *relata* of which one is eternal and the other temporal. We have to be able to characterize such a relationship coherently if we are to be able to claim that there is any connection between an eternal and a temporal entity or event. An eternal entity or event cannot be earlier or later than, or past or future with respect to, any temporal entity or event. If there is to be any relationship between what is eternal and what is temporal, then, it must be some species of simultaneity.[9]

In order to avoid the objection of Swinburne and Kenny discussed earlier, Stump and Kretzmann distinguish between eternal simultaneity and temporal simultaneity. And they introduce an idea of simultaneity ("ET-simultaneity") that in their view can relate what is eternal and what is temporal: any eternal event is ET-simultaneous with any temporal event. But unlike "ordinary" simultaneity *simpliciter,* the relation of ET-simultaneity is not transitive, since in order for two things to be related by ET-simultaneity there must be either an eternal or a temporal stand-

---

[7]This and other related points are discussed by Katherin A. Rogers in "Eternity Has No Duration," *Religious Studies,* 1994, reprinted in *An Anselmian Approach to God and Creation* (Lewiston, N.Y.: Edwin Mellen, 1997).
[8]Eleonore Stump and Norman Kretzmann, "Eternity," *Journal of Philosophy* 78, reprinted in *The Concept of God,* ed. T. V. Morris (New York: Oxford University Press, 1987). Page references are to this reprint. See also Brian Leftow, *Time and Eternity* (Ithaca, N.Y.: Cornell University Press, 1991), chap. 8.
[9]Stump and Kretzmann, "Eternity," p. 226.

point from which such simultaneity is observed. This view requires what is (to my mind) the obscure claim that an eternal observer observes a temporal event as temporally present, and so requires that divine eternity should have some of the features of temporality. These are rather opaque ideas, and their difficulty is compounded by the fact that the idea of ET-simultaneity appears to be devised simply to stipulate the absence of transitivity and hence the absence of the *reductio ad absurdum* of the idea of timelessness, rather than offering an account showing why such transitivity cannot occur in these circumstances.

Not only are these ideas of Stump and Kretzmann difficult to grasp, there is reason to think that the modification they propose to the classical idea of divine timelessness is not actually coherent. Katherin Rogers argues that it is a "puzzling concept." How could we make sense of the idea that divine eternity is a timeless *duration?* If there is duration, then presumably it is possible to denote points along that duration. But then any such point will have temporal relations to the points of temporal duration and another such point will have different temporal relations to temporal duration. There will be points in eternal duration that are simultaneous with a certain point in temporal duration. Although Stump and Kretzmann say that "no temporal entity or event can be earlier to, later than or past or future with respect to the whole life of an eternal entity,"[10] their willingness to introduce the idea of *duration* suggests the exact opposite. As noted earlier, Brian Leftow develops a very similar idea of eternal duration, which he calls quasi-temporal eternity (QTE). But if QTE is an extension that has no proper parts and is indivisible, but is nevertheless an extension in which points are ordered as earlier and later, these claims look self-contradictory.[11]

Rather than attempt, in the manner of Stump and Kretzmann or of Leftow, to explicate eternality as involving aspects of duration, it is perhaps wiser, though no doubt intellectually less satisfying, for the eternalist to think of the assertion of divine timeless eternity as a piece of negative thinking about the divine essence, a fragment of negative theology. For divine eternality is time*less*ness, and it cannot be expected that

---

[10]Ibid., p. 225.

[11]As Philip Quinn argues in "On the Mereology of Boethian Eternity," *International Journal for Philosophy of Religion*, 1992.

human analogies and models will throw much light on what more positively it is or is like. For any analogies must be drawn from our own
temporal existence. It is certainly no part of the claim that God is timelessly eternal to say that we can imagine what existing in such a timeless
fashion must be like, nor is any such ability necessary to make the idea
cogent.

We can say with some confidence what timeless eternity is not, and
we can use analogies, such as the relation between the center of a circle
and its circumference, or someone at the summit of a hill taking in at a
glance what is occurring beneath her. But the hilltop analogy of Boethius has been shown to be strictly speaking, unsatisfactory, because the
person at the top of the hill and those beneath her are all in time.[12] And
the idea of God as the center of a circle with time being represented by
the circumference is also defective, because of course the temporal
order is linear and not circular. But it is surely not a reasonable require-
ment for a satisfactory articulation of a doctrine such as timeless eternality that one must be able accurately to describe what it is like to be
timeless. Part of what it means to say that God is incomprehensible is to
say that though we believe that God is timeless we do not and cannot
have a straightforward understanding of what his timeless life is. We
cannot echo God's self-knowledge.

Eternity and Impassibility

It is frequently objected that the idea of divine timeless eternity is unacceptable because it has the consequence that God is impassive, without
feeling, and indeed that he is incapable of feeling. For feelings of affection and emotion, at least as we experience them, are episodes. They
start, last for a time and then finish. I am pleased when I've completed
mowing the lawn, but that feeling of pleasure does not last. I am angry
when a carelessly driven car smashes into the back of mine, but this
anger does not last. And even a deep-seated love for one's nearest and
dearest may ebb and flow. But a timelessly eternal God is immutable
and so impassible in a very strong sense; he *necessarily* cannot change,
for change takes time, or is in time, and a timelessly eternal God by def-

---

[12]See, for example, Martha Kneale, "Eternity and Sempiternity," *Proceedings of the Aristotelean Society,* 1968-1969.

inition is not in time, and so his actions cannot take time, nor can he experience fits of passion or changes in mood. But how—the opponents of eternality ask—could such an impassible God be a person (or a Trinity of persons), and how could he be a God to whom we can relate?

In reply, it must be noted that there is an initial linguistic source of misunderstanding that may give the impression that such questions have more force than in fact they have. When used of a human being, the term *impassible* suggests someone who is without feeling, perhaps as a result of some psychological abnormality. And of course it is unthinkable that the eternal God, the One who has fullness of being, should be withdrawn and unfeeling in this sense. A further source of misunderstanding is the idea that, being timelessly eternal, God is "static" in a way which, in a human being, would be regarded as an incapacity—so that God does not, so to speak, move a muscle in the face of human evil and misery. Does not impassibility imply impassivity? And is not impassivity often vicious? We need to remind ourselves at this point that the idea of timeless eternality is based on the idea that God has fullness of being, that he is "pure act," and not that he is like a withdrawn, sadly incapacitated human being. Impassibility in God is not a defect but a perfection; it signals fullness, not deficiency.

So how, more positively, are we to understand the idea of God's impassibility? We can begin by dismissing from our minds the idea that God might have anything that corresponds to what in us is a sinful or unworthy passion or affection—lust, envy or vengefulness, say. And we must also rule out feelings or affections that require change and that require the possession of a body; hunger or thirst or tiredness. For passions in us change us; they are affections. And many of our passions arise because we are embodied. If we rule these out in the case of a timelessly eternal God who is pure spirit, what is left?

There is a great deal left, if we think of God's having, in a manner suitable to his own perfection, what corresponds to us when we have emotions. What corresponds in God to such emotional states in ourselves is much more attitudinal, or dispositional, in character than a fitful human passion or emotion. Joy, care, pleasure and love in a timelessly eternal God are much more like deep-seated attitudes or dispositions in us. They are fundamental states of mind, part of the divine fullness and glory, and of the engagement of that divine fullness with his creation.

These permanent states of the divine being are differently experienced by God's human creatures according to their various situations and conditions.

If we think not only of God himself, in isolation, but of a Creator God, then we can see how it is reasonable to think of God's having pleasure or joy or peace not only in himself but also in his works as they reflect himself; he has the joy and pleasure and contentment of seeing fitfully in others what he has in full measure in himself alone. And the same delight he has in the delightful may be experienced as mercy by the penitent and justice by the impenitent.[13]

This is not the place to list exhaustively such divine states of mind; drawing on their own preferred sources, readers may have their own ideas as to what the list might contain. What I have tried to establish is that far from being psychologically or spiritually impoverished, an "impassible," timelessly eternal God may have a fullness of character of which our fitful human emotions are but inadequate shadows.

Timeless Eternity and Omniscience

One currently fashionable argument against divine timeless eternity is that a timelessly eternal God could not be omniscient. And since God is omniscient, necessarily so, God could not be timelessly eternal. Those of us who are in time know that some particular day is now. We know, say, that June 9, 1999, is now, that June 8 is now past and that June 11 is now future. But a timelessly eternal God can know none of these things, for since he is not in time there are no segments of time that are past and present and future for him. Eternalists such as Boethius and Augustine say that to an eternal God everything is present *all at once.* God, for the eternalist, can know that some event E is before another event F, and that F is in turn before another event G. But God cannot know that one of these events is occurring now, because it isn't true, as far as he is concerned, that one of these events is occurring now. So God cannot know what we know. So God cannot be omniscient.

What are we to say to this argument? In the first place it is worth noting that many temporalists are in any case content to adopt a weakened or

---

[13]This discussion owes much to Norman Kretzmann's account of divine impassibility in Aquinas in *The Metaphysics of Theism* (Oxford: Clarendon, 1997), chap. 8.

modified account of divine omniscience, usually on the grounds that God's infallible knowledge of the future is incompatible with human free action.[14] So even if we have to tailor our initial intuitions about omniscience in the light of God's eternity, eternalists are in no worse case than many temporalists. And so, thinking in purely dialectical terms, it is not that temporalists have an account of divine omniscience that eternalists may find it difficult to match and so, on this matter at least, have the advantage. They have no advantage. Each, for different reasons, may find it necessary to qualify the strictest understanding of divine omniscience.

But what of the argument itself? I shall reply to it by offering several possible counterarguments to the claim that eternalism and divine omniscience are incompatible, leaving the reader to decide which is the more cogent. One response—if it may be called that—is simply to concede the point and give up strict omniscience. One might concede the strict point of metaphysics but claim that God may nevertheless know sufficiently to enable him infallibly to deduce the occurrence of all true indexical expressions about time, expressions using words such as *now, then, yesterday, tomorrow.* The occurrences of such expressions in utterances are, after all, events that God, in virtue of his vast knowledge, must know. He does not know that 1999 is now for him, because it isn't. But he knows all the times when each of us make true utterances such as "It is now . . ." and he knows that whenever in 1999 we say "It is now 1999" we are speaking the truth. So God can know that "It is now 1999" is true for us whenever in that year it is uttered, and he knows when it is uttered, for he knows that it is uttered at some particular time during 1999.

If this response is not considered satisfactory, one may point out that (quite apart from the question of divine omniscience and human freedom touched on earlier) the temporalist is in a parallel position with respect to the issue. For if God is in time, then there are also types of propositions that such a temporal God cannot know—propositions that express knowledge of the universe from the perspective of timeless eternity. This must be so, if temporality and eternality are exclusive positions. And each person is in a similar position with respect to God's

---

[14]See, for example, Swinburne, *Coherence of Theism,* pp. 174-78, and William Hasker, *God, Time and Knowledge* (Ithaca, N.Y.: Cornell University Press, 1989), chap. 10.

knowledge of each of us. For it is plausible to suppose that each of us has unique knowledge of ourselves—call it "me-ness." I know that it is I who is typing this paper. You can know that it is Paul Helm who is typing, but you cannot know that fact as I know it; and similarly with you; and similarly with God's knowledge of me. He is in rather like your position with respect to my me-ness, and in something like my position with respect to your me-ness. But if this is a problem, a problem generated by the uniqueness of each individual, including God himself, then it is one that all theists share.

Finally, one may argue that the "knowledge" we possess when we say truly "It is raining now" is not propositional knowledge in the strict sense but more like know-how. Take an analogy. Suppose that from a map of London I know the position of the Strand. Suppose I want to get to the Strand. I need to know something else. I need to know not only where the Strand is but also that I am *here,* and that *here* denotes a particular point on the map. Then, and only then, can I use the map to get to the Strand. But what I know when I know that I am *here* (pointing to a particular place on the map) is not an additional fact about the geography of London; it is knowledge of my relation to certain bits of that geography, and this is more like a case of know-how than it is like knowing that. Knowing that I am here (pointing to the map) and being able to read the map enables me to get to the Strand. So that what God lacks when he lacks "knowledge" of indexicals is a certain sort of skill. He does not lack knowledge but power. And since the concept of omnipotence is hard to define for both temporalist and eternalist, the eternalist may be more comfortable with denying a power to God than with denying some kinds of knowledge.

Timelessness and Biblical Language
Earlier on I said that the idea of eternality, if not founded in Scripture, is certainly consistent with it. But any reader of Scripture is forcefully struck by the language of time and change as applied to God. In fact, there are at least two kinds of language in the Bible about God. There is, first of all, language that asserts, say, God's all-encompassing knowledge, including knowledge of matters that are future to us and that encompasses the free decisions of human agents. Such a view is implied

by texts such as the following:

☐ "And Joseph said to them, 'Do not interpretations belong to God? Please tell [your dreams] to me'" (Gen 40:8).

☐ "'O LORD, the God of Israel, your servant has heard that Saul seeks to come to Keilah, to destroy the city on my account. And now, will Saul come down as your servant has heard? O LORD, the God of Israel, I beseech you, tell your servant.' The LORD said, 'He will come down'" (1 Sam 23:10-11).

☐ "The LORD searches every mind, and understands every plan and thought" (1 Chron 28:9).

☐ "In your book were written all the days that were formed for me, when none of them as yet existed" (Ps 139:16).

☐ "I have aroused Cyrus in righteousness, and I will make all his paths straight; he shall rebuild my city and set my exiles free" (Is 45:13).

☐ "I am God, and there is no one like me, declaring the end from the beginning" (Is 46:9-10).

☐ "The former things I declared long ago, they went out from my mouth and I made them known. . . . I declared them to you from long ago, before they came to pass I announced them to you" (Is 48:3-5).

☐ "Thus says the LORD, the God of hosts, the God of Israel, If you will only surrender to the officials of the king of Babylon, then your life shall be spared, and this city shall not be burned with fire, and you and your house shall live. But if you do not surrender . . .'" (Jer 38:17-18).

☐ "For Jesus knew from the first who were the ones that did not believe, and who was the one that would betray him" (Jn 6:64).

☐ "This man, handed over to you according to the definite plan and foreknowledge of God, you crucified and killed by the hands of those outside the law" (Acts 2:23).

☐ "Before him no creature is hidden, but all are naked and laid bare to the eyes of the one to whom we must render an account" (Heb 4:13).

And then there is biblical language about God that implies that God learns, that he is surprised at what happens (because apparently he does not know what is going to happen before it does) and that he changes his mind. How, from an eternalist perspective, can we make sense of the biblical language of change that implies that God is in time? In trying to answer this question we shall first glance at the answer Aquinas gives and then at some remarks of John Calvin.

Aquinas is emphatic that God's will is unchangeable. And so words ascribing change to God, or words ascribed to God which entail change:

> have a metaphorical turn according to a human figure of speech. When we regret what we have made we throw it away. Yet this does not always argue second thoughts or a change of will, for we may intend in the first place to make a thing and scrap it afterwards. By similitude with such a procedure we refer to God having regrets, for instance in the account of the Flood, when he washed off the face of the earth the men whom he had made; to speak of God as repenting is to use the language of metaphor. . . . The conclusion to this argument is not that God's will changes, but that he wills change.[15]

These remarks of Aquinas's help us from a logical point of view; by invoking the idea of metaphor, they enable us to say that while certain things are nonmetaphorically true of God, for example that he knows that *p,* other things are only metaphorically true of him, for example that he changes his mind as a result of learning that *p,* and that there corresponds to this metaphorical truth a nonmetaphorical truth of the matter about God's cognitive state. But such an account hardly tells us, or even hints at, why such metaphors are needed in the first place. Why is the Bible so full of such language about God, language that implies change in God and therefore suggests that God is in time?

For help in trying to answer this further question we may turn to what John Calvin says. Here is part of his famous (or infamous) treatment of divine repentance from his *Institutes of the Christian Religion:*

> What therefore, does the word "repentance" mean? Surely its meaning is like that of all other modes of speaking that describe God to us in human terms. For because our weakness does not attain to his exalted state, the description of him that is given to us must be accommodated to our capacity so that we may understand it. Now the mode of accommodation is for him to represent himself to us not as he is in himself, but as he seems to us. Although he is beyond all disturbance of mind, yet he testifies that he is angry towards sinners. Therefore whenever we hear that God is angered, we ought not to imagine any emotion in him but

---

[15]Thomas Aquinas, *Summa Theologiae,* trans. Thomas Gilby (London: Spottiswoode, 1966), 1a.19.7.

rather to consider that this expression has been taken from our own human experience; because God, whenever he is exercising judgement exhibits the appearance of one kindled and angered. So we ought not to understand anything else under the word "repentance" than change of action, because men are wont by changing their action to testify that they are displeased with themselves. Therefore, since every change among men is a correction of what displeases them, but that correction arises out of repentance, then by the word "repentance" is meant the fact that God changes with respect to his actions. Meanwhile neither God's plan nor his will is reversed, nor his volition altered; but what he had from eternity foreseen, approved and decreed, he pursues in uninterrupted tenor, however sudden the variation may appear in men's eyes.[16]

On the theory of divine accommodation, statements such as "God repented" are in a sense false, false if taken literally. For God does not literally repent and cannot do so. Calvin and Aquinas agree. But if such words are false when taken strictly, why is such language needed in the first place? Here Calvin can help us.

The language that asserts or implies change in God invariably has to do with divine-human dialogue, where God speaks to and acts on behalf of his people and his people speak and act in return. At the heart of Calvin's idea of divine accommodation is, I believe, a logical point about such dialogue: it is a logically necessary condition of dialogue that each of the partners in the dialogue should appear to act and react in time. If dialogue between God and humankind is to be real and not make-believe, then God cannot represent himself (in his role as dialogue partner) as wholly immutable, for then dialogue, real dialogue, would be impossible. His purposes for his people on whose behalf he intervenes in time cannot be expressed in fully immutable fashion. The language of change in God is not for rhetorical or ornamental effect, therefore, but its use takes us to the heart of biblical religion.

The fundamental point is that such language is not dispensable but necessary, not necessary only for the plowman but necessary for us all,

---

[16]John Calvin, *Institutes of the Christian Religion,* trans. Ford Lewis Battles, ed. John T. McNeill (Philadelphia: Westminster Press, 1960), 1:227 (1.17.13). Calvin's commitment to both divine eternality and divine impassibility is clearly affirmed in this passage.

in view of our moral and metaphysical position vis-à-vis God.[17] If a timelessly eternal God is to communicate to embodied intelligent creatures who exist in space and time and to bring about his purposes through them, and particularly to gain certain kinds of responses from them, then he must do so by representing himself to them in ways that are not literally true. How could God put Moses to the test, apart from testing him step by step and so appearing to change his mind? So the impression we may form, reading the biblical narrative, that God changes is an illusion that arises because we learn of God's purposes for the actors in the narrative (and perhaps for others) only bit by bit.

On the theory of divine accommodation, statements such as "God repented" are false if taken literally, because God does not literally repent and cannot do so. But although they are literally false, some truth about God may nevertheless be conveyed by them. Someone who upholds the principle of noncontradiction in logic nevertheless may, when asked if it is raining, say "It is and it isn't." In uttering what is literally self-contradictory he does not believe that he has actually flouted the principle, and moreover he succeeds in conveying something intelligible using language that, strictly speaking, is incoherent. Similarly, someone who denies geocentrism as a theory about the heavenly bodies may nevertheless say, "It's warmer in the garden now that the sun has come out from behind the clouds."[18]

Each of these sentences, though literally false, may be taken to convey a truth. Sometimes looseness in speech signifies waffle and incoherence. But at other times language may be loose (when judged from the standpoint of some theory) but economical, the very opposite of waffle. It is hard to believe that such language, the language of accommodation, is typically misleading or wrong any more than it is misleading to say that it is and it isn't raining. It is language that records the appearance of things in an unpedantic and vivid way.

Does the use of such language involve God in insincerity then? Not necessarily. (And if not necessarily, then necessarily not.) What is sincere is,

---

[17]Accommodation is a recurring motif in Calvin's thought. But unlike some who have used the idea he does not do so for elitist purposes, to make a distinction between the real and the merely superficial. (I have discussed this point further in "John Calvin and Moses Maimonides on Divine Accommodation," in *Referring to God*, ed. Paul Helm (Surrey, U.K.: Curzon Press, 1999).

[18]For these examples, see Peter Van Inwagen, *Material Beings* (Ithaca, N.Y.: Cornell University Press, 1990), p. 101.

say, his desire to test Moses and also his desire that Moses pass the test. For this sincere intention to be carried out it does not follow that each separate element in his dialogue with Moses, when isolated from all the other components, should take the form of a sincerely uttered truth, but that the entire testing should be sincerely intended.

Eternity and Creation

Earlier we touched on the idea of God as the Creator. We need now to spend some time looking at the compatibility of divine timeless eternity and the idea of *creatio ex nihilo*. In particular I shall have in mind the fundamental Christian claim that the universe, the creation of God, is metaphysically contingent. Although God is in some sense necessary, at least to the extent that he has his existence from himself and not from any other, the universe has its source in God, and had God willed it, no universe, or some universe other than ours, would have occurred. I shall look at this idea of contingent creation and defend its consistency with the idea of divine timeless eternity by looking at a recent treatment of God, time and creation by William Lane Craig.

We might begin by distinguishing between the absolute idea of divine timeless eternity, such as is being defended here, according to which God is timelessly eternal without qualification, and Bill Craig's modified understanding of divine timeless eternity, according to which God is timelessly eternal but only until the moment of creation; at this point he becomes temporal. Bill argues against absolute divine timelessness. He thinks that given the fact of the creation of the universe, the absolute timelessness of God is an impossible idea on the grounds that since the creation is contingent, God must have relations with his creation that he would not have had had there been no creation, and so he must come to have these relations and so be in time when he has them. Bill states his position as follows:

> But once time begins at the moment of creation, God either becomes temporal in virtue of his real, causal relation to time and the world or he exists as timelessly with creation as he does *sans* creation. But this second alternative seems quite impossible.
>
> Even if the beginning of the temporal world is the result of a timeless volition of God, the fact that the world is not sempiternal but began to

exist out of nothing demonstrates that God acquires a new relation at the moment of creation.[19]

It is certainly true that God has relations with something, the universe, with which he would not have had relations had there been no universe. But by itself this is hardly sufficient to cast doubt on the idea of absolute timeless eternity. For the way in which Bill characterizes God's relation to the creation is not a way that the eternalist can accept or need accept.

Bill couples this objection to the idea of divine timeless eternity in the absolute sense with a discussion of Thomas Aquinas's rather obscure doctrine of real relations. According to Aquinas, though the universe is really related to God, God is not really related to the created universe.

> Whenever two things are related to each other in such a way that one depends upon the other but the other does not depend upon it, there is a real relation in the dependent member, but in the independent member the relation is merely one of reason—simply because one thing cannot be understood as being related to it. The notion of such a relation becomes clear if we consider knowledge, which depends on what is known, although the latter does not depend on it.
>
> Consequently, since all creatures depend on God, but he does not depend on them, there are real relations in creatures referring them to God. The opposite relations in God to creatures, however, are merely conceptual relations; but, because names are signs of concepts, certain names we use for God imply a relation to creatures, even though, as we said, this relation is merely conceptual.[20]

But this reference to Aquinas is in my view an unnecessary entanglement. There is only a contingent connection between divine timeless eternity (understood in absolutist fashion) and Aquinas's doctrine. And since I do not have to, I do not here wish to defend any account of God's creation that maintains that his relation to the creation is not a "real" relation. Rather I shall defend my account by objecting to the way Bill has set up the problem—he represents the coming into existence of the universe as a temporal event. Of course if it is a temporal event

[19]William Lane Craig, "The Tensed vs. Tenseless Theory of Time: A Watershed for the Conception of Divine Eternity," in *Questions of Time and Tense,* ed. Robin Le Poidevin (Oxford: Clarendon, 1998), p. 222.
[20]Thomas Aquinas *De Veritate* 4.5, quoted by Craig, "Tensed vs. Tenseless," p. 225.

then we can raise the question whether God exists before (temporally) that event, or at the time of that event, and if the answer to such questions is yes (as it appears that it would have to be) then God's timeless eternity would be fatally compromised. But then God would not cease to be timelessly eternal, for he would never have been so.

But according to the eternalist,[21] there need be no temporal first moment of creation, and so the universe need not have begun (temporally) to exist, for from the divine standpoint the universe is eternal, even though it exists contingently. And even if we suppose a first moment of creation it does not follow that God existed before the creation, before that first moment. For if there was a first moment of creation, then there was no time prior to the first moment during which God might exist.

So an eternalist should deny Bill's claims that "God acquires a new relation at the moment of creation. At the moment of creation, God comes into the relation of sustaining the universe or at the very least that of coexisting with the universe, relations which he did not before have."[22] The last phrase betokens misunderstanding of the eternalist position, if the "before" is intended as a temporal before, as it clearly is. For there are no relations that an eternal God could have before (temporally) anything else, since he does not exist "before" (temporally) anything else. Therefore there need be no "moment at which the temporal world springs into being." The universe is contingent, and within that contingent temporal order it makes sense to talk of an event *A* being before another event *B*, but for the eternalist it makes no sense to talk in this way of the contingent order as a whole.

If one wishes to use the language of time about God and the creation, then it must be said that God has always stood in the relation of being the Creator of the universe. But this language is itself misleading and therefore needs to be used cautiously. It is better, more accurate to eternalism, to say that God has a timelessly eternal relation with the temporal world, but a relation that is nevertheless contingent.

The eternalist argues that God has a relation to the universe that he

---

[21]To save trying the reader's patience, from now on (unless otherwise stated) by *eternity* I shall mean divine timeless eternity understood in the absolute sense that Bill denies.
[22]Craig, "Tensed vs. Tenseless," p. 222.

might not have had, and that nevertheless this relation is eternal. As a result we can say that had God decreed a different world, or no world at all, then his relations would have been different. But this is not inconsistent with eternalism. Without getting entangled in Aquinas's distinction between real and nonreal relations we can say that God has a relation with the temporal universe that happens, as a result of his contingently decreeing it, to be as it is. Whether, if this is true, there remains any reason for denying God's temporality is a question not of this fact per se, which is quite consistent with divine eternality, but of the cogency and rationale of divine eternality more generally. So an eternalist may consistently deny that God's being the eternal Creator of a temporal universe is inconsistent; and deny that if God is related to the temporal world by virtue of creating it, then God is temporal.[23]

Aquinas discusses the question whether something that has always existed may nevertheless be wholly caused by God. And in particular, is it possible for something to come to be that always was? He answers in the affirmative, taking the view that an efficient cause does not necessarily precede its effect in time.[24]

There is a tendency to confuse time with contingency. Scripture implies, if it does not affirm, the contingency of the universe in two respects: that its existence is not logically necessary, and that it owes its existence to the agency of God—it depends on him. But it does not follow from the contingency of the universe in these senses that there was a time when the world was not, only that there might not have been a universe. If the universe is beginningless,[25] without a first event, it does not follow from this that it is not contingent; and if it is contingent then it has a cause, though not a temporal cause, but someone on whom it depends for its entire existence.[26]

---

[23]See ibid., pp. 222-23.

[24]Thomas Aquinas, *On the Eternity of the World*, in *Selected Writings*, ed. and trans. Ralph McInerny (London: Penguin, 1998).

[25]It is probably true that most eternalists, like Augustine, take a relational view of time. Suppose that an eternalist took a nonrelational view of time. Then there may exist an expanse of time before the creation of the physical universe. Does it follow that that expanse of time must be backwardly everlasting? Perhaps not.

[26]For a fascinating account of one medieval debate about this, see Norman Kretzmann, "Ockham and the Creation of the Beginningless World," *Franciscan Studies* 45 (1985): 1-31. See also Anthony Kenny, *Wyclif* (Oxford: Oxford University Press, 1985), p. 34.

So the question whether the universe had a first moment or not can be approached by the eternalist in the following way. Either there was a first beginning of time or there was not. If there was, then God eternally decreed the existence of such a universe. If there was not, then, as Aquinas claimed in the discussion just referred to, God brought about a universe that has always been. In other words, assuming that each of these alternatives is coherent, eternalism can accommodate either.[27]

There is also a temptation to confuse what we are able to conceive with how things must be. Perhaps for any time t_1 prior to the present it is possible to conceive an earlier time than t_1. If this is possible, what does it show? What it shows is not that it is possible to establish a moment of creation, but rather the reverse. For any such putative moment it is possible to imagine an earlier moment than that, and so any supposed first moment of creation is in indefinite retreat. On the other hand, the fact that we can think in these ways goes no way toward establishing that the universe is not contingent, though it may be without temporal beginning. Perhaps we must recognize the strongly regulative influence that conceptions of time and space exert on individuals such as ourselves who are necessarily temporal and spatial.[28]

For the eternalist, temporality is an essential feature of creatureliness; the universe is created by God with time, not in time—"all at once" only in the sense that the creation is the product of a divine timeless decree. The universe could not have begun with an event such as the "big bang," since the big bang is itself a physical effect. Thus for the eternalist God's creation of all that is ("the universe") is not a scientific event, like the exploding of a star or the splitting of an atom, nor a series of such events; nor is it a unique historical event, like the Battle of Hastings or the coronation of the queen. It is the bringing of the universe into being from a standpoint outside it. For this reason the idea that God exists (timelessly) "before" the universe cannot mean that God exists temporally before it. He exists before the universe, I argue, rather in the way the queen exists before the prime minister, age comes before beauty, or

---

[27]The issues involved in taking each alternative of the disjunction are discussed by W. Newton Smith, *The Structure of Time* (London: Routledge, 1980), chap. 5, "The Topology of Time III: The Beginning of Time."

[28]Whether such regulative procedures recognize regularities objectively present or construct or impose regularities is of course a further interesting philosophical question.

duty comes before pleasure. These "befores" are not temporal "befores"; they are another kind of priority, betokening a constitutional or hierarchical or normative arrangement. There was no time when the Creator was not, any more than there was a time when the creation was not. And yet the Creator exists "before" the creation. It is in some such way as this that we may interpret the apostolic claim that Christ is before all things (Col 1:17).

So God is before the creation not by virtue of existing at a time when the universe was not yet in existence, but by virtue of his necessity and the creation's contingency and of the universe's causal dependence on him. Everything created (except the temporal order itself) is necessarily in time, mutable and (so) corruptible; anything that exists uncreatedly is necessarily eternal, immutable and incorruptible. By contrast, for the temporalist the creation has a beginning in time, even though (in the view of at least one temporalist[29]) before the regularities of the creation were established such time was unmetricated. On this view God's necessity is partly expressed in terms of his everlastingness, and such changefulness as he possesses does not imply corruptibility.

I am quite content to suppose that in talking about a timeless God's causing or bringing about the universe we are using *cause* in an unusual sense. The action is not temporal, occurring before its effect. But then arguments that causality entails time fail to compel; nor is the effect a temporal event or a series of such events, though the effect has temporal features. And in virtue of the divine power the cause is noncontingently related to its effect; that is to say, given divine power it could not be that God could will F and that F would not come to pass. But these significant departures from the usual ways we talk of one event's causing another do not result in a sense of "cause" that is so stretched that it makes no sense.

God's Action in the World

The idea of timeless creation leads very naturally to a consideration of a timeless God's actions in the world. To many the idea has seemed incoherent, and God's timeless eternity has seemed to entail a form of deism according to which such a God may timelessly create the entire tempo-

---

[29]Richard Swinburne, *The Christian God* (Oxford: Clarendon, 1994), chap. 4.

ral order and all that it contains but not be able to act within it. I shall argue that this is a mistaken view; that not only may such a God act within time but he may also be said to act in response to what happens in time.

What is it to act, to perform an action? I shall, somewhat crudely no doubt, suppose that to act is to bring about something as the result of intending or desiring or willing that thing, and to do so for a purpose. (Here we are ignoring the special problems raised by acts of omission.) It would, of course, be fatal to God's timeless eternity to imagine that in acting in the world God wills in time to do something at a later time. For this would be to suppose that God exists at a time. But there seems to be nothing incoherent about the idea that God eternally wills that some event—say the miraculous burning of a bush—occur at some particular determined time. That is, we need to distinguish between

(a) God eternally decrees (to will A at t_1 and to will B at t_2 and to will C at t_3 . . .)

and

(b) God eternally decrees (A at t_1 and B at t_2 and C at t_3 . . .)

The correct way to think of God's eternally willing something in time is to think of one eternal act of will with numerous temporally scattered effects. As an analogy, we may think of a person's action in setting the timer on her central heating system. This is (we may suppose) one action, analogous to God's eternal willing. But this one action has numerous temporally scattered effects, analogous to the effects in time of God's one eternal act of willing; as a result of the one act, the system fires at 7:00 a.m., goes off at 12:00 noon, fires again at 2:00 p.m., goes off again at 10:30 p.m. day after day. The basic point is: there can be one decision to bring about different effects at different times. This decision may be in time, as in our example, but it may also be timeless. Aquinas put the point well: "Note that to change your will is one matter, and to will a change in some thing is another. While remaining constant, a person can will this to happen now and the contrary to happen afterwards. His will, however, would change were he to begin to will what he had not willed before, or cease to will what he had willed before."[30]

---

[30]Aquinas, *Summa Theologiae*, 1a.19.7 (p. 33).

Further, it is consistent to suppose that not only can a timelessly eternal God will things in time without changing his will, but he may also eternally will his own reactions in time to some human action. God might both eternally will some event *E* knowing that *E* will elicit a certain reaction *R* and eternally will *F* in response to *R*. Thus God may know: that his willing *E* will elicit *R* and that if R then his willing F is best. And as a result (not a temporal result of course) he may eternally will *E* and *F* while eternally knowing of *R*. Thus God may eternally will the burning bush and his temporally subsequent utterances to Moses, eternally knowing that Moses' attention will be attracted by the burning bush.

The incarnation is a unique case of God's acting in time. One thing to note is that if God the Son is timelessly eternal and yet incarnate in Jesus Christ, there is no time in his existence when he was not incarnate, though since he became incarnate at a particular time in our history there were times in that history before the incarnation, and times since. This does not mean that the incarnation was logically necessary, any more than it means that the creation was logically so.

The incarnation is the "projection"[31] of the eternal God. There is therefore no sense in talking of the eternal Son of God apart from the incarnation except to make the point that the incarnation was logically contingent. That is, there is no point to it if by this we mean there was a time when the eternal Son of God existed unincarnated. It is of course possible for us to *think* of the eternal Son of God as unincarnated, by an abstraction of thought, but that is a different matter. The point is, as Herbert McCabe says, there is no preexistent Christ with a life history independent of and prior to the incarnation. There was no time when the eternal God was not Jesus of Nazareth.[32] There is no other life story—story in time—of God than the story of the incarnation. There was no time when the Son of God was not willing himself to be incarnate, but only decided at a particular time to become incarnate in our history. God did not exist and then at some later point decide to become incarnate, for there is no change or succession possible in the timeless eternity of God's life.

---

[31]The word is used by Herbert McCabe in his stimulating discussion of the incarnation understood from an eternalist perspective in *God Matters* (London: Chapman, 1987), p. 48.
[32]Ibid., pp. 49-50.

The Son of God is conceptually or ontologically prior to the incarnate Jesus, but not temporally prior. He is conceptually prior because being the Son of God he is not created, and he took our flesh, in just the same way in which, though there was no time when the creation was not, God eternally willed the universe, and hence is logically and ontologically prior to the universe.

But could it not happen that Moses could say, "Jesus does not exist yet but the Son of God does"? And would this not give some sense to the idea that the Son of God exists before the incarnation? Not really. For as McCabe says, it is necessary to distinguish between saying "It is true now the Son of God exists" and saying "The Son of God exists now." There is no time at which the Son of God exists in a preincarnate form.[33]

The Two Standpoints

There is an inclination to confuse the standpoint of the Creator with that of the creature. From the Creator's standpoint his creation is a timeless whole, including, as it does, the incarnation. However, from the standpoint of an intelligent creature the universe may be thought to be coeternal with God, for there may be no time when the universe is not. For such a creature the universe unfolds as a temporal sequence and because such an agent is in time, he is able to represent the universe as having a past, a present and a future. As Augustine put it, "In the first instance, God made everything together without any moments of time intervening, but now He works within the course of time, by which we see the stars move from their rising to their setting."[34]

As paleographers and geologists and cosmologists investigate the past, they investigate past phases of what is (from the Creator's standpoint) the one creation. But from the divine standpoint the universe is one whole that exists by the eternal will of God.

We may elucidate this idea of the two standpoints, the divine and the human standpoints, by thinking of two physical standpoints. A building may be viewed from more than one standpoint—let us say, from the

---

[33]Ibid., p. 50.
[34]Augustine, quoted in E. McMullin, ed., *Evolution and Creation* (Notre Dame, Ind.: University of Notre Dame Press, 1985), p.10.

respective standpoints occupied by two individuals at the same time. But while any building must be viewed from some standpoint or other, such viewings are contingent in the sense that one viewer, *A*, could occupy the standpoint of another viewer, *B*, or vice versa, as well as the fact that there is an infinity of such standpoints.

In the case of temporal standpoints, the contingency is a little less obvious than in the case of space, because of the unidirectionality of time. It follows from the unidirectionality of time (and here I am ignoring the possibilities of retrocausation, time travel and suchlike) that what has happened cannot now not have happened. Someone living in 1994 could not now take up Napoleon's temporal standpoint (though he could view the pyramids, say, from exactly the same spatial standpoint as Napoleon did), and perhaps such a person could never have had Napoleon's standpoint (if, say, having a certain genetic history is essential to an individual's being the individual that he or she is).

The distinction between the eternal and the temporal standpoints is even more entrenched than that between two temporal standpoints, with even fewer elements of contingency, in that anyone who occupies a temporal standpoint occupies some definite temporal standpoint or other willy-nilly. If June 10 is now present, then June 11 could not now be present. And similarly an occupant of the eternal standpoint has no choice. If God is timelessly eternal then he is necessarily so, and he could not occupy any temporal standpoint, though in Christ he is united to a nature that necessarily does have some temporal standpoint. No temporal creature could be timelessly eternal. For to be a temporal creature is to have the possibility of changing, while to be timelessly eternal is necessarily not to change and so not to be able to change. So it is necessarily the case that God, if he is timelessly eternal, cannot translate his eternal standpoint into ours, nor can we, creatures of time, translate our various successive temporal standpoints into his.

Given these necessary truths, and given the reasonable supposition that any standpoint is either temporal or eternal, and that we exist in time and that God exists in timeless eternity, it would appear to follow that for such a theist there cannot be a standpointless truth of the matter about events and actions in time, any more than there can be standpointless truth of the matter about timeless eternity. The temporal order that is the created universe is necessarily to be understood either from a timeless standpoint, as a timeless God understands it, or from a temporal vantage point, as you and I understand it.

The contrast in the standpoints can be brought out starkly as follows. From our standpoint God's creation is continuously unfolding, a *creatio continua*. The state of the universe at time t_1 does not logically necessitate the character or even the existence of any phase at t_2 or later, even though there are discovered regularities between different past phases, and promised continuations of them, for as long as the created order persists. So from our perspective the Creator may be said to be continuously creating the universe, in that more universe has unfolded today than had yesterday, for the present builds on and is made intelligible by the past. But from the divine standpoint what is created is one temporally extended or ordered universe.

In *The View from Nowhere*[35] Thomas Nagel draws a contrast between two irreconcilable points of view, the external and the internal. Insofar as a person adopts an internal view she is a subject of experience, and what she learns about the world and does to the world (and what the world does to her) depends on the place and the time that she occupies in it. Were she to lose this perspective, she would lose her identity as a particular person. To take up an external view, the view from nowhere, she must depersonalize herself and strive to understand the world from no particular place or time, something she can do with only limited success, partly because it is logically impossible to act, even to think, within such a world.

I am suggesting something similar in the case of the Creator God and ourselves. Besides the externalism that Nagel draws attention to, and that we may fitfully strive to attain, there is, for the theist, the externalism of God's standpoint. We may even say that our objective, external way of understanding the world, insofar as we accurately discern it, approximates more closely God's standpoint vis-à-vis the material universe than does the internal way of understanding. Insofar as we understand the world, including ourselves, in this objective or external way, our thought approaches the shape of the thought possessed by God in his eternal vantage point.

God's is not the view from nowhere or nowhen, but the view from

[35]Thomas Nagel, *The View from Nowhere* (Oxford: Oxford University Press, 1986).

his own unique where and when, the "where" and "when" of timeless (and spaceless) eternity. For not only are we subjects, God is also a subject, with a unique epistemic and volitional standpoint, though he is not a subject of experience in quite the way that we are. God as a subject stands outside space and time and views his creatures in a manner that is best expressed by us (though not fully comprehended by us) in ways that are free from either temporal or spatial indexicals. God's view is not, of course, a literal viewing; nevertheless God has a unique perspective on the world, a perspective necessarily free of temporal and spatial indexicals. And so, saving the case of the incarnation, he does not take up the cognitive standpoint of any one of his creatures more than that of any other.

To understand the idea of two standpoints further, we may refer to two fundamentally distinct ways of referring to time, by treating it as either an A-series or a B-series. On the A-series view of time, time is to be understood from a point within the temporal series; thus expressions like *yesterday, today, now, then* are A-series expressions. One can refer to a particular day as yesterday only from a standpoint within time; if September 14 is yesterday, then today is September 15, and so on. On the B-series view time is to be understood from an atemporal perspective, by expressions such as *earlier than* and *later than, before* and *after.* Thus on the B-series view of time Napoleon's defeat at Waterloo is earlier than Field Marshall Bernard L. Montgomery's victory at El Alamein; the event of the Battle of Waterloo occurs before that of El Alamein. But Napoleon's victory is in the past only from the standpoint of someone who exists later than that date; and only in the future from the standpoint of someone who exists earlier than that date.

If God had created the temporal order as an A-series from his standpoint, then God would himself be in time. So it makes better sense for the eternalist to suppose that God created the temporal order as a B-series. From the divine standpoint no one moment of the series would be privileged by being present, but as regards presentness, pastness or futurity, all moments would be in exactly the same position, even though some moments would be earlier in relation to others in the series, some later. It is a temporal order, in which causal powers operate. And yet it is a B-series of a rather special kind, whose every moment is also eternally present to God.

Is this idea of two standpoints, a divine and a human standpoint, a case of having one's cake and eating it? I suggest not, for the following reason. It depends crucially on the idea of two different subjects, eternal God and temporal creatures, with two irreducibly different standpoints, and this enables us to give accounts of the world from the two standpoints which are complementary rather than contradictory.

Let us suppose that God eternally knows

(1) Helm is writing his paper on September 15, 1999,

and that I know both that

(2) I am now writing my paper today

and that

(3) Today is September 15, 1999.

Are the two states of affairs represented by 1 and 2, and by 3 respectively, contradictory or incompatible in some way? It is hard to see how they could be.

Divine Eternity and Human Spirituality

This chapter has developed and defended the idea of divine timeless eternity chiefly by attempting to respond to objections to it. I shall round off my discussion by considering an objection from a rather different quarter from those so far discussed.

We have seen that divine timeless eternity, based as it is on a particular intuition about divine fullness of being, entails divine impassibility. Such a timelessly eternal, impassible God is the object of a Christian's worship and devotion. It might be thought that given such a conception of God, the ideal for the Christian is to detach himself as far as possible from the world of change and to attach himself to the unchanging, impassible God—as far as possible, to be like God. Since God does not feel emotion, nor should we. Since God is unaffected by the vicissitudes of time, so should we be.

This is certainly one possibility. Let us suppose that a life free of emotional disturbance is to be desired, but that it is not to be desired in a situation in which there are legitimate objects of such disturbance. It is right to grieve when there are fitting objects of grief, right to fear when fear is appropriate, and so on. But just as we should strive for the objects of grief and fear to be removed, and so the grief and fear itself become inappropriate and eliminable, so we should not be content with spasms of joy and love but seek the displacement of such spasms by states of unalloyed joy and bliss.

This may be the most desirable ideal from a Christian point of view. Nevertheless, since in considering the timelessness and impassibility of God we are considering what is his necessarily, and our being in time and liable to change is a necessary truth about ourselves, it is surely inappropriate, even were it logically possible, that we should model ourselves on God to the extent of striving to be as free of change and disturbance of any kind as he is. The distinction between the eternal God and his time-bound creation remains.

But there is another possibility. For while it may be thought that divine timelessness, entailing as it does divine impassibility, presents to us a picture of God that is grotesque, one in which God remains unconcerned and unaffected by the miseries of humankind, this is to neglect the vital ingredient of spirituality as far as the Christian is concerned. For this impassible God is (as we noted earlier) eternally united with human nature in the person of Jesus Christ. It is here, in what Jesus came for, what he did and suffered and achieved, that the unchangeably glorious heart of God is shown and known. And according to this second possibility it is in knowing and striving to be like this Jesus that the moral and spiritual aspirations of men and women will find their true fulfillment.

RESPONSE TO PAUL HELM

ALAN G. PADGETT

*D*espite the seeming disagreement, there is much that I agree with in Paul Helm's chapter on God and time. I agree that the idea of atemporal eternity is the traditional view of God in Christian thought (although as Bill, Nick and I argue, it is not the biblical view). Further, I accept his basic intuition that God must in some way transcend time, and I attempt to spell out carefully the sense in which I am willing, against Nick, to see God's being as "beyond time."

However, on the view of "relative timelessness" I represent, it is still true that God has a life, and that God undergoes the passage of time from past to present to future. This troubles Paul. On such a viewpoint, "those bits of his life that he remembers are over." This is true, but why is it a problem? True, God does not possess the whole of his life together, that is, all at once. But such a notion is coherent only if God is absolutely timeless. Why is a historical life any less "perfect" than a timeless, changeless "life" that is not lived out in time? Is not the absolute changelessness of the traditional view just as problematic as the historical life God lives in relative timelessness? Is not this God in a box, a changeless Being that "lives" only in a very stretched sense of the word? The "life" of a changeless, atemporal being is lived only in the "space" of logical order, not in real time. Is this not also a problem? Does this kind of God seem anything like the biblical God?

There are two points where Paul does misunderstand the viewpoint I defend. He notes that, on such a view, "God is subject to the vicissitudes of temporal passage, with more and more of his life irretrievably over and done with." While I agree that God's life undergoes temporal passage, I deny that God is in any way subject to the "vicissitudes" of temporal passage. *Vicissitude* is a negative term for change, and I deny that God changes in his basic attributes, those essential characteristics that he holds as divine Being. God is immutable in nature (viz., essential properties), I would argue. God changes only in real relation to ourselves—that is, in the kinds of actions he carries out at different times. Such action and the changes it brings are not imperfections, but rather the perfection of a loving Creator.

Second, it is not the case that more and more of the life of an infinite, eternal God is over and done with. God's time is infinite and immeasurable. At every moment of time there is an *unlimited* (nonfinite) past eternity. The addition of one more day does not increase the length of God's past, since God has lived forever!

The real place where Paul and I disagree is in the philosophy of time. It becomes clear at the end of his chapter that Paul relies on the stasis (tenseless or B) theory of time for the coherence of his viewpoint. I have argued that this philosophy of time is dubious and we have no real reason within the philosophy of science to embrace it. Here is the real place where he and I would disagree. Interestingly, our disagreement does not take place in the discipline of theology, but rather in philosophy, specifically the philosophy of science and of time. I discuss this disagreement more fully in my own chapter and in other books, and see no reason to rehearse this discussion here. It is in fact so complicated that it takes a good, long chapter just to review it.

I find Paul's traditional notion of divine eternal action at bottom incoherent. But this is not because it is incoherent in itself. Rather, it is incoherent with the process (tensed, or A) theory of time, which I believe is true on grounds outside of theology and the philosophy of religion.

RESPONSE TO PAUL HELM

WILLIAM LANE CRAIG

S ince I myself believe that God, existing alone without creation, is time-less, and since I have said that Paul Helm is the one defender of divine timelessness who has consistently defended that doctrine against objections by appealing to the static theory of time, it is not surprising that I find much to agree with in Paul's essay. Let me focus on a few points of contention.

Argument from the Incompleteness of Temporal Life

Paul rightly sees the argument from divine fullness as the most powerful consideration in support of God's atemporality. But he fails to see the import of the distinction between static and dynamic views of time for this particular argument. For it is only on a dynamic view of time that it is true to say of a temporal God that there are segments of his life that are objectively "over and done with." For as A. N. Prior showed,[1] the notion of "being over" is inherently a tensed notion, which on a static theory of time corre-sponds to no objective reality. On a static theory of time, earlier segments in

---

[1]A. N. Prior, "Thank Goodness That's Over," *Philosophy* 34 (1959): 12-17.

the life of a temporal deity are over only in his subjective experience. The argument, then, is essentially experiential: a perfect being must *experience* his life all at once. But then considerations of divine omniscience mitigate the argument's force. It is not so obvious that a being with perfect recall and complete foreknowledge must experience his life all at once. Still, I agree that the argument could justifiably motivate a doctrine of divine timelessness were it not for more powerful arguments on the other side.

Argument from God's Knowledge of Tensed Facts

The only way to beat the argument from God's knowledge of tensed facts is to adopt a static theory of time and thus deny that there are any tensed facts. This Paul does. But he also attempts to turn the tables by asserting that the defender of divine temporality "may find it necessary to qualify the strictest understanding of divine omniscience" too, because divine foreknowledge may be incompatible with human freedom. An adequate discussion of this issue would require another book, but suffice it to say that such arguments for fatalism have been rejected as fallacious not only by most philosophers of religion but also by philosophers working in fields where analogous fatalistic arguments have been broached.[2] Paul also alleges that "if God is in time, then there are also types of propositions that such a temporal God cannot know—propositions that express knowledge of the universe from the perspective of timeless eternity." I deny the parallel. A timeless being cannot be coherently said to know tensed truths, but there is no incoherence in a temporal being's knowing tenseless truths (like "The Battle of Hastings is earlier than the Battle of Waterloo" or "2 + 2 = 4"). Indeed, a being who knows all tensed truths *must* know such tenseless truths, since he must know of any tenselessly true proposition P that "P presently has the property of being true" or "Truth presently inheres in P."

Paul also alleges that God cannot know such facts as "I am Paul Helm." Even if this allegation were correct, however, it hardly justifies further attenuating God's omniscience by denying him knowledge of tensed facts as well! But the vast majority of philosophers do not think that the difference between knowing "I am Paul Helm" and knowing "He is Paul Helm"

---

[2]See William Lane Craig, *The Only Wise God* (reprint, Eugene, Ore.: Wipf & Stock, 2000).

is a matter of differing propositional content (in terms of which omni-science is usually defined). These sentences express the same proposi-tional content but are differently grasped by or presented to different persons. Moreover, if God were to hold the belief "I am Paul Helm," it would impugn rather than enhance his omniscience; but just the opposite is the case for tensed facts. Paul suggests that knowledge of tensed truths is also nonpropositional (like knowledge how to ___ rather than knowl-edge that ___). But even if we agree that indexical elements in a sentence like *I, now* and *here* merely reflect the subjective perspective of the speaker, it is not so easy to dismiss the verbal tense of a sentence as carry-ing no propositional content. In any case, a person who has maximum cognitive excellence as God does cannot plausibly be ignorant of what is presently going on in the universe. Thus, if time is dynamic, God must know tensed facts, however these are construed.

Argument from God's Real Relation to the World

Paul's commitment to a static theory of time emerges most clearly in his response to the argument from God's real relation to the world. His response also serves to expose the theological inadequacy of the static theory with respect to the doctrine of creation. Paul agrees that if the creation of the world is a temporal event, then God must be in time. He is therefore led to deny that the creation of the world is a temporal event. Paul does not mean thereby that the big bang event at $t = 0$ was not a temporal event; rather he means to deny that there ever was any event of God's bringing the universe into being at all. The picture of God existing alone without the universe and bringing the universe into existence at $t = 0$ presupposes the reality of temporal becoming and thus a dynamic theory of time. But on the static theory, God and the universe are coeternal; even the incarnation of the second person of the Trinity is an unchanging state. The four-dimensional space-time universe is tem-poral only in the sense that one of its internal dimensions is time; extrin-sically it exists as timelessly as God. Creation is reduced to the ontological dependence of the universe on God.

I claim that this leaves us with an emasculated doctrine of *creatio ex nihilo*. A robust doctrine of creation involves both the affirmation that God brought the universe into being out of nothing at some moment in the finite past and the affirmation that he thereafter sustains it in being moment by moment.[3] Now the static-time theorist can make the first affirmation only ingenuously. For him *creatio ex nihilo* means only that the world depends immediately on God for its existence at every moment. The static-time theorist's affirmation that God brought the universe into being out of nothing at some moment in the finite past can at best mean that there is (tenselessly) a moment that is separated from any other moment by a finite interval of time and before which no moment of comparable duration exists and that whatever exists at any moment, including the moments themselves, is tenselessly sustained in being immediately by God. All this adds to the doctrine of ontological dependence is that the tenselessly existing block universe has a front edge. It has a beginning only in the sense that a yardstick has a beginning. There is in the actual world no state of affairs of God existing alone without the space-time universe. God never really brings the universe into being; as a whole it coexists timelessly with him.

Such an emasculated doctrine of *creatio ex nihilo* does not do justice to the biblical data, which give us clearly to understand that God and the universe do not timelessly coexist but that the actual world includes a state of affairs that is God's existing alone without the universe. Typically such a state is described in the ordinary language of the biblical authors as obtaining "before" the world began (Jn 17:24; Eph 1:4; 1 Pet 1:20; cf. Mt 13:35; 24:21; 25:34; Lk 11:50; Heb 9:6; Jude 25; Rev 13:8; 17:8). The notion that God and the universe timelessly coexist in an asymmetrical relation of ontological dependence is not only foreign to but actually incompatible with the biblical writers' conception of *creatio ex nihilo*, of God's existing alone and bringing the world into being out of nothing.

Not only so, but the idea that God and creation tenselessly coexist seems to negate God's triumph over evil. On the static theory of time, evil is never really vanquished from the world: it exists just as sturdily as ever at its various locations in space-time, even if those locations are all earlier than some point in cosmic time (for example, judgment day). Creation is never really purged of evil on this view; at most it can be said that evil infects only those parts of creation that are earlier than cer-

---

[3]For more on this distinction, see William Lane Craig, "Creation and Conservation Once More," *Religious Studies* 34 (1998): 177-88.

tain other events. But the stain is indelible. What this implies for events like the crucifixion and resurrection of Christ is very troubling. In a sense Christ hangs permanently on the cross, for the dreadful events of A.D. 30 never fade away or transpire. The victory of the resurrection becomes a hollow triumph, for the spatiotemporal parts of Jesus that were crucified and buried remain dying and dead and are never raised to new life. It is unclear how we can say, "Death has been swallowed up in victory" (1 Cor 15:54) when death is never really done away with on a static theory of time.

A robust doctrine of creation, then, involves more than just the tenseless ontological dependence of the world on God. It involves the affirmation that God brings it about that the world comes into being at some time t. Something comes into being at a time t if and only if the following three conditions are met: (i) the thing exists at t, (ii) t is the first time at which the thing exists, and (iii) the thing's existing at t is a tensed fact.[4] The static-time theorist cannot affirm that the world came into being at the first moment of its existence and therefore cannot affirm that God created the world in the full sense of the word *create*. It seems to me, therefore, that a robust doctrine of creation requires a dynamic theory of time.

The Two Standpoints

I have understood Paul to be advocating a static theory of time. But as a result of what he writes about the two standpoints, I wonder if I have correctly understood him. When he says that from God's standpoint time is a B-series, but from our standpoint time is an A-series, does he mean that time *appears* to us as an A-series or that it really *is* an A-series? The former is uncontroversial; but if he means the latter, how can this be the case? The states of affairs described by his 1, 2 and 3 definitely are incompatible if we try to combine them by saying that the members of the B-series of events are all equally real (static-time theory) and that the property of presentness moves along the series (dynamic-time theory), as J. M. E. McTaggart showed.[5] So how can both standpoints be correct?

---

[4]If God can re-create things, then we would have to add to condition (ii) "or t is preceded by a time at which the thing did not exist."

[5]See William Lane Craig, "McTaggart's Paradox and the Problem of Temporary Intrinsics," *Analysis* 58 (1998): 122-27.

Is not God's standpoint privileged? If there really are tensed truths, must not God know them? How can these two incommensurable standpoints be united in one reality? Would not God from our standpoint exist temporally? I ask for clarification of Paul's two standpoints doctrine.

RESPONSE TO PAUL HELM

NICHOLAS WOLTERSTORFF

*P*aul Helm's argument for God's timelessness is that it would be incompatible with the fullness of God's life for God to be in time. What's characteristic of those of us who live in time is that there are experiences we have had that are over, "irretrievably over and done with." We cannot "live them again." We may remember them with greater or lesser vividness. But as experiences, they are "forever lost." This is not an accidental feature of experience in time; it belongs to its essence. Of course certain experiences endure for a while. But for us human beings, who must sleep, no experience lasts all that long; all of them are rather quickly over. And if there be persons who need no sleep and for whom, accordingly, experiences can in principle last a long time, it will still be the case, even for enduring experiences, that parts of them will be over and forever lost. So once again: intrinsic to the experience of a person in time is that, at any moment in that person's life, many of her life's experiences have this quality of irrevocable overness. Such irrevocable overness, so Paul argues, is incompatible with the fullness of God's life and experience. So it must be that God is outside of time.

Before I say anything about the substance of this argument, let me make a few comments about its form. Where does this concept of *the fullness of life* come from, according to which, at least as Paul sees it, one's having had an experience that's over is incompatible with enjoying fullness of life? And why should we accept the thesis that God's life is necessarily full in that sense? Paul remarks that "those who defend the idea of divine timeless eternity appeal to an intuition about the divine fullness and self-sufficiency." What epistemological status does this "intuition" have?

Let's recall the "dialectic" of the argument, as I describe it at the beginning of my own essay. Scripture pervasively represents God as having a history of action, knowledge and response. The eternalist argues that Scripture's representation of God as having a history must not be taken as literally true. The person who accepts Scripture as canonical will concede, in advance, that the eternalist might just possibly have good reasons for this view; after all, everybody who accepts Scripture as canonical thinks that certain aspects of how Scripture represents God should not be taken as literally true. However, the burden of proof lies on the eternalist; in general it's the case, if one takes Scripture as canonical, that the burden of proof lies on the person who holds that in some particular respect Scripture's representation of God is not to be taken as literally true. The relevant question, then, is whether Paul's argument for eternalism bears the burden of proof.

I asked what is the epistemological status of Paul's intuition, that God's life is necessarily of that sort of fullness which is inherently incompatible with having had experiences, or parts of experiences, that are over. Paul does not reply that the proposition in question is a self-evident truth. As indeed it surely isn't. It's not one of those propositions that a person cannot grasp without seeing it to be true and believing it; I, for one, grasp it without believing it. Neither does Paul hold that the thesis is affirmed in Scripture; indeed, he thinks it's not even implied by what's affirmed in Scripture. He remarks that "it would be unwise for the eternalist to claim that divine timeless eternity is *entailed* by the language of Scripture."

Rather, what Paul claims for eternalism is that, in the first place, it is "consistent with the biblical data about God and time"; and second, that it helps "to summarize and epitomize the thought of the canonical writers in ways that, because of their situation, they were not able to do themselves" and helps "to rule out certain types of inferences about God that are unscriptural." Scripture itself is "underdetermined" on the issue of eternalism versus temporalism; its language "about God and time is not sufficiently precise so as to provide a definitive resolution of the issue one way or the other."

One thing that puzzles me here is the following: given his argument for eternalism from the fullness of the divine life, one would expect Paul to say that one way to arrive at a synoptic interpretation of Scripture that fits the biblical data without being compelled by them is to affirm the thesis that God's life is *maximally full;* what he says instead is that one way to arrive at such an interpretation is to affirm the thesis that God is *timeless.* His argument leads one to expect him to discuss what Scripture has to say about the *excellence* of God; in fact he discusses not that but what Scripture has to say about the *temporality* of God.

What perplexes me even more, however, is how little Paul claims concerning the epistemological status of his core thesis. He claims that the thesis, that God is timeless, is a component in a synoptic interpretation of the biblical data which fits those data without being compelled by them. This leaves open the possibility that an interpretation incorporating the thesis that God is in time fits the data at least as well. But if all that's to be said in favor of the eternalist interpretation is that it fits the biblical data, leaving open the possibility that temporalist interpretations do so at least as well, then surely we should reject the eternalist interpretation; for then the eternalist has not succeeded in bearing the burden of proof against taking as literally true Scripture's representation of God as having a history.

Even more important than these two considerations is the following, however: one of the biblical "data" we have to take account of is the pervasive representation of God as having a history. The issue is whether we are to take that representation as literally true or not. Paul remarks that "the biblical data are consistent with eternalism." But in saying this, what does he take "the data" to be? Scripture's representation of God as having a history? the *literal truth* of Scripture's representation of God as having a history? the *metaphorical truth* of Scripture's representation of God as having a history? I don't see that it is at all helpful here to think of the biblical data as underdetermined with respect to the issue before us, and to try accordingly to find an interpretation that, while not compelled by the data, nonetheless fits the data. The dispute is over what we take the data to be.

Late in his essay Paul discusses an issue that, though it seems to me important for eternalists to confront, is nevertheless neglected by almost all of them. He asks (this is my way of putting it) why it is that Scripture represents God as having a history when God in fact has none. Why does Scripture use this metaphorical mode? His answer is that "if dialogue between God and humankind is to be real and not make-believe, then God cannot represent himself (in his role as dialogue partner) as wholly immutable, for then dialogue, real dialogue, would be impossible. His purposes for his people on whose behalf he intervenes in time cannot be expressed in fully immutable fashion. The language of change in God is not for rhetorical or ornamental effect, therefore, but its use takes us to the heart of biblical religion."

I find this an interesting, though ultimately baffling, answer to the question. I understand Paul to be saying that "dialogue, real dialogue," is impossible between two persons unless both are mutable; if one is not capable of change, then it's only "make-believe" dialogue that can take place between them, not "real" dialogue. If we now add to this thesis about dialogue—which seems to me eminently correct—Paul's thesis that God is immutable, then it follows that, on Paul's view, there can be no genuine dialogue between God and human beings. Nonetheless— this seems to be his view—it was indispensable to God's achievement of "his purposes for his people on whose behalf he intervenes in time" that the people *believe* that they were engaged in genuine dialogue with God.

Now I find it troubling to suppose that God engaged in deception of this sort. But what I find baffling is this: Paul and his fellow eternalists claim, as it were, to have seen through the deception; they have seen that God cannot change and that, accordingly, there cannot be real, genuine dialogue between God and human beings. But if it is important, or even essential, to God's accomplishment of his purposes that we *believe* we can engage in genuine dialogue with God, what happened to God's purposes when, until our own time, almost the entire theological tradition held that God is immutable? In all likelihood I'm missing something in Paul's thought here. He can hardly be saying that God's purposes cannot be achieved when human beings believe that God is immutable—and hence incapable of genuine dialogue!

All this pertains, more or less directly, to the form of Paul's argument. Let me conclude my scrutiny of his argument in favor of eternalism with a comment on its substance. The point I wish to make here is one I also make in my response to something that Bill Craig says in his essay.

What would be required for my life to be lacking in any experience that has the quality of irrevocable overness? It would at least have to be totally devoid of change. Would it also have to be momentary? Strictly speaking, yes. For if it were not momentary, then a segment of it would be over at a certain time. I do not suppose, however, that those who think that the overness of some experience or segment thereof is incompatible with maximal fullness of life would be bothered by such overness. Suppose my experience is confined to that of seeing an unaltering patch of vivid green. Yes; after ten minutes of this the first ten minutes would be over—irrevocably, irretrievably and all of that. But since my experience would continue to be more of exactly the same, surely there would be no cause for lament in the fact that the experience of the first ten minutes was forever "lost."

Now why would anyone imagine that unchanging experience, be it momentary or durational, is a more excellent form of life—or if you will, fuller—than that which I do experience? Consider how little of what we actually experience could be gotten into a changeless state. Watching my children grow up would be something I could not experience, listening to a piece of music would be something I could not experience, walking through Hagia Sophia so as to see it from a variety of different angles would be something I could not experience, building a piece of furniture or designing a house would be something I could not experience; and so forth, on and on. To me it seems just bizarre to suppose that such a life would be more excellent, more full. It seems, on the contrary, appallingly impoverished. Were I offered such a life as an option, I would reject it out of hand. Change, and the changing experience of change, makes possible a fullness in the totality of one's life experiences that would be impossible without change. One cannot possibly pack all that's rich and excellent in experience into one unchanging state; it needs to be strung out over time. In short, Paul's argument for God's timelessness has, on me, no "tug" whatsoever.

Let me move on to some reflections on Paul's response to certain of the fairly standard objections to the eternalist view. Here's a problem for the eternalist. Suppose that God exists at some time x and also exists at some time y. And now suppose, in addition, that x precedes y. Then, on the assumption that God does not go out of and come back into existence, God endures from x to y, and that establishes that God is in time. On the other hand, if God does not endure, then x and y must be the same time. But that would imply that if God exists now, then God did not also exist yesterday—since yesterday is not the same time as today. The only way out for the eternalist would seem to be to deny that God exists at any time; for any time whatsoever, it's not the case that God exists at that time.

Now let's consider that thesis: never is it true to say that God now exists; always the true thing to say is that it's not the case that God now exists. Why isn't that just atheism?

The eternalist might reply that the reason it's not just atheism is that, though he agrees with the atheist that it's never true to say "God now exists," he disagrees in holding that it's nonetheless always true to say, "God exists." "God doesn't exist now; but it's nonetheless now true that God exists": that's always the true thing to say.

All attempts on my part to understand this proposal in such a way that it comes out true have failed. To me it seems that for an entity to exist "at" a time just is for it to be true at that time that the entity exists. So I conclude that eternalism is incoherent. The well-known attempt by Stump and Kretzmann to escape the difficulty with their concept of ET-simultaneity seems to me to fail—for roughly the reasons Paul cites.

Paul's own proposal, as I understand it, is to concede the incoherence but to insist that it doesn't really matter. We should see ourselves as engaging here in negative theology. Why should we suppose that "human analogies and models will throw much light" on what divine eternality is *positively* like? Why should we suppose that "we can imagine what existing in such a timeless fashion must be like"? Why should we insist that being able to imagine what it's like is a condition of conceding that God's life is indeed timeless?

This response seems to me not to the point. The source of the difficulty over simultaneity is not our inability to imagine a timeless life; the source of the difficulty is our inability to understand how it could be false that God exists now while it's nonetheless now true that God exists.

Apart from some brief comments on the relation of eternity to impassibility, the other objection to timelessness to which Paul devotes some attention is that timelessness is incompatible with omniscience; more specifically, if God were timeless, God could not have knowledge of tensed states of affairs. I develop this argument against timelessness in my essay in this collection.

Paul holds that the distinction between past, present and future is not an objective feature of time; there are no objective tensed states of affairs. Though perhaps it's not entirely clear from his essay in this collection that this is his position (until very near the end), it is abundantly clear from his book *Eternal God*. Paul's view in this present essay seems to be that even though there are no objective tensed states or affairs or propositions, it may nonetheless well be true that there are true propositions that we each express with tensed sentences that God cannot know. As I read him, he does not want, on this occasion, to take a position one way or the other on this matter. Rather, his argument is that even if this is the case, nothing alarming follows.

One point he makes is this:

> God may nevertheless know sufficient to enable him infallibly to deduce the occurrence of all true indexical expressions about time. . . . He does not know that 1999 is now for him, because it isn't. But he knows all the times when each of us make true utterances such as "It is now . . ." and he knows that whenever in 1999 we say "It is now 1999" we are speaking the truth. So God can know that "It is now 1999" is true for us whenever in that year it is uttered, and he knows when it is uttered, for he knows that it is uttered at some particular time during 1999.

This seems to me not true. If God didn't know last year (I am writing this in the year 2000), that the year then present was 1999, how could God know that whenever we said, last year, "It is now 1999," we were speaking the truth? If I have no idea which year is the present year—and no idea, accordingly, as to which year was last year, which year is next year and so on—then I have no way of knowing whether when someone says "The present year is 2000" they are speaking truth. Of course the person who doesn't know which year is the present year does know that by assertively uttering the sentence "This present year is 1999," one asserts something true if and only if this present year is 1999. But that's not enough to know the truth of the assertion; one also has to know whether 1999 *is in fact the present year.*

Paul's other point is that even if this is true, nothing of any significance follows. The temporalist too is likely to hold that there are true propositions that God does not know. It is "plausible to suppose," he says, "that each of us has unique knowledge of ourselves—call it 'me-ness.' I know that it is I who is typing this paper. You can know that it is Paul Helm who is typing, but you cannot know that fact as I know it; and similarly with you; and similarly with God's knowledge of me." I think this is an interesting and important point, and true. But I do not think that God's ignorance of all tensed propositions would be as bland and insignificant a fact about God as Paul here suggests it would be.

If God never had any idea what's happening *then,* then God could not respond to what happens in human affairs; for God to respond to Moses' protestation that he was no good at public speaking, God would have to know when Moses was presently making that protest. Paul rejects the charge that eternalism is "a form of deism according to which such a God may timelessly create the entire temporal order and all that it contains but not be able to act within it." He insists that "not only may such a God act within time but he may also be said to act in response to what happens in time." It seems to me, on the contrary, that if the eternalist view were correct, then God would not respond to what happens in time, and that the way God acts within time would simply be the way that deists have always held that God acts within time. I see the crux of the debate as located at this point: An eternalist God is necessarily a deistlike God.

Think of God's action in the world, says Paul, on the model of one of us setting the timer on our central heating system. As the result of my one act of setting the timer, the system may go on at 7:00 in the morning, go off again at 10:30 in the evening, day after day. Let us add that the system has a thermostat that I set at 65 degrees Fahrenheit—so that when the system is on during the day, if the temperature dips a bit below 65 in the room the furnace will light, and if it gets a bit above 65 degrees the flame will go out.

I agree that this is a rather good model of how the eternalist thinks of God's action vis-à-vis the world. So let us ask, first, whether on the model I *respond* to the time of day or the temperature in the room. It seems to me obvious that I do not. I program the *timer* so that *it* responds to the time of day, and I program the *thermostat* so that *it* responds to the temperature in the room. That is to say: I program the timer so that *it* responds to the event, on Thursday, of it's becoming 7:00 in the morning, and I program the thermostat so that *it* responds to all events, during the day, of its becoming a bit cooler or a bit warmer than 65 degrees. But I myself don't respond to those events. Probably a good many of them I don't even know about. And in any case, when I set the timer and the thermostat, those events hadn't even occurred yet; they weren't available for responding to. If I walk into the room, find it too cool for my taste and turn the thermostat up to 70 degrees, *then* I respond to the actual event of its being 65 degrees.

And what's to be said concerning my action regarding the temperature in the room some time after I have set the timer and thermostat—a week later, let's say? Can it be said that *I* turned the system on at 7:00 in the morning? Can it be said that *I* turned the flame on at 2:10 in the afternoon? I think we would all find this an odd, if not downright misleading, way of speaking. What can be said is that a week earlier I did something that brings it about that now the system goes on and the flame lights. Suppose we make use here of the concept, common in action theory, of a *basic action:* a basic action is an action one brings about without bringing it about by bringing about some other distinct action. I performed some basic actions a week earlier when I programmed the timer and the thermostat; but those are the last basic actions I performed relative to the heat in the room. Having performed those then, I may well have gone off on vacation.

On the eternalist's picture of God's action in the world, God in eternity formulates a plan for world history, initiates the first stage of the plan and then watches the scroll unroll. God does not respond to the actual events of history any more than I respond to the actual events of temperature fluctuation when I set the thermostat in advance. And the only basic actions God performs are whatever basic actions are necessary for instituting the first stage in cosmic history. After that, God acts "in" history only in the sense that I act "in" my room by doing something a week before which has the consequence that now the flame turns on at 2:10.

I do not suppose I have to argue that in Scripture God is represented as acting in a very different way: as responding to the actual events of history and as intervening with ever new "basic actions." Thus I do not see that Paul, or any other eternalist, has succeeded in bearing the burden of proof that, within the Christian community, is laid on those who think this biblical representation of God should not be taken as literally true.

RESPONSE TO CRITICS

PAUL HELM

I shall try to respond to the comments of my fellow participants by taking up three or four issues that particularly Nick and Bill raise. In doing this I hope I may also allay some of Alan's concerns that the view that God exists in timelessly eternal fashion is incoherent.

The Idea of Dialogue and of Two Standpoints

Nick finds the account of dialogue that I (briefly) offer baffling, and Bill asks for clarification of the idea of the two standpoints. On the eternalist view, in revealing his will God must accommodate himself to human spatiotemporal conditions by the use of sensory, figurative, anthropomorphic language about himself, particularly by using the language of change. So at the heart of the idea of divine accommodation is a logical point: it is a logically necessary condition of God's dialogue with his creatures that the divine dialogue partner must recognize that such creatures must act and react in time. If dialogue is to be real and not make-believe, then God cannot represent himself to such creatures by only revealing one immutable thing, for then dialogue, real dialogue, would be impossible.

Suppose that God wishes to convey some truth about himself to his creatures existing in space and time—in particular, some truth about his relation to them, seeking in doing so to elicit a response from them. Suppose that he wishes to test his people in some way. Then it would seem that he is bound to represent to his creatures his will about this matter in the only terms that will serve as a test to them, in terms of sequential divine action in space and time, and not to disclose his purposes for them all at once. So God must accommodate himself in these ways if he is faithfully to represent his intentions to humankind and carry out his intended purposes on their behalf. The "must" here is an ontological or metaphysical "must." Given the metaphysical distinction between changeless Creator and the changing creature, there is nothing else for it but that God represent himself to them in such ways if, in dialogue with them, he seeks to test them or to instruct them. A person could not be tested if God were to disclose to him the outcome of the test before it occurred.

Despite all this, one may still be left with the nagging feeling that given the idea of divine accommodation, the divine action and reaction in the world which the Scriptures recount is only shadow action, and that the real action, or the real inaction, is God's immutable will for his people. It is all very well to invoke the idea of divine accommodation, but does God really change his mind, or not?

To try to answer this question let us take a concrete case, the story of Hezekiah's sickness and recovery (Is 38). The Lord tells Hezekiah that he will die and then, in answer to a prayer from Hezekiah about this, promises recovery. Here is a case not simply of God's apparently changing his mind, but of his apparently changing his mind having implied that he will not change his mind. What are we to make of this? Can this be made consistent with what the Bible elsewhere says about God's immutability and steadfastness? If God is steadfast, how could God's first utterance, that Hezekiah will not recover, be sincere?

Does Hezekiah have to believe what (for the eternalist) is false, that God is capable of changing his mind? No, there would be nothing to stop Hezekiah from believing the following: *Either God has eternally decreed my death imminently, or he has eternally decreed that I will live for I don't know how many further years, if I pray to him and mend my ways.* And because Hezekiah does not know which of these (and indeed of other) possible outcomes has in fact been decreed, and because he (naturally enough) wishes to live longer, he prays accordingly. What Hezekiah's story does require, however, if he is genuinely to enter into dialogue with God on the matter, is that he believes that what God says on one occasion is not necessarily a *full* account of what God has decreed. And maybe Hezekiah recognizes that one rationale for this partial disclosure of his mind is that God wishes to bring about certain changes in the lives of his time-bound and space-bound creatures, perhaps (as in the case of Hezekiah himself) to put them to the test. So there is no need for Hezekiah to believe that God changes, only that there may be a certain dislocation between what God has willed in total and what he says he has willed as the dialogue unfolds, and that there may be a sufficient reason for this dislocation.

But does not Hezekiah react to God's word to him supposing that God may change? Is this not the only supposition on which his reaction to what God says makes sense? If so, how can this supposition be an appropriate one if (as eternalists aver) God does not and indeed cannot change? Let us try to examine why and how it is that sometimes our language about God is changeful even if God is necessarily changeless. Suppose that at t_1 God announces A, which X notices at t_1 and that at t_2 he announces not-A, which X notices at t_2. Then from the point of view of this cognizer of A and then not-A, there is a change, in precisely the same sense in which a human person may be said to have changed her mind if she sincerely declares she believes A at t_1 and then sincerely declares that she believes that not-A at t_2. That is, over the period of time in question God is perceived to have willed what, had this been a human action, would make it reasonable to say that the person in question has changed her mind. And this is because what has been successively announced by God is truly though perhaps rather loosely expressible in contrary or contradictory terms. It is *loosely* expressible in such ways because these loose ways of speaking omit the temporal indexing of God's actions. One can temporally index God's announcements, just as one can index human actions, and so account for the language in which change is asserted, by highlighting the fact that the successive announcements are indeed successive; each of them possesses a different temporal index. By temporally indexing the divine announcements to Hezekiah, one can see that announcing A to

Hezekiah at t_1 and announcing not-A to Hezekiah at t_2 is not necessarily contradictory even though the utterance at t_1 is a formal contradiction of the utterance at t_2. Furthermore, with the recognition that God might eternally will both the announcement of A at t_1 and of not-A at t_2 one can see that such successive announcements do not even require a real change in the will of God.

So if God eternally decrees the recovery of Hezekiah at t_2, having eternally decreed to announce his death at t_1, then God has not changed (since, we might suppose, his eternal will was to bring about the recovery of Hezekiah through both the announcement and the recovery), and his announcement that Hezekiah will die and then that he will live can be expressed as component parts of one eternal will. Putting the point even more fully, what God in fact decreed (it emerges) was not the recovery of Hezekiah but the recovery of Hezekiah *upon request,* the request being a component part of the entire decree, for the eliciting of which the original sentence of death was announced. Having said all that, it is nevertheless natural, unpedantic and economical in thought to think and talk as if God changes, to use the language of accommodation.

So while one reason for the use of accommodated language is for God to be able to interact with his creatures in temporal sequence, another part of the explanation, though a subsidiary one, is the desire for economy in expression, as when we utter falsehoods such as "The sun has moved behind the clouds, so it'll be cooler in the garden now." We might ask what truth is communicated by the manifestly false claim that the sun has just moved behind the clouds. But the answer is obvious, isn't it? Are we deceived by such language?

In summary, while the justification for using the language of accommodation is partly pedagogical, the Lord's speaking to his people in vivid and unpedantic ways, at the center of the idea is a logical or metaphysical point. It is a logically necessary condition of dialogue between people, or between God and humankind, that the partners in the dialogue should appear to act and react in time. If dialogue with God is to be real dialogue, then God's language cannot be restricted to characterizing himself and his will in eternal and immutable fashion; though his accommodation is certainly not inconsistent with God's being eternal and immutable, he must accommodate himself to speak in ways that are characteristic of, and essential to, persons in dialogue with each other.

And behind this logical point is the fundamental fact of theism, that whatever God's essential properties are, whether he is timelessly eternal or in time, he has not chosen any of them, nor has anyone else chosen them for him. So if God is (as a matter of brute fact) timelessly eternal, and if he wills to create a world of creatures in time and to teach them by *(inter alia)* testing them, then he must represent himself to them in such a way that it is natural for them to think of him as changing even though (strictly speaking) he does not change and even though those who are in time can see, on reflection, that he does not change.

Nick is also baffled by the fact that I and my fellow eternalists claim to have seen through God's deception in using the language of change about himself. But as we have just seen, God is not deceiving us; he is certainly not intending to deceive us, and we need not as a matter of fact be deceived. On an eternalist reading of the story of Hezekiah, the king would be being deceived only if he believed that God's announcement that he would die was unconditional. But why need Hezekiah believe this?

But then Nick says something that for once I'm not sure that I understand. "What happened," he says, "to God's purposes when, until our own time, almost the entire theological tradition held that God is immutable?" If he means to suggest that the tradition of ascribing to God timeless eternality had no place for a positive account of dialogue, then I think that this is a mistake. While almost the entire theological tradition held that God is (timelessly) immutable, Christian thinkers also believed that (in some sense) God engages in dialogue with his people, as can be seen, for example, in the way the notion of accommodation has been used down the ages.[1]

Christian thought about God and the world must always reckon with the standpoints of the transcendent Creator and of the time-bound and space-bound creature. Bill is bothered by this because he thinks that it may be inconsistent for a B-theorist such as myself to introduce such

---

[1]For an account of this tradition see Stephen D. Benin, *The Footprints of God: Divine Accommodation in Jewish and Christian Thought* (Albany: State University of New York Press, 1993).

standpoints. But it is evident that it is perfectly consistent with the B-theory of time that agents employ temporal indexicals in their action on and reaction to their world. This represents and expresses their temporal standpoint. B-theorists proceed to affirm that this is not, ontologically speaking, the most basic standpoint, but nonetheless they recognize that the use of temporal indexical language is vital for the agency of someone who is in time. When eternalists invoke the idea of divine accommodation, it is to cater to the fact that God condescends to speak in terms that creatures who employ such indexical language, creatures with a time-bound and a space-bound standpoint, require if they are to respond appropriately.

God, Creation and Conservation (with a Remark on Evil)

Bill is also concerned with what he thinks is the theological inadequacy of the static theory of time with respect to the doctrine of creation. The eternalist cannot have a "robust" doctrine of creation because he cannot say that God brought the universe into being at some moment in the finite past and affirm that he thereafter sustains it moment by moment.

Bill is not quite correct when he says that "Paul agrees that if the creation of the world is a temporal event, then God must be in time." In the paper I deliberately oscillate between the views that the universe has a first temporal moment and that it is timelessly eternal. Each seems to me to be compatible with eternalism. If, for example, the world had a first temporal moment, then God could have eternally willed this, for he can eternally will a first moment of time just as he can eternally will events in time. And since there cannot have been a moment before the first temporal moment, there was no time before that moment for God to exist in. So I do not hold that if the first moment of the creation of the world is a temporal event then God is in time, for that moment could be the first moment of time.

But let us continue to suppose that the universe is sempiternal, at least backwardly everlasting; we certainly shan't make things any easier for the eternalist if we do so. If one were persuaded of the merits of an account of the creation of the universe which was consistent with the universe's having always existed, and that the "beginning" of Genesis 1:1 referred not to a beginning in time but merely to the idea of the divine causal origin of the universe, then the expression "In the beginning God created the heavens and the earth" would be equivalent to "God is the sole causal origin of the heavens and the earth." And if God cannot exist in time before the first moment of the creation, then the "befores" that occur in the texts Bill cites will also have to be interpreted not as temporal befores but as ontological or hierarchical befores. Such a reading of all these texts does not seem to me to be implausible. But such a view may give rise to Bill's theological objection that it will then be impossible for a distinction to be made between creation and conservation.

The objection is this: If the universe begins to exist, if there is a first moment, then God's creating the universe is his causing to be whatever came to be at that instant, and his conservation of the universe is whatever happened at each subsequent instant. But what if the universe exists beginninglessly? There is no instant of creation. If the universe has no beginning, then the distinction between creation and conservation appears to be conflated. This seems to be Bill's point.

So is it not possible in this case to maintain the distinction between creation and conservation? It may seem that Bill is correct and that one cannot on this view distinguish between God's creating of the universe and his conserving of it. But why not? In his discussion of these questions William of Ockham claims that there is a sense of "create" which is distinct from "conserve" even on the supposition of beginningless existence.[2] To create is to produce from nothing, to conserve is to keep in being what is thus created. So there is a conceptual distinction between the two even if we allow that creation out of nothing does not imply a period of time when there was nothing.

But we might go further than this, or so it seems to me. We might, in the first instance, agree with Norman Kretzmann in his comment on Ockham at this point, that the notion of creation implies the contingency of what is created, that it might not have existed, while the conserving of something implies that it already exists. And we might go further still, as Kretzmann suggests. From the fact that the universe is beginningless it does not follow that the universe is endless. It is perfectly consistent

---

[2] I rely here on Norman Kretzmann, "Ockham and the Creation of the Beginningless World," *Franciscan Studies* 45 (1985). See also the discussion in his *The Metaphysics of Creation* (Oxford: Oxford University Press, 1999), chap. 5.

that the universe should have no beginning but have an end. And so if it does not have an end, or if it has not had an end yet, this is because God has conserved in being what, though it had no beginning, he none-theless made to be. So I don't see that the eternalist is deprived of the distinction between creation and conservation even if he believes that the universe is without a beginning, though I leave to the reader to decide whether or not this distinction is theologically "robust" enough.

Bill is also concerned about evil. He says that on the eternalist view the stain of evil is indelible, because on the static view of time, evil is never vanquished from the world. Perhaps, as an A-theorist, Bill holds a nonrealist view of the past and the future, though I'm not sure of this. But if so, then past evil is no longer real, nor is past goodness. But the view that only the present is real seems to me to be a hard saying. If the past is real, then the evil that occurred in the past is always real, even in heaven. What has happened cannot now not have happened. In that sense its stain is indelible. But if the death and resurrection of Jesus have immense causal consequences, as for the Christian eternalist they undoubtedly do have, then how can the resurrection be a hollow tri-umph? And if there is to come a time for a Christian when there is no subsequent time at which she will die, then at that time death is swal-lowed up in victory for that person. Here again the distinction in stand-points is apposite. Perhaps Bill has a tendency to confuse a static universe with a purposeless universe.

The Intuition of Divine Fullness

Nick is worried by the slim epistemological basis for my appeal to the idea of the divine fullness. Of course I don't think that God's fullness or excellence or perfection is restricted to his being timeless, but that it is a part of it, and is implied by the intuition that God is a maximally excel-lent being. Nick thinks that an appeal to such an intuition is epistemo-logically weak and unsatisfactory, and I agree with him that it would be better if such an intuition were universally self-evident. Well, though *tu quoque* arguments are not really very satisfying, the same criticism could be made of his view that a life of immutability is impoverished, for (as far as I can see) he supports this only by an appeal to his own less-than-self-evident intuition.

More to the point, perhaps, Nick believes that the one who makes the appeal to divine fullness in support of eternalism should accept the burden of proof in the face of the prima facie scriptural data to the contrary. In fact I did try to shoulder some of this burden in the paper. I started by agreeing with Nick that it would be a pretty weak defense only to say that eternalism is consistent with the data of Scripture. But not only did I say that eternalism is consistent with Scripture but also that it rules out (for example) certain types of inferences about God that (I believe) are unscriptural and that it would be hard, though not impossible, for the temporalist to rule out. Take the scriptural data that claim that God foreknows all things, and indeed that he foreordains all things.[3] It is interesting that Nick denies the truth of these claims, as do many temporalists. But if one believes them to be scriptural claims, as much of traditional Christian teaching has done, and as I do, then part of the defense of divine eternality is that that notion enables us to safeguard such teaching with economy and ease. No doubt one could give a temporalist account of (what I believe is) the scriptural teaching about the reach of God's knowledge and power, but there would be no point in doing so, and so why would one go to the trouble?

On the scriptural data, I don't see the force of Nick's query about what exactly the data of Scripture are. In this context, the data are certain linguistic forms that prima facie imply temporal change in God, and certain linguistic forms that do not. The question then—for temporalists like Nick and eternalists like me—is which of these linguistic forms take priority, and so are to be taken literally, and which not.

Atheism and Deism

Nick thinks that eternalism is committed to atheism and also to deism, though not, presumably, to both together. On atheism, he says that he cannot understand the sense of the eternalist's saying "God doesn't exist now; but it's nonetheless now true that God exists." But what the eternalist in fact can say (or must say) is not this but something rather different:

---

[3]Incidentally, I do not think that the argument that divine foreknowledge is incompatible with human indeterministic freedom is an argument for fatalism, as Bill implies, but concur with Augustine that "we neither deny an order of causes wherein the will of God is all in all, neither do we call it by the name of fate" (*City of God* 5.9). But I do agree with Bill that adequate discussion of this point would require another book.

"It is true now that God eternally exists"[4]—that is, the present utterance "The eternal God exists" is true. (A Platonist might say about numbers, "It is true now that the number five exists," and this does not, as far as I can see, commit him to denying the existence of the number five.) So this does not seem to me to have the consequence that eternalism is incoherent, or of atheism. I agree with Nick that my remarks on negative theology are not to this point, but then they were not offered as remarks on this point.

On deism, Nick says that an eternalist God is necessarily a deistlike God and that this is the crux of the debate; that is, "God in eternity formulates a plan for world history, initiates the first stage of that plan and then watches the scroll unroll." According to Nick, God does not respond to the actual events of history any more than I respond to the actual events of temperature fluctuation when I set the thermostat in advance. (Nick pushes the analogy of the timer and thermostat-setting to God's eternal decree in a direction that it was not intended to apply—to what we would say about the thermostat-setter's action some time *after* he had set the timer and the thermostat. Clearly there is no "after" for God's eternal decree. But we may let that pass.) Certainly it's odd to say that I turned on the flame at 2:10 p.m. on Thursday afternoon when what I did was set the timer and the thermostat a week earlier. But suppose that something went tragically wrong on Thursday as a result of my setting the timer and the thermostat in the way that I did. Surely it would be no defense to the charge that I was at least partly responsible for this tragedy for me to say, "It's not me, guv, it's my timer and thermostat." Surely in these circumstances the firing of the boiler on that Thursday was my action. So the deistic picture that Nick paints does not apply to the eternalist's God, but even if it did God would not be a mere bystander watching the scroll unroll.

But—to push the analogy a little further—suppose that I set the timer and the temperature (at 70 degrees) knowing that you'll otherwise find the room chilly. Am I not responding to you? There is nothing in eternalism to preclude such a view, a view of logically ordered components in the one eternal decree, some being conditioned on what is eternally

---

[4]What religious or theological use such expressions serve or might serve is of course another question.

foreknown. But as Bill points out in his comments, on the eternalist view God does not initiate (present tense) and then (later) watch (present tense) the scroll unroll. He eternally creates and conserves the scroll.

God's Knowledge of the Present

Nick is also concerned that God could not know that we were ever speaking the truth when we say (in 1999, say) "It is now 1999." But we know that someone is speaking the truth when they make that utterance in 1999 and only then. And the eternal God (if he is omniscient) knows for any year all the utterances made in that year, and is able to distinguish the true from the false. And God can eternally decree to respond to Moses at some time by knowing that the present for Moses is the moment immediately after those times that he can have memories of. At such a moment we may suppose that Moses prays to God, and God, eternally knowing this, eternally wills to respond to his knowledge of Moses' cry at that moment. So God did know that when, in 1999, I say "It's now 1999," I'm speaking the truth, for he knows that I'm saying this in 1999, and that's sufficient. Such an utterance, though never temporally present for God, is present for me sometime in 1999, and this ensures the utterance's truth, and (if he is omniscient) God's knowledge of its truth.

Bill raises a rather similar problem. He thinks that my effort to show that temporalists also have difficulty with the idea of divine omniscience fails because though a timeless being cannot know tensed facts a temporal being can know tenseless truths. I agree with him that a temporal being can know tenseless truths, and so perhaps I wasn't careful enough to make clear what I meant by knowing the universe from the perspective of timeless eternity. The point I should have stressed is that in my view there are propositions available to a timeless God which are not available to anyone in time, including temporal knowers' knowledge of tenseless propositions. I'll bring these remarks to an end by trying to make the distinction between timelessness and tenselessness clear.

On the B-series view of the temporal order, each event is tenselessly related to each other. The Battle of Hastings has a fixed, tenseless but nonetheless temporal relation to the Battle of Waterloo. It is earlier than the Battle of Waterloo. But God does not have such a tenseless relation to the universe, for he is not earlier than it, he has a timeless relation to it. How do timelessness and tenselessness differ? A timeless standpoint entails a tenseless standpoint but is not entailed by it. Being timeless, God has ways of knowing facts that are not open to us in time, even when these facts are tenseless facts. There is the equivalent for a timeless knower of temporal indexicals for a temporal knower. Let us call this equivalent the eternal indexical. God's timeless knowledge of all truths, and especially (for our purposes) of contingent matters of fact, knowledge that must be tenseless, is eternal indexical knowledge, knowledge indexed to timeless eternity. Here the distinction between the divine and the human standpoints is once again applicable. The two standpoints generate two different kinds of indexicals, temporal indexicals for those in time, an atemporal indexical for God. Obviously at this point the resources of negative theology need to be employed in answer to the question, what is eternal indexical knowledge of contingent truths like? Answer: We have and can have no positive idea; but it is certainly not like our temporal indexical knowledge of contingent truths, or our temporal indexical knowledge of tenseless truths.

But is there a cognitive difference between the eternal indexical knowledge of a contingent truth and a tensed indexical knowledge of the same fact? Do ways of knowing facts generate further facts? If they do not then Bill is correct; with respect to any tenseless truth a timeless God and a temporal God are in precisely the same cognitive state. However, the temporalist (typically) claims that ways of knowing facts do give rise to further facts; in fact it is a central plank of his account of divine knowledge. Thus being present with John when he is mowing the lawn enables us truly to utter, "John is mowing the lawn now," and to know that fact, a fact unknowable to a timeless God. Hence, the temporalist typically argues, those in time can know truths that an allegedly omniscient atemporal God cannot know.

So here's a dilemma for the temporalist. Either ways of knowing facts give rise to further facts, or they do not. If they do not, then the temporalist's objection to the eternalist's account of omniscience—that there are facts, like the fact that it is 9:22 a.m. now, which a timeless God cannot know—falls. For on this horn of the dilemma its being 9:22 a.m. on May 28 is not cognitively distinct from its being 9:22 a.m. now, when the "now" is uttered on May 28. If on the other hand these two expressions are cognitively distinct, one conveying different information from the other, then I argue that in similar fashion God's eternal indexical way of knowing tenseless facts gives rise to further facts, facts necessarily not available to anyone in time. And then the parallel that Bill denies in fact holds, for there are types of propositions that a temporal God cannot know: those propositions that are eternally indexed, that express knowledge of the universe from the perspective of timeless eternity.

3

ETERNITY AS RELATIVE TIMELESSNESS

ALAN G. PADGETT

*T*he relationship between God and time may seem an obscure subject. Yet the more one studies it, the more convinced one becomes that this doctrine plays a key role in our grasp of the relationship between God and the world. How we understand God's relationship to the world, in turn, is a central part of any theistic worldview. So despite the seeming obscurity of the topic, the doctrine of divine eternity is an important part of any fully developed theology.

Normally scholars distinguish between two views of the relationship between God and time, the everlasting model (sometimes called "sempiternal") and the absolute timelessness or atemporal model. The debate has been framed, historically, between these two views, with problems being pointed out for each position by its opponent. In this chapter I will outline a third proposal, a model I call "relative timelessness."[1] Nei-

---

[1]I develop this model in Alan G. Padgett, *God, Eternity and the Nature of Time* (1992; reprint, Eugene, Ore.: Wipf & Stock, 2000).

ther the everlasting nor the atemporal model is finally satisfactory; the relative timelessness model preserves the best of both—so I shall argue.

The Problem with Everlasting Eternity

What are the problems with the everlasting viewpoint? It does have the virtues of being easy to grasp and clearly consistent. Moreover, it is the view clearly consistent with a straightforward reading of the Bible, although the Scriptures do not clearly favor any one developed philosophical model.[2] But there are problems with this theory. We do seem to have some sense of the transcendence of God, requiring that God be outside of any merely created category. Because God is beyond gender, for example, it seems equally proper to call God "he" or "she" (but not "it" since God is a person). Sex and gender are created categories, which God transcends. We also hold that God is beyond space, or spaceless, and is infinite in Being while all other things are finite.

The main problem with the everlasting model is not logical consistency but theological inadequacy. Given our notion of God as an infinite, personal Creator, we would expect God to transcend time in some way. Merely knowing the future and living forever is not enough to satisfy this demand. Recent developments in physics would join with St. Augustine and many traditional philosophers to insist that time is a created category that came into existence with the physical universe.[3] Space-time as we know it has a beginning—but God does not. Space-time is warped by the presence of matter—but God is not. Thus God must be beyond time as we know it, in some sense. David Braine may overstate the case when he writes, "If we understand eternity as mere everlastingness, then it seems that we are in danger of reducing him who is worshiped to the level of the creature," but he is giving voice to a common and powerful objection to a merely everlasting eternity for God.[4] Proponents of an everlasting view of eternity have difficulty overcoming this objection, in my view.

---

[2]For a brief discussion of some key biblical texts, see ibid., chap. 2; and the key text of modern times on this issue: Oscar Cullmann, *Christ and Time*, trans. F. V. Filson, rev. ed. (London: SCM Press, 1962).

[3]Augustine *Confessions* 11, and many recent works on time by physicists, e.g., Stephen W. Hawking, *A Brief History of Time* (New York: Bantam, 1988).

[4]David Braine, "God, Eternity and Time" (review essay), *Evangelical Quarterly* 66 (1994): 337-44, quoting 337.

Problems with Timeless Eternity

What, then, of an absolutely timeless God? This traditional view does pay attention to—indeed embodies—the intuition that God must transcend time. There is a great deal of attachment to the traditional notion of a timeless God. In a fine recent article on this topic, Katherin Rogers writes, "Criticisms of the tenseless view of time are not powerful enough to necessitate abandoning the venerable tradition of an eternal God."[5] In the face of such attachment, we will need to give powerful reasons to abandon the timeless God of traditional theism. I will argue that it is possible to continue to hold to a timeless model of eternity, but only when other important truths are abandoned.

Unlike some critics, I believe that the atemporal model is logically consistent.[6] However, sometimes a theological doctrine must be rejected not for incoherence within itself but for incoherence with other truths, or for a better fit with other theories. For example, the doctrine that God determines every event "from eternity" is incoherent with a libertarian understanding of human free will. For this reason many have rejected (rightly in my view) the notion that God determines every event. The doctrine that God determines every event is not incoherent in itself, but it conflicts with other ideas that we believe are true and important.

The traditional philosophers who have developed the idea of timeless eternity, such as Augustine, Boethius and Aquinas, believed that God was alive. Most modern defenders would agree with this position. But if God has a life, it must have different instants or points to it. Thus sometimes theologians and philosophers have spoken of a "timeless duration." Now I object to the term *duration* (*duratio* in Latin, from the verb *durare,* to endure or last), since it means an interval of *time* through which something endures. But this objection is a semantic one, since modern defenders of the doctrine are willing to substitute "atemporal extensive mode of existence."[7] This longer phrase is what

───

[5]Katherin Rogers, "Omniscience, Eternity and Freedom," *International Philosophical Quarterly* 36 (1996): 399-412, quoting 408. This is also found in her book *An Anselmian Approach to God and Creation* (Lewiston, N.Y.: Edwin Mellen, 1997).
[6]Padgett, *God, Eternity*, pp. 76-81.
[7]Eleonore Stump and Norman Kretzmann, "Atemporal Duration: A Reply to Fitzgerald," *Journal of Philosophy* 84 (1987): 215. Stump and Kretzmann later insist that their terms "timeless now," "timeless simultaneity" and "timeless duration" are meant to be analogies, in Eleonore Stump and Norman Kretzmann, "Eternity, Awareness and Action," *Faith and*

was meant by the ill-chosen "timeless duration."

But what can this longer phrase mean? Can we make any sense of an atemporal extensive mode of existence? I believe so. An extension is a "spread" of something. What is eternity a spread of? It must be an atemporal extension of the being or nature of God. What we have, then, is a nontemporal order in the mind of God, or a series of nontemporal "instants" in the life of God, ordered in succession. As was argued by John Duns Scotus in the Middle Ages, God's Being has "succession" only in a conceptual sense, not in a temporal one.[8] One can think of the nontemporal succession of the letters in an alphabet, say, or the points in an argument, as analogies to the atemporal conceptual succession in the life of God.

Even though this doctrine is self-consistent, there is hidden within it a serious flaw. The main objection I have to the timeless model is simply stated: It is true only if the stasis theory of time is true. Since the stasis theory of time is false, we should reject the timeless view because we should, whenever possible, bring coherence to theology. As theologians, we should be attached to the truth, not to any favorite doctrine, no matter how traditional or trendy. Since I believe the stasis theory of time is false, I cannot use it in theology. I use the term *stasis* because it is not pejorative, like "block universe" and other names. Also, it is a word with some meaning, whereas the usual term "B-theory" is without meaning— B is just a letter. Finally, I suggest we avoid *tenseless* since we wish to avoid confusing grammar and ontology. Thus I will call the "tenseless" theory of time "the stasis theory."

With respect to the reality of past, present and future, there are in fact two sets or types of theories: the stasis and the process types. Process viewpoints may differ in some ways but will all affirm the reality of tem-

---

Philosophy 9 (1992): 463-82, esp. 464-65. Stump and Kretzmann use terms like *duration, now* and *simultaneity,* all modified by *timeless,* because they wish to retain some aspects of the ordinary predicates. But why not use ordinary words when possible? Especially in specialist publications (like theirs), it is better to use ordinary terms in univocal predication, to avoid confusion and hasty conclusions. For example, if they had used "timeless coexistence" instead of "ET-simultaneity" in the publications, a great deal of confusion (and a few errors on their part) could have been avoided.

[8]John Duns Scotus *Ordinatio* 1.d9, d43. This work is sometimes entitled *Opus Oxoniense,* but it is called "Ordinatio" in the beautiful modern critical edition of Scotus, *Opera Omnia,* ed. C. Balic et al. (Vatican City: Typis Polyglottis Vaticanis, 1950).

poral passage—that is, past, present and future. On process theories, temporal passage is a real part of the physical universe. Stasis theories of time all deny the reality of temporal passage, although they too will differ among themselves as to why this is so. For convenience, I will continue to write about *the* process or *the* stasis theory, even though there are many types of each. It is not always easy to grasp the difference between these two points of view.

The main difference between process and stasis theories has to do with temporal passage. Imagine a time T in the far future, and an event E which (let us say) will certainly happen at T. If we take the combination E-at-T, we can get a sense of the difference between the process and stasis views. For the stasis view, E-at-T is real always. Of course E is not real now, but then neither view thinks it is.[9] Rather, the stasis view believes that E is always real *at* T (and only at T). The process theory, however, denies that E is always real at T. E is fully real only when T is now. Nothing is real-at-T unless T is present. Of course on the process theory you can contrast the abstract set of all things past, present and future that will ever be real with illusions, myths and other nonreal things. But within that set, for the process view, only present things are fully real. Past things used to be real, and future things will be real.

To return to my argument against atemporal eternity, two propositions need defending in order for the objection to be sustained. First, one needs to show that the atemporal view of eternity depends on the stasis theory of time.[10] Second, one needs to show that the stasis theory of time is false. I believe the best path to this conclusion is to use a doctrine so essential to theism that it is simply more important than the timeless model of eternity. The doctrine I use for this purpose is the idea that God sustains the universe (that is, everything that has being) in its being, as long as it exists. God also gives it whatever basic properties and causal powers each thing possesses. A very short version of a long argument goes like this:

---

[9]In her very helpful book *The Dilemma of Freedom and Foreknowledge* (New York: Oxford University Press, 1991), p. 48, Linda Zagzebski makes a rare slip, misunderstanding these two views.

[10]Many defenders of an atemporal eternity simply assume the stasis theory in their discussion, e.g., Leslie Walker, "Time, Eternity and God," *Hibbert Journal* 18 (1919): 36-48; Richard Sturch, "The Problem of Divine Eternity," *Religious Studies* 10 (1974): 487-93; or Paul Helm, *Eternal God* (Oxford: Clarendon, 1988).

1. On the timeless view, God cannot have any real change. This follows from the very idea of a timeless being.

2. Since God sustains all things, God is responsible directly for the being of all things, at all times.

3. On the process theory of time, things come into and pass out of existence with the passage of time.

4. On the stasis theory of time, nothing that ever has existed or will exist passes out of existence from a timeless perspective. God creates/sustains the whole of the universe "tenselessly" or timelessly.

5. On the process theory, bringing something into existence, or ceasing to sustain something, is a real change in the Creator, not the creature.

Since the creature does not exist at all (yet), it cannot undergo any changes. Only existing things can change. Many philosophers think of the future as "already there" in some sense and smuggle the stasis theory of time into their notion of an unchanging, timeless Act by which God created and sustains the world. But this will not do. On the process theory of time, the future does not exist. When God creates something, that can be a change only in God, not in the creature, for the creature does not exist yet. Even a timeless God must await the present moment to act on really existing (present) things, if the process theory of time is true. This fact has been overlooked by numerous defenders of a timeless God. Likewise, if something is annihilated, then God ceases to act directly upon that object. This, too, is a real change in God, not in the creature.

A. On the process theory of time, God undergoes real change (from [2], [3] and [5]).

B. Only the stasis theory of time is compatible with (A) (from [2] and [4]).

Since the stasis theory of time allows every event to "exist" (using this word without tense) at the time it "occurs" (again, tenseless) in the spread of space-time, this theory and only this theory makes atemporal eternity compatible with God's creating and sustaining all things.[11]

Certain defenders of atemporal eternity, especially Brian Leftow and Eleonore Stump, will object that their view of eternity is compatible with

---

[11]For the long version of this argument, see Padgett, *God, Eternity,* chap. 4.

a process theory of time. They often fail to realize that even a timeless God must wait for the present to occur, in order to act upon real things, if the process theory of time is true. But, they will object, is not God timeless? Does not God's life abstract from such things as "waiting" for the present moment to arrive? The answer is no, not if the process theory is true. The definition of something's being timeless is (a) that it exists, (b) that it does not exist at any time and (c) that its existence has no extension in time.[12] God can be all these things and still have to wait for a temporal world to pass by. What follows from God's timelessness is that God never changes, but it does not mean that all times can now be "present" to God. All times' being present to God, while a traditional idea, is incoherent. Being past, being present and being future are temporal properties that God cannot partake of, if God is absolutely timeless. What we might say is that God *coexists* with every moment in time. This is true, but only in one sense.

We might mean that God coexists with every moment of time, in the sense that for each present moment, however long time lasts, God coexists (timelessly) at that moment. There should be no problem with this meaning. On the other hand, we might mean that all times coexist timelessly with God (or in eternity). This second sense is incoherent. First of all, things that exist in time cannot coexist timelessly. Nothing that is temporal can also be timeless. In the second place, all times cannot and do not coexist in any sense—and certainly not "timelessly" or "in eternity." Different times are not all present, and only present things are fully real (on the process view). Things have happened in the past, and things will happen in the future, but those things are not real. Therefore they cannot coexist with present things.

The Special Theory of Relativity does not change this logical fact, but it forces us to ask, "Present according to what system of measurement?" An event may be present in one system of measurement but past in another. However, a timeless God does not have a system of measurement. God coexists with the true present—that is, the real moment of Becoming, in the life of everything in the universe. If the physical universe as a whole is in the process of Becoming (as the process theory demands), then so is each object (really existing thing)

---

[12]Nelson Pike, *God and Timelessness* (London: Routledge & Kegan Paul, 1970), p. 7.

in it. Even a timeless God must await the future of any and all objects in the universe, in order to act directly upon future (nonexistent) episodes of that object. But what can a timeless God do in the future that he doesn't do now? Nothing. This argument, of course, presupposes a process theory of time.

Defenders of God's timeless Being are often captured by a picture. This is a picture of God, high and lifted up, seeing all of time at once, in the way an observer on a high hill can see the whole of a road at once. The problem here is that only one step of the road exists, even for the observer. The typical abstraction of thinking about all events forever in space-time is just that: an abstraction. In reality, on the process theory, time is not like space. As I have shown elsewhere (and cannot repeat here), Stump and Leftow can defend God's timelessness only because of a misunderstanding of the Special Theory of Relativity.[13] Once this misunderstanding is removed, their claim of coherence falls apart. In particular, it is hard to accept Leftow's notion of all events' being both in a timeless eternity (which he calls God's "frame of reference") *and also* in our temporal world of process.[14] First of all, God does not have a "frame of reference." Leftow misuses this term from the Special Theory of Relativity, which is about inertial frames of reference in motion relative to each other. Is God in motion too? But even if we use the term "frame of reference," on a process theory all events cannot coexist in any frame of reference—not even God's. Interestingly, John Duns Scotus considered and rejected just this idea in his *Lectura* centuries ago, because of its incoherence. "If all future beings were present to God according to their actual existence, it would be impossible for God to cause them to exist anew."[15] Since timeless existence is so very different from temporal being, even if every event existed in God's timeless "frame of reference"

---

[13]Alan G. Padgett, "Eternity and the Special Theory of Relativity," *International Philosophical Quarterly* 33, no. 2 (1993): 219-23. Some of these same criticisms can be found in William Lane Craig, "The Special Theory of Relativity," *Faith and Philosophy* 11 (1994): 19-37.

[14]Brian Leftow, *Time and Eternity* (Ithaca, N.Y.: Cornell University Press, 1991), pp. 234-35.

[15]"Si omnia futura essent praesentia Deo secundum eorum actualem existentiam, impossibile esset Deo causare aliquid de novo" (John Duns Scotus *Lectura* 1.d39.q5.sec28 [*Opera Omnia*, 17:487]. There is an English translation and commentary on this distinction, titled *Contingency and Freedom*, trans. A. Vos Jaczn et al. (Dordrecht, Netherlands: Kluwer, 1994).

then God would have to re-create all events within the flow of temporal passage—which is absurd.

That Stump and Kretzmann's view of timeless eternity is coherent only given the stasis theory of time I have argued elsewhere.[16] Their (in)famous notion of "ET-simultaneity," when stripped of its problematic elements, boils down to the idea that God timelessly coexists with a temporal world. A critical analysis of this theory uncovers a problem with a timeless God's causing temporal things to happen without a change to God's own being. In a recent attempt to defend their view, Stump and Kretzmann develop a philosophical story.[17] The purpose of this story is to show the coherence of their notion of ET-simultaneity. On the contrary, an examination of this story will support my basic claim that they have been assuming the truth of the stasis theory of time all along.

They tell a possible world story of Aleph. Like E. A. Abbott's *Flatland* (1884), the possible world of Aleph has fewer spatial dimensions than our world. In fact, it has a single linear dimension, inhabited by inch-long intelligent beings who are ordered in the relation "in front of" or "behind" each other. None are in the same place, however. Each Alephian moves from A1, where the line begins, to a high point of "here" and then to the end of the line at A2.

Monica, however, exists outside of Aleph and can see all of the living Alephians along with their entire world-line. Notice what this means, however. The absolute quality of "here" for the Alephians is contradicted by Monica's point of view. If the story of Aleph were to really follow the process theory of time, *only the inch at "here" would be real*. Monica should be able to see only one Alephian at a time (even though she is outside their spatial dimension altogether) because only one "here" is real on Aleph. This is because "here" on Aleph is supposed to mirror "now" in our world. Thus it would be impossible for Monica to see more than one Alephian at a time, even though she is spatially outside Aleph. In fact, Stump and Kretzmann write in a footnote to this story, "this way of looking at eternity and time need not conflict with the idea that there is an absolute temporal present, that temporal passage is real rather than mind-dependent." I believe they are fooling themselves at this point, as

---

[16]Padgett, *God, Eternity*, pp. 66-73.
[17]Stump and Kretzmann, "Eternity, Awareness"; the story of Aleph is on 470-73.

the next sentence makes clear: "One frame of reference in respect of which to determine presentness might be all of time itself."[18] This sentence makes sense only when "presentness" is reduced to "existence," as it usually is for Stump and Kretzmann. All times cannot be present, because the same time cannot have incompatible properties (in the same manner). So in the end, the story of Aleph is coherent only when we assume (as Stump and Kretzmann have all along) a stasis theory of time.

I argue, then, that the traditional idea of God's timeless life is compatible with God's sustaining everything only if the stasis theory of time is true. There is another avenue to this same conclusion, starting from divine omniscience. If we assume that God has knowledge of concrete states of affairs (and not merely abstract, propositional knowledge) concerning an indeterminate future, then one can argue that these doctrines are coherent only given the stasis theory of time. Katherin Rogers has independently come to this conclusion.[19]

This argument will be convincing to the extent that we have independent reasons to reject the understanding of omniscience typical among analytical philosophers. In this group, divine foreknowledge is often framed in terms of propositions. However, I believe that a great deal of trouble comes from this definition.[20] Since God is God, God's knowledge should not be limited to the abstract world of propositional truth. I agree with William Alston, and Jonathan Kvanvig, who in different ways have pointed out several problems with a merely propositional notion of omniscience.[21] Since God is the Creator and Sustainer of the universe, God's knowledge includes an "insider's view" of everything, a concrete

---

[18]Ibid., p. 481, n. 33.

[19]Rogers, "Omniscience."

[20]Nelson Pike, in his famous article "Divine Omniscience and Voluntary Action" (*Philosophical Review* 74 [1965]: 27-46; reprinted in *God, Foreknowledge and Freedom,* ed. J. M. Fischer [Stanford, Calif.: Stanford University Press, 1989]), wrote that it was a virtue of his definition that it was in terms of propositions rather than causation, thus avoiding some problems (*God, Foreknowledge,* p. 64). The subsequent discussion of Pike's article (e.g., in Fischer) makes this claim rather doubtful.

I am happy to note that in his recent, retrospective article on the debate, Pike has emphasized the importance of reflecting on the causes of God's knowledge of future contingent states of affairs: Nelson Pike, "A Latter-Day Look at the Foreknowledge Problem," *International Journal for Philosophy of Religion* 33 (1993): 129-64, esp. 145-48.

[21]William P. Alston, "Does God Have Beliefs?" *Religious Studies* 22 (1986): 287-306; Jonathan Kvanvig, *The Possibility of an All-Knowing God* (London: Macmillan, 1986).

and direct grasp of all physical states of affairs (along with all abstract knowledge). Traditional philosophers understood (rightly, I have come to believe) that God's knowledge is of the actual existence of things, because God is the cause of the being of everything. This perspective was held by both Aquinas and his critic Duns Scotus. For example, in the *Summa Theologiae,* Aquinas wrote: "God knows all contingent events not only as they are in their causes but also as each of them is in actual existence in itself" (1a.q14.a13).

How can a timeless God have a concrete and direct grasp of all physical states of affairs? If the process theory of time is true, that is impossible apart from present things. Such states of affairs do not exist, not even for a timeless God. If the stasis theory of time is true, however, then it is possible. Those future or past states of affairs do exist (not now of course, but that will not matter to a timeless God). Thus God can know them in a concrete way.

Just what is so bad with the stasis theory, then? If we have a strong attachment to atemporal eternity, can we not choose to hold on to a stasis theory of time? Not, I would argue, if we seek coherence and consistency in our metaphysics. While the term *metaphysics* is sometimes used in a pejorative way, it is possible to develop a careful, critical and coherent metaphysics. Metaphysics, as Aristotle rightly saw, should begin with experience.[22] But metaphysics cannot ignore logic and natural science. Rather, good metaphysical methods will seek a balance between these sources of knowledge.[23] Of course experience can lead us astray, but so can logic or science!

With respect to the philosophy of time (one aspect of metaphysics), our daily experience is of primary importance to our grasp of time. Our interaction with the real world through action and sensation forms an indispensable avenue for our knowledge of time. In fact, temporal passage cannot be known through either classical physics or symbolic logic.[24] These symbol systems are abstractions that are intended to avoid the pas-

---

[22]Aristotle *Metaphysics* A.1.98
[23]See Robert J. Henle, *Method in Metaphysics,* Aquinas Lecture (Milwaukee, Wis.: Marquette University Press, 1951), and E. J. Lowe, *The Possibility of Metaphysics* (Oxford: Clarendon, 1998).
[24]Modern physics, especially thermodynamics, quantum mechanics and cosmology, has been forced to take past, present and future more seriously.

sage of time. But when we walk with our daily experience, our common sense or "wisdom," this avenue leads straight to a process theory.

The broad, general problem with the various types of stasis theory is that they rely too heavily on abstractions. These abstractions are mere human creations, useful in a limited way but not the be-all and end-all of metaphysics. The two abstractions that have particularly led philosophers astray are mathematical physics and logic. In these all-too-human domains—useful, important, and true as they are—thinkers are tempted to forget that their symbol systems *are* abstractions. The temptation is to make the symbols real, or at least more real than the only real world, which is the world we live in day to day. This error goes by many names, such as "the fallacy of mistaken concreteness" (A. N. Whitehead) or "the fallacy of confusing the logical with the physical." It is a prominent error in the field of philosophy of time. Now the broad claims I have made need careful justification, but there is no space for it in this chapter, and I have justified them elsewhere.[25]

A second major reason I believe we should reject all stasis theories of time is that they cannot account for important facts. They may attempt to explain away these facts, but their explanations are rather unsatisfactory. The class of facts I have in mind are "process facts" that almost any competent adult is aware of: facts about what dates and times are past, present or future right now. Take today's date, the date you are reading this sentence. Assign this date a number, using the calendar system of your culture (e.g., January 1, 2001). Let [D] stand as the name for this date in your language. Now it is true for you, reader, that "today is [D]." If you ask anyone on the street, or listen to radio or television, they may tell you that "today is [D]." You might say that everyone knows "today is [D]"—yet stasis theories cannot account for this important fact. Because they rely on abstractions from the real world, stasis theories cannot account for process facts. Their attempts to explain away process facts are not very convincing.[26]

I am not here arguing in a circle, assuming the process theory in order to defend it. Rather, I claim that common sense and ordinary

---

[25]See Padgett, *God, Eternity,* chap. 5.
[26]See Richard Swinburne, "Tensed Facts," *American Philosophical Quarterly* 21 (1990): 117-30; and Padgett, *God, Eternity,* pp. 100-107. For a recent attempt to defend the stasis view on this point, see D. H. Mellor, *Real Time II* (London: Routledge, 1998), pp. 25-38.

experience teach us certain facts about time, facts that I am calling "process facts." My claim is that stasis theories give us dubious explanations of these facts (not that they have *no* explanations, just that they have rather poor ones). Thus the argument is not circular, contrary to some critics.[27]

Finally, while I argue that the stasis theory of time is wrong to reject the reality of past, present and future, there is nothing wrong with assuming a stasis perspective on time. It is often useful to abstract from temporal passage and assume an abstract perspective on reality. A stasis *perspective* can be very useful in symbolic logic or theoretical physics. However, philosophers go astray when they turn this abstract, conceptual perspective into the only "right" way to understand time.

We are wise, then, to reject the stasis theory of time as the correct one. That is, we are wise to accept the reality of past, present and future as our senses present temporal passage to us. Despite the work of numerous philosophers to the contrary, there is no sound reason to reject the evidence of our senses with respect to temporal passage. But this means that the traditional notion of God's timeless life must be rejected. Are we then left in the everlasting camp?

Eternity as Relative Timelessness

So far our investigation has been a negative one. We have found reasons to reject both of the normal theories of eternity. Is there any other alternative? In the space left, we will explore a third theory of divine eternity: relative timelessness.[28] I will further argue, theologically, that God is the "Lord of time."

This third view starts with time rather than with God. That is, while most theories of eternity develop a rich conceptual notion of God, few have taken the time (!) to develop an equally careful understanding of

---

[27]I have in mind here conversations and e-mail correspondence with Nathan Oaklander, for which I am most grateful.

[28]I develop this theory in Padgett, *God, Eternity,* chapter 6. For similar views, see Richard Swinburne, *The Christian God* (Oxford: Clarendon, 1994); Lawrence Osborn, "Space-Time and Revelation," *Science and Christian Belief* 8 (1996): 111-23; and two recent articles by William Lane Craig, "Timelessness and Creation," *Australasian Journal of Philosophy* 74 (1996): 646-56; "Divine Timelessness and Necessary Existence," *International Philosophical Quarterly* 37 (1997): 217-24; and his forthcoming set of books on God and time.

time. Yet as the issue of time and eternity comes more to the fore in contemporary philosophy of religion, scholars are giving more thought to the nature of time.

There are many meanings to the word *time* and many possible meaning to the word *timeless*. *Timeless* in a strict sense means that no duration ever occurs in the life of that which is timeless (using the word *duration* to mean "an interval of time"). Something timeless in the strict sense will lack both temporal extension and temporal location. However, this is not the only sense of the term.

We can and should distinguish between time as a pure duration, which can flow without any changes taking place in the world, and time understood as the measure of change. Aristotle, for example, defined time as "the numbering of change according to before and after."[29] This is the time of ordinary life, the time of clocks and calendars, the time we know through physical science. Let us call the first kind of time "pure duration" and the second kind "measured time."

Modern physical science can teach us a great deal about measured time, some of which corrects (but does not entirely refute) our knowledge of time through ordinary experience and common sense. For one thing, measured time is not absolute. If I stand near a very powerful gravity source, or travel at speeds close to that of light (relative to your different inertial frame of reference), then my measure of time will be quite different from yours. In fact, there is no absolute measure of time. All temporal measure is dependent on the laws of nature, and on the choice of some clock to act as the standard for temporal measure.[30]

According to relative timelessness, God is the Creator of space-time, which God transcends. In this way, relative timelessness attends to the intuition that God cannot be "contained" within any created category. It also fits with the idea that time is created. But the time of "space-time"— created time—is physical, measured time. It is time as we know it through physical science that is created. But God's own time is not made at any time. It is not created in the same sense.

Because God really does change in order to sustain a dynamic,

---

[29]Aristotle *Physics* 4.220a.

[30]Our discussion here is about the actual world, not about any and all possible world stories we could tell. In a different world story, God's relationship to time might well be different.

changing world (assuming the process theory), there must be some sense in which God is temporal. But I reject the phrase "God is in time," because of its negative theological connotations. Rather, I want to argue that God is the metaphysical precondition for the existence of eternity (understood here as a pure duration that is relatively timeless). Our time, created time, exists within the pure duration of God's time, which is relatively timeless. And God's time exists because God exists (not the other way around). What many people seem to imply by "God is in time" is that God exists only if time exists—and this is what I deny.

I argue for this latter point by telling a possible world story. Imagine a strictly timeless world. God exists in that world and is the Creator of all things in it. This ontological dependence is not in any temporal order. The relationship of dependence of all things in this world upon God is conceptual, not temporal. God's creating in this world does not take any time; it is instantaneous. Now such a world is logically possible. Since God is capable of doing anything that is logically possible, God could have created a timeless world (instead of the actual, temporal one). Yet God did not. The difference between the timeless possible world and our world is so fundamental, so ontologically basic, that it can only be God that brings this difference about.

This leaves us, logically, with two possibilities. The first is that God's time is a *necessary precondition* to God's Being. The second is that God's Being is a necessary precondition to God's time (eternity). In the first case, God could exist only in possible world stories where time occurs. Brian Leftow has in fact raised this as an objection to any kind of temporality in God.[31] However, Leftow at this point confuses an essential property with an eternal one. Temporality is not essential to God in a logical sense (in other words, God is not temporal in all possible worlds), and Leftow has no argument to show that it is. If God is temporal, then in the actual world God is eternally temporal. But Leftow confuses what is eternally true with what is true in all possible worlds (i.e., with what is true of logical necessity).

The second option is that, in some sense, God's own temporality is dependent on the Being of God rather than a necessary precondition of God's existence. I wish to draw on the distinction between temporal and

[31]Leftow, *Time and Eternity*, p. 273.

conceptual order that we discovered above, in understanding the traditional notion of divine timelessness. God is not contained within time, not even God's own time. Rather, God's Being is *conceptually prior* (in terms of ontological dependence) to eternity, even though God's life is not temporally prior to God's time. God's eternity is thus similar to other divine attributes that are always part of God's existence but are not logically essential to the divine Being. Thus, God remains the Lord of time and the Creator of our (measured) time.

God's time is infinite, but it is also immeasurable. This is another sense in which God is *relatively* timeless. In other words, God is timeless *relative to* the created time of our space-time universe. As we saw above, any temporal measure depends on the laws of nature (which in turn depend on the created structures and regularities of natural objects). Temporal metrics are relative to inertial frames of reference; they change with strong gravity or great speed. There is no reason to assume that such metrics apply to God.

To summarize, then, I have argued that God is relatively timeless—that is, timeless relative to our created, measured time. This means, first, that God is the Creator of our time (space-time universe). Our time takes place within (and only because of the prior existence of) God's own time. Second, even God's own time, eternity, exists only because God exists (and not the other way around). Even eternity is dependent, ontologically, on God's very Life and Being. The Being of God is thus rightly at the heart of the whole of reality in history or eternity, in heaven and on earth. Third, God's own time is infinite and cannot be measured by our time. Eternity is infinite and immeasurable.

There are three theological points I would like to add to round out the notion that God is Lord of time. First, God is not limited by time. For an omniscient, all-powerful God, time cannot press or get in the way of the divine plan. God could accomplish any series of events in any amount of time, no matter how small. The rate at which things happen, the causal structure of the world, and the laws of nature are in God's hands. Time is not the master here.

Second, God's life is not limited by time. God's life is from eternity to eternity. While humans may fear the passage of time, because it brings them closer to death, God is the ever-living Fountain of being itself. God's existence is *a se*, not dependent on anything else. God is immutable also, unchanged in basic powers and attributes, living forever and ever. God cannot die and does not change in fundamental nature and power.

Finally, God is the Lord of time because God has a plan. Things do not surprise the infinite Mind who is Lord of time and eternity. Even if humans or subatomic particles have some limited freedom, all possibilities and eventualities are anticipated from eternity by Providence. Time brings nothing outside the will and purposes of God. Even human free will, so often abused, is the gift of God and exists because God wills it to be so.

The fact that God is the Lord of time I have interpreted to mean that he has a plan or design for history, that nothing takes place outside of the divine will; that he is not limited or changed in any fundamental way by the passage of time, and that God is a metaphysically necessary Being who lives forever and ever. To this I would add the metaphysical properties of relative timelessness. By "relative timelessness" I mean that God is the Creator of our (physical, measured) time; that in contrast to our time, God's eternity is infinite and immeasurable; and finally that God's time is dependent on God's Being, not the other way around.

I believe, then, that this third notion of eternity preserves the best of the two normal conceptions of eternity. It has the coherence of the everlasting view but respects the intuition of the traditional notion of timeless eternity, by pointing to several ways in which God "transcends" time.

Problems with Relative Timelessness

There are difficulties in any view of eternity, including the third view developed in this chapter. I would like to anticipate some problems that might arise for my preferred conception of eternity, and answer them in this short concluding section.

A very old problem, noted by Augustine in his *Confessions*, has to do with the moment when God created the universe. Since God's own time exists before our created time, it does make sense to talk about a time before the first moment of our time (which we currently associate with the big bang). What was God up to before creation?

We should first notice that since God's time is nonfinite and immeasurable, there is no *amount* of time that passed before creation. Temporal measure (hours, days, millennia) depends on created things and structures (laws of nature). Before creation, no amount of time passed. Before creation, God existed in a nonfinite temporal duration, but not in a finite (or even infinite) *amount* of time. Second, before the change in God that brought about the first moment of time (and with it created reality) there is no reason to believe that any change took place in God. Thus time as we know it—that is, a time with change and measure—did not take place before creation. We can, if we like, consider all of the infinite past before the first change as a single "moment" of eternity. Also, since eternity has no beginning or end, at any time in which God begins to create, there would be a nonfinite, changeless prior eternity. God's time really is different from our own!

Closely associated with this problem is the charge that Leftow makes, that a temporal God cannot act at any time to create time.[32] However, his argument rests on the idea that time is a precondition of God's existence, and I have already rejected this assumption above. God brings about God's own infinite, immeasurable time by simply living. This is because God's time is dependent on God's own Being (not vice versa).

We can also anticipate an objection from modern followers of Anselm, who insist that God must be a perfect Being. A perfect Being would not change, since any change would either be for the better or for the worse. A perfect Being cannot get better, neither can a perfect Being get worse. So God cannot change. I deny the premise of this argument. That is, I deny that a change must always be for the better or for the worse. God is immutable relative to essential divine attributes, those powers and properties that constitute a perfect Being. God changes only in relational ways, in order to create and care for that creation. The ability to change in response to others is part of what makes God a perfect Being.

Finally, some might object that if God is only *relatively* timeless, God cannot be fully omniscient.[33] I am not quite persuaded that this is the case. There are complex issues involved in Molinism, Ockhamism and related topics.[34] The Boethian way out of the dilemma of divine omni-

---

[32]Ibid., pp. 273-75.

[33]William Hasker has come to this conclusion. See his *God, Time and Knowledge* (Ithaca, N.Y.: Cornell University Press, 1989) and his chapter in Clark Pinnock et al., *The Openness of God* (Downers Grove, Ill.: InterVarsity Press, 1994).

[34]See the excellent surveys of this problem by Zagzebski, *Dilemma,* and William Lane Craig, *Divine Foreknowledge and Human Freedom* (Leiden, Netherlands: Brill, 1991).

science and human freedom may not be the only road available to us. In any case, since we should reject the traditional notion of absolute timelessness, the Boethian avenue is a dead end. We must find another way forward. But that is a journey for another day.[35]

---

[35]I want to thank Greg Ganssle for his helpful criticisms of an earlier draft of this chapter.

RESPONSE TO ALAN G. PADGETT

PAUL HELM

I applaud the positive things that Alan says regarding the intuitions about the divine sovereignty and transcendence which motivate many who argue for divine timeless eternity. I also agree with him that the logical ordering of intentions in the divine mind is compatible with timeless eternity of God's existence. And in common with many others, I find myself in agreement with much of what Alan says by way of criticism of the Stump-Kretzmann account of ET-duration.

What I wish first to focus upon is the following claim, which is central to Alan's own position, which he calls relative timelessness: "Our time takes place within (and only because of the prior existence of) God's own time." Let us call this statement *P*. I shall leave aside the difficult question whether time has an intrinsic metric, except to say this. If, as Alan says, "all temporal measure is dependent on the laws of nature, and on the choice of some clock to act as the standard for temporal measure," then how could we ever know that the intervals measured by the laws, or by the clock, are intervals of the same temporal length?

But here's a dilemma for this view that God is "the Lord of time."

Either our time is backwardly everlasting or it is not. If it is backwardly everlasting then it is hard to see how *P* could be true, because it is hard to see what sense could be given to one stretch of time's existing within another, if both stretches of time are backwardly everlasting. Perhaps Alan will agree. But then let us suppose that time is not backwardly everlasting, and that our time begins to exist in God's own time. Then God's pure duration, duration without change, is not so pure; it is divided into intervals, the interval occurring before the creation, and the interval existing contemporaneously with our time, and perhaps (if we were to suppose that the universe might cease to be) the interval that occurs after the universe stops existing. There are times before the creation, the event of the creation, and times contemporaneous with the continuance of the creation, and (possibly) times after. So it looks hard to sustain the idea of divine pure duration, a central feature of Alan's account.

Here I shall try to understand some further remarks of Alan's on the relation between God and such pure duration. He says, "God's time exists because God exists." God is the metaphysical precondition for the existence of eternity. God's own temporality is dependent on the Being of God. So God's Being is a necessary precondition of God's time (eternity), the time of pure duration. But not a sufficient condition? So God's time is a contingent feature of God. And so, despite the parallel Alan attempts to draw between God's eternity and other divine attributes, God's eternity is crucially different in one respect, for these attributes are always and necessarily a part of God's existence, since on classical views of God's existence goodness and omnipotence are necessary or essential properties of God. While God exists conceptually prior to the eternity of pure duration (according to Alan) in that it depends on him, he cannot exist conceptully prior to being good or omnipotent.

According to Alan there could not be created time unless God was in his own time; hence according to *P* only if God wills his own eternity can he will created time. But if divine pure eternality is contingent, why does God need it? On Alan's view God is timelessly eternal but chooses to create pure time, within which created time exists. This looks unnecessarily cumbersome. Why not say what is simpler, that a timelessly eternal God creates the universe *cum tempore?* All that Alan well says, in concluding his paper, about God's lordship of time and his plan of providence can just as well be accommodated within classical Augustinianism, with much less machinery than Alan introduces.

Alan uses both a philosophical argument and a theological argument against the stasis view. Let us look at each of these in turn.

While I concur with Alan that the atemporal view of eternity depends on the stasis theory of time, I find his philosophical defense of the process view of time unconvincing. He defends it by one argument, by an appeal to experience. But of course stasis theorists do not deny the experience of processes—how could they?—but they offer a different account of it. Alan also chides Hugh Mellor, a leading B-theorist, for failing to explain away process facts. He asserts that according to Mellor the true sentence "Jim races tomorrow" spoken on June 1, does not entail that June 2 is tomorrow, and that this is clearly mistaken. But Alan fails to appreciate that we can say of any date that, with respect to that date, the immediately subsequent date is tomorrow. But it does not follow that the date in question is actually tomorrow—the date that is immediately after the date that is now. There are, therefore, two senses of "tomorrow": tomorrow with respect to the date that immediately precedes it (whatever that date may be) and tomorrow as the day after today.

Alan also makes remarks that stasis theories rely too heavily on abstractions, human creations. But I doubt that logic has quite the metaphysical power that Alan supposes. The fact that Arthur Prior's strongly held views about human freedom and the openness of the future (expressed, for example in his *Papers on Time and Tense* [Oxford: Clarendon, 1968]) led him to pioneer the development of tense logic (as found, for example, in *Past, Present and Future* [Oxford: Clarendon, 1967]) is one piece of evidence to suggest that it is not the logic that drives the metaphysics but the other way round. There is certainly no one-way street from logic to metaphysics.

Second, on the theological appeal, it is not at all clear to me what the argument is that is intended to demonstrate that the very idea of God sustaining the universe shows that the stasis theory of time is false. Alan claims that God's sustaining of all things means that he is responsible directly for the being of all things, at all times, and that on the stasis theory of time nothing that ever has existed or will exist passes out of existence from a timeless perspective. But in the course of arguing this Alan may reveal some confusion; for while on the stasis view nothing that ever has existed or will exist passes out of existence from a timeless perspective, this does not imply that what exists in the universe does so necessarily or for all times. If a flower blooms from t_1 to t_2 then on the stasis view that blooming starts at t_1 and ceases at t_2. But that it ceases at t_2 is due to God's eternally sustaining the blooming precisely from t_1 to t_2. Had the flower bloomed until t_3 then of course it would have bloomed for longer, and God would in that case have sustained the blooming from t_1 to t_3. But though he would have sustained this blooming timelessly, the blooming thus sustained is not metaphysically necessary, nor does it occur for all time. So the stasis view is perfectly consistent with things' coming into and passing out of existence, with temporal change, but it gives an account of such change in terms of the possession or lack of temporally indexed properties, as in our example. And it is perfectly compatible with the contingency of the creation. So it is hard to see how the idea (accepted by all Christian theists) that God sustains the universe, giving to each thing whatever basic properties and causal powers that thing possesses, trumps the very idea of God's timelessness.

So I believe that Alan goes wrong in misunderstanding the idea of God's sustaining all things, on the eternalist view. God is responsible directly for the being of all things at all times. But God timelessly gives being to a thing for a period of time. At any time anything exists, God sustains it. God does so timelessly, not "at all times."

What it means for a timeless God to act on really existing things is for God timelessly to will the existing of a thing, and timelessly to will different temporally indexed properties in temporally successive fashion. If (to continue the botanical theme) God eternally wills the existence of a bush at t_1, then to say that he acts on the bush (to make it burn, say, at t_2) is to say that he eternally wills its burning at t_2. So the bush is acted upon and changes, and (for a theist) it changes in virtue of God's eternally willing its existence at t_1 and eternally willing its combustion at t_2. So a proponent of the stasis view of time can give a perfectly consistent and intelligible account of what it means for a timeless God to act upon the creation he sustains without having to make the fatal concession that such a God must wait for the present moment to act on really existing things.

RESPONSE TO ALAN G. PADGETT

WILLIAM LANE CRAIG

O f the four views discussed in this book, Alan Padgett's view of divine eternity most closely resembles my own. I well recall, upon reading his doctoral thesis, my sense of gratification mingled with alarm that someone had anticipated virtually every one of the conclusions in my own developing work on God and time! The chief difference between Alan and me concerns the issue of metric conventionalism with respect to time, which in turn affects how we understand God's temporal status sans creation.

Alan draws an important distinction between "pure duration" and "measured time." But his characterization of this distinction is ambiguous, and his employment of it leads me to think that he has conflated a number of separate distinctions here.

First and foremost is Isaac Newton's famous distinction between time itself and our sensible measures thereof. Newton characterizes time itself as "absolute, true, and mathematical . . . duration," whereas our measures of time yield a "relative, apparent, and common time."[1] Like Alan, Newton

---

[1] Isaac Newton, *The Principia*, trans. I. Bernard Cohen and Anne Whitman (Berkeley: University of California Press, 1999), p. 408.

thinks of time itself as grounded in God, although Alan seems to think of time as dependent on God's free volition, whereas Newton takes it to be a concomitant of the very being of God.[2] Measured time for Newton as for Alan is the time registered by time-keeping devices, which is subject to distortion due to physical influences. Newton speaks of the motion of our clocks as being fast or slow,[3] and there is no reason to doubt that he would have agreed with Alan, had he been confronted with the evidence that measured time so defined is affected by the motion of one's clock and the presence of gravitational fields. Thus Alan's initial explication of the distinction between pure duration and measured time sounds like vintage Newton. In this sense "relative timelessness" is a complete misnomer; "true temporality" would have been a more accurate label of Alan's view.

The great French physicist Henri Poincaré drew a quite different distinction between "absolute" and "conventional" metrics of time.[4] The metric of time has to do with the comparative extents of nonoverlapping temporal intervals. For Newton time has an objective metric; for two temporal intervals *ab* and *cd* there is an objective fact of the matter concerning their comparative extents: either *ab=cd,* or *ab>cd,* or *ab<cd.* But on Poincaré's view, the metric of time is a convention adopted for the sake of convenience only. There literally is no fact of the matter concerning the comparative lengths of separated temporal intervals. Thus on Poincaré's view it is neither true nor false that the Indy 500 lasted longer than the running of the Kentucky Derby.

Now Alan, in differentiating God's time from measured time, sometimes really means to endorse metric conventionalism with respect to God's time. This is what he means, for example, when he says that God's time is immeasurable. His claim that temporal measure depends on the laws of nature, which in turn depend on created structures and regularities, must be an assertion of precisely Poincaré's conventionalism; otherwise he would be involved in the self-contradiction of holding that measured time is not a measure of time. He must mean that God's time is immeasurable in

---

[2] Ibid., p. 941.
[3] Ibid., p. 410.
[4] Henri Poincaré, "The Measure of Time," in H. Poincaré, *The Value of Science,* in *The Foundations of Science,* trans. G. B. Halstead (Washington, D.C.: University Press of America, 1982), p. 228; Henri Poincaré, "Sur les principes de la géometrie," *Revue de métaphysique et de morale* 8 (1900): 80; Henri Poincaré, *Science and Hypothesis,* in *Foundations of Science,* p. 92.

the sense that it has no objective metric. It is on this basis that he claims that prior to creation God's time was neither finite nor infinite in extent.

Here is where confusion sets in. Newton's distinction between absolute time and measured time has nothing to do with and in no way implies Poincaré's distinction between absolute and conventional metrics of time. The fact that Newton's measured time depends on clocks that are determined by the laws of nature does not imply that temporal intervals have no objective measure (metric) in the sense of comparative extent. Similarly, in relativity theory the metric of time is not relative to inertial frames; on the contrary it is invariant. If $ab > cd$ relative to one frame, the same holds in all frames, and the proper time recorded by a clock (that is, the physical time actually ticked off by the clock between two events) is the same for all observers, regardless of their inertial frame. Similarly with gravitational fields: only the quantity of time elapsed is affected by such fields, not the comparative extents of intervals.

Metric conventionalism is a radical view rooted in a verificationist epistemology and rejected by the vast majority of philosophers of time and space. Certainly there are no good arguments for it. So why think that time has no metric structure? Is not such a view outrageously implausible? As Michael Friedman points out,[5] our scientific theoretical concepts must connect with our pretheoretical understanding if we are to know what we are talking about. For example, thermodynamics deals with temperature phenomena. If we set up measuring procedures as part of such a theory which yielded the result that an ice cube has the same "temperature" as a blast furnace, then we just are not dealing with a theory of temperature. Similarly, if we develop a theory of temporal congruence using measurement procedures such that the era of galaxy formation turns out to have the same temporal duration as my lunch break, then we are just not talking about temporal duration. Any property shared to the same degree by the era of galaxy formation and my lunch break simply is not duration.

Moreover, if we deny that time has an objective metric, then, as Peter

---

[5]Michael Friedman, "Grünbaum on the Conventionality of Geometry," in *Space, Time and Geometry*, ed. Patrick Suppes, Synthese Library (Dordrecht, Netherlands: D. Reidel, 1973), pp. 231-32.

Kroes points out, our temporal metrics as determined by, say, mechanical, gravitational or electromagnetic clocks may not stay in synchronism, and the unity of time becomes a mere assumption.[6] Lawrence Sklar notes that there are natural measures of time which yield simple, elegant laws of nature and that a wide variety of clocks not only will agree with each other in their metric of time but will measure time in a way that approximates the natural measure. But if the metric of time is a mere convention, then *any* process has equal right to the status of the standard measure, regardless of how sporadic it might be relative to the concordant "natural" measures. But would Alan really think that the metric of time determined, say, by Richard Swinburne's periodic visits to Sainsbury's would be as equally valid a choice for the standard measure as the periods of an atomic clock? The fact that we think that time has an objective metric is witnessed by our willingness to correct our clocks. As J. R. Lucas says, "If we really regarded time simply as the measure of process, we should have no warrant for regarding some processes as regular and others as irregular. . . . So long as we are prepared to assess the time-keeping qualities of a clock, and are prepared in principle to replace it by a more regular one, if it could be obtained, we are committed to an idea of absolute time which is not simply what the clocks actually say."[7]

A third distinction that may be lurking behind the scenes is that drawn by the French philosopher Henri Bergson between what he called "real duration" *(durée réelle)* and mathematical time. Bergson held that the analysis of time on the model of a geometrical line composed of points (in this case instants) is a mere conceptual construct that we impose on time, whereas time itself is not composed of instants but is an uncomposed flowing or duration. The "mathematization" of time is a convenient fiction for scientific purposes, but the metaphysician should not take literally the concept of time as a point-set of instants. Alan's contrast between "pure duration" and time as "the numbering of change according to before and after" makes me wonder whether he is not also endorsing Bergson's view. I think that Bergson is, in fact, correct, and

---

[6]Peter Kroes, *Time: Its Structure and Role in Physical Theories*, Synthese Library 179 (Dordrecht, Netherlands: D. Reidel, 1985), p. 8.
[7]J. R. Lucas, *A Treatise on Time and Space* (London: Methuen, 1973), p. 91.

his ontology can be useful in dealing with certain metrical puzzles about time (e.g., how long is the present?). But again it needs to be understood that Bergson's view does not imply metric conventionalism. Once we do specify conceptually instants in time, then there is no reason to doubt, for example, that the duration of the Clinton presidency was shorter than the duration of the Jurassic Age.

It seems to me, therefore, that Alan has conflated a number of independent distinctions and that once we get clear on these no reason remains for adopting metric conventionalism with respect to God's time, which is crucial for Alan's claim that prior to creation God did not endure through any interval of time. We may agree that God's time is distinct from the sensible measures that stand in for time in the physical sciences and may see time as the freely willed creation of God. We may further regard the analysis of time on the mathematical model of a geometrical line as a conceptual construct rather than a realistic description of time. But there is no reason to follow Alan in embracing the bizarre doctrine of chronometric conventionalism.

RESPONSE TO ALAN G. PADGETT

NICHOLAS WOLTERSTORFF

I fail to see that Alan Padgett's "relative timelessness" proposal is really a third model of the relation of God to time. It appears to me definitely to be a variant on the everlastingness view. It is, in fact, fully compatible with my own articulation and defense of the everlastingness view. In some respects it goes beyond my own commitments; at no point does it go against them.

Before I get to that, however, I want to say something about Alan's grounds for rejecting the timelessness view. He argues that the timelessness view of God can be true only if the stasis, or nonprocess, understanding of time is correct. He furthermore shares my own commitment to the "process" understanding of time; what J. M. E. McTaggart called the A-series of past, present and future, is just as objectively real as what he called the B-series of succession and simultaneity. From these premises Alan concludes that the timelessness view of God cannot be correct.

Alan tacitly acknowledges that whether or not the timelessness view of God is compatible with the process view of time depends crucially on what else one takes to be true of God; it's possible to understand God in such a way that the two views are compatible. What he himself adds is "the idea that God sustains the universe (that is, everything that has being) in its being, as long as it exists." His argument is that if one takes this to be true of God, and if one holds to a process understanding of time, then one cannot hold that God is timeless.

Insofar as Alan's objection doesn't beg the question, this seems to me not true, however. His argument hinges on there being "a problem with a timeless God's causing temporal things to happen without a change to God's own being." But Aquinas, in the passage I quote in my own essay, gave what seems to me a satisfactory answer to what Alan sees as the problem here. The problem, as he sees it, is that "bringing something into existence, or ceasing to sustain something, is a real change in the Creator." "Even a timeless God must wait for the present to occur, in order to act upon real things, if the process theory of time is true." Aquinas would respond that this way of phrasing the objection begs the question. Distinguish, says Aquinas, between the time of one's decision to bring about some event and the time that one decides shall be the time of its occurrence; to illustrate Aquinas's point, I use an example of a child's toy. Of course it's perfectly clear from Alan's way of framing the objection that he is operating with an interventionist understanding of God's action, whereas Aquinas is committed to a noninterventionist view; it's really the interventionist understanding of God's action that is incompatible with the timelessness view. But since Aquinas and other eminently respectable Christian theologians held the noninterventionist understanding, Alan, if he wishes his argument to have polemical force, cannot simply take the interventionist understanding for granted.

Something similar has to be said for Alan's attempt, later in his essay, to get an argument against God's timelessness from the fact of God's knowledge. I too think that a right understanding of God's knowledge leads to the conclusion that God is everlasting rather than timeless; but I think that that right understanding of God's knowledge, in the face of those who defend timelessness, requires considerably more articulation and defense than Alan gives it.

Mainly, though, I want to speak of Alan's theory of "relative timelessness." Much of the time in his discussion it sounds as if the core of his thesis is that there are two times, "God's time" and "created time," and that, compared to created time, God's time is relatively timeless. The core of the difference is that though in God's time there is duration, so that in that way it is genuinely temporal, nonetheless there is no metric for God's time. The possibility of a metric for time comes along with creation.

Alan objects to the straight everlastingness view that it compromises God's transcendence, whereas his own view allows for transcendence in three ways: God is the Creator of our time, God's own time is infinite in that it is not susceptible to our metrics or any others, and God's time is grounded in God rather than God being grounded in God's time.

It seems to me, however, that Alan's view cannot really be that there are these two times. For one thing, if that really were his view, it would be incumbent on him to explain to us how these two times are related; he gives no such explanation whatsoever. But second, the view that God has a time distinct from ours which is metric-free seems to me clearly incompatible with the argument that Alan mounted against the timelessness view. Remember that he took for granted an interventionist understanding of God's action. That implies that God does one thing at this time and another thing at that time. And this implies, in turn, that our metric does apply to God: God brings about this event a hundred years before God beings about that event, and so forth.

It seems to me, then, that Alan's view has to be that there is just one time. That time is a feature of God's own life. There's no metric for it, however, until God creates this world of ours with its various cyclical processes making possible a metric for time.

Whether it's true that time is an inherent feature of God's own life I do not know. But in any case, it's fully compatible with my articulation and defense of the everlastingness view to hold that it is. Furthermore, if time is a feature of God's own life, then obviously God is ontologically more basic than this feature of God's life. In addition, any Christian would hold that God is the Creator of this world of ours, with its cyclical processes which can serve as metrics for time. It's for these reasons, then, that I conclude that Alan has not really given us a third model for the relation of God to time. His model is a version of the everlastingness model, in which he commits himself to a thesis—about which I have remained uncommitted—concerning the place of time in God's life apart from creation.

Early in his essay Alan remarks that God must be "outside of any merely created category." The suggestion is that God must be outside of "our" time. But in the very same paragraph Alan insists that God is not outside the category of personhood; personhood is thus not a *merely* created category. I think the best interpretation of his view is that time, the one and only time there is, is likewise not a *merely* created category but characterizes the very life of God.

RESPONSE TO CRITICS

ALAN G. PADGETT

*I*t is good of Nick, Paul and Bill to reply to my chapter with their usual insight and energy. Even when I disagree with them, I admire each of them as philosophers, and I am happy for this opportunity both to clarify my position and to respond to their comments.

The position I outline depends crucially on the difference between pure duration and time as we know it in physics and everyday life. Nick denies that this is a real distinction, thinking that for me "there is just one time." Well, this is both true and false. There is only one ontological time, true. That is pure duration, which is God's own time. But our experience and knowledge of physical time, created time as we know it, is different in some important ways. Pure duration is a rather thin ontological category without the robustness of changing things to make it concrete and to measure it. I see these as differing aspects of time, or approaches and experiences of time. Because this distinction makes sense to me, I do think that I offer an alternative to his view, in which God is wholly within time. I pay attention to the intuition (which Paul applauds!) that in some manner the Creator must transcend time. Nick does not; in fact he is forced to admit that time is *not* a created category, on pain of incoherence. And this seems rather odd. Surely some aspect(s) of time must be created, when God first begins to make the universe. Or does that incredible event make no difference to time?

I cannot explain at this time my views on divine action and the laws of nature (a current project which I hope to have time to finish). But I accept the medieval notion that God both creates the universe and does special acts beyond natural powers with his absolute omnipotence *(potentia Dei absoluta)*. However, it is just as important that God contin- ues to uphold the common course of nature, throughout time, by his ordained power *(potentia Dei ordinata)*.[1] The issue is not about "inter- vention," whatever one thinks of that. Rather, it is about God's ordained power, by which (moment by moment) he upholds the universe through secondary causes like the laws of nature. Of course Aquinas, like all the great medieval Christian philosophers, thought this was com- patible with God's complete simplicity and atemporality. But I disagree.

The issue between Nick, Paul and myself (not to mention St. Thomas) depends on what we mean by "will." If the "will" of God is a *plan* or *intention*, fine: that does not have to change, given God's foreknowl- edge. But "will" also includes the use of power, especially among medi- eval philosophical theologians. So if the "will" of God is a *concrete action*, then I think they are in trouble. For if the process theory of time is true, and the blooming flower is far in the future, then God's "will" has to change in order to sustain that flower as a *concrete act*. Assuming a process view of time, either God does the same thing throughout time or God does *new* things. Atemporal eternity is compatible only with the first position, as I argued fully against Aquinas (and Eleonore Stump) in my previous book.

I think I had better explain myself again concerning "our time," given the fact that Paul misunderstands my position. By "our time" I always mean physical time, time as we know it because of the creation. This is not ontologically distinct from God's own time, eternity or pure duration (which is infinite and immeasurable). But "our time," which is physical

[1]See, e.g., William of Ockham *Quodlibeta Septem* 6.q1; English translation by A. J. Fred- doso and F. E. Kelley, *Quodlibetal Questions*, 2 vols. (New Haven, Conn.: Yale University Press, 1991), 2:491-92. See further William J. Courtenay, *Covenant and Causality in Medi- eval Thought* (London: Variorum, 1984).

time or measured time, exists only with physical things. And so "our time" has a beginning, even though every moment of our time is simultaneous with a moment of God's time.

Paul notes that God's time is divided into intervals. And it is true that, on my view, God undergoes temporal passage from past to present to future. And so yes, intervals are part of God's eternity. What I deny is that there is any sense to the measure of those intervals. This is what distinguishes the vast majority of philosophers of time (who accept temporal metric as a convention) from Bill. Bill writes as if my view were the minority: when in fact almost all philosophers of time hold—for excellent reasons!—that temporal measure is a convention. Choosing a good clock, of course, is not purely arbitrary. There are rational values like simplicity which guide our choice of clocks. But time of itself, like space, has no objective and intrinsic metric. To believe that is does is a rather odd notion, given the relativity of temporal measure in modern physics.

Paul wants to know if temporality is a necessary property for God. I am not as sure as he is that God's goodness and omnipotence are logically necessary divine attributes. But he is right, this is the traditional view, and so other examples would have been better. Deciding to become incarnate, for example, depends on God's prior existence. If God the Son knows from eternity that he will take up human flesh, then the property of "willing to become human" is a property God the Son always has, but does not have of necessity. God's temporality, I believe, is similar.

The next problem Paul raises is more difficult. On the stasis theory of time, God sustains the flower at t_1-to-t_3 and does so "always" (here we must take the tense out of "always" to get the point). This is an act that an atemporal God can do, since he does not have to change to bring it about. The flower "always" (tenselessly) exists at t_1-to-t_3; it does not pass out of existence just because mere humans experience t_4 as the "present" moment. My critique of the stasis view of time is more fundamental than the rather simple error Paul attributes to me.

Finally, Bill's viewpoint is almost the same as my own. The minor differences between us are almost not worth debating. Since this is true, I find it odd that he uses such rhetorically loaded, emotional terms in his comments. So I turn with some reluctance to the only major issue between us.

Bill seems to equate metric conventionalism with a kind of arbitrariness or antirealism with regard to temporal measure. That is certainly *not* the issue. And I believe Bill misunderstands the position he labels "metric conventionalism," which is the view I (and most philosophers of physics today) would hold. For one thing, Bill completely confuses *comparative size* with *metric*. This is like confusing "greater than" and "lesser than" with actual *numbers*. Let us take an example from space and distance. Let's say that there is a tower 26'6" tall. I stand in front of this tower, which is taller than I am. And this comparative size will be invariant for all possible observers (inertial frames). So far so good. However, the fact that I am 6'6" will not be measured to be the same by all observers. And the fact that the tower is twenty feet taller than I am is also relative. High speed, or powerful gravity, can alter our *spatial metric*. I don't see how the invariance of comparative size (one thing's being longer than another in time or space) helps Bill at all in his quixotic quest for an intrinsic *metric*.

On my view, the measure of time is stable, and our choice of "clocks" is rational. We do not live in a chaotic world. The stability of our temporal measure is based on the regularities of nature, created by God, and hence is just as stable as they are. We choose the best "clock" on rational principles, not caprice. To say that our measure of time is true within our inertial frame of reference is not the same as saying these measures are "rooted in a verificationist epistemology," or that "*any* process has equal right to the status of standard measure." Instead of such rather hasty generalizations, my view is in fact this. We have come to know, in the light of Special Relativity, that exactly the same temporal interval (say, the time between my birth and Bill's) can be *measured* as being very different, if we are in a different inertial frame of reference. Those measurements are true and valid within that frame but cannot be properly extrapolated into an absolute or intrinsic metric. As a matter of fact, I do agree with Bergson that mathematical time is a (very useful and important) scientific conceptual construct. But even if I did not, my main point would be the same. Bergson is irrelevant to our debate. This is because the measure of time (metric) is what is at stake, not its mathematical modeling. That measure is different for different "observers" moving at high speeds relative to each other, in the world that God has in fact created. The measure of time is created along with the physical universe and is just as stable as the other principles and laws of nature that God upholds moment by moment. But temporal measure does not apply to God any more than the laws and principles of nature do. God's own infinite, pure eternity is not measured by physical reality.

4

TIMELESSNESS & OMNITEMPORALITY

WILLIAM LANE CRAIG

God, Isaiah proclaims, is "the high and lofty one who inhabits eternity" (Is 57:15). But the nature of divine eternity is left unclear. Minimally, it may be said that God's being eternal means that God exists without beginning or end. He never comes into or goes out of existence; rather his existence is permanent.

But there agreement ends. Is God temporal or timeless? Oftimes laypeople, anxious to affirm both God's transcendence and God's immanence, assert that God is both timeless and temporal. But in the absence of some sort of model or explanation of how this can be the case, this assertion is flatly self-contradictory and so cannot be true. One cannot affirm both.

Now the question is: does the biblical teaching on divine eternity favor either one of these views? This question turns out to be surprisingly difficult to answer.[1] On the one hand, it is indisputable that the biblical writers typically portray God as engaged in temporal activities, including fore-

---

[1]See Alan G. Padgett, *God, Eternity, and the Nature of Time* (1992; reprint, Eugene, Ore.: Wipf & Stock, 2000), chap. 2; Paul Helm, *Eternal God* (Oxford: Clarendon, 1988), pp. 5-11.

knowing the future and remembering the past, and when they speak directly of God's eternal existence they do so in terms of beginningless and endless temporal duration (Ps 90:2; Rev 4:8).

But the biblical data are not wholly one-sided. Genesis 1:1, which is neither a subordinate clause nor a summary title,[2] speaks of an absolute beginning. This absolute beginning, taken in conjunction with the expression "And there was evening and there was morning, the first day" (v. 5), may very well be intended to teach that the beginning was not simply the beginning of the physical universe but the beginning of time itself and that consequently God may be thought of as timeless.[3] The most striking New Testament reflection on Genesis 1:1 is, of course, John 1:1. Here the uncreated Word, the source of all created things, was already with God and was God in the beginning. It is not hard to interpret this passage in terms of the Word's timeless unity with God—nor would it be anachronistic to do so, given the first-century Jewish philosopher Philo's doctrine of the divine *Logos* and Philo's belief that time begins with creation.[4]

Or again, Proverbs 8:22-23 is certainly capable of being read in terms of a beginning of time. The passage, which doubtless looks back to Genesis 1:1, is brimming with temporal expressions for a beginning.[5]

---

[2]See exegesis by Claus Westermann, *Genesis 1-11,* trans. John Scullion (Minneapolis: Augsburg, 1984), p. 97; John Sailhamer, *Genesis,* Expositor's Bible Commentary 2 (Grand Rapids, Mich.: Zondervan, 1990), pp. 21-22.

[3]This conclusion is rendered all the more plausible when the Genesis account of creation is read against the backdrop of ancient Egyptian cosmogony (John D. Currid, "An Examination of the Egyptian Background of the Genesis Cosmogony," *Biblische Zeitschrift* 35 [1991]: 18-40).

[4]On the beginning of time with creation, see Philo of Alexandria, *On the Creation of the Cosmos According to Moses,* trans. with introduction and commentary by David T. Runia, Philo of Alexandria Commentary Series 1 (Leiden, Netherlands: E. J. Brill, forthcoming); cf. Richard Sorabji, *Time, Creation and the Continuum* (Ithaca, N.Y.: Cornell University Press, 1983), pp. 203-9. For a discussion of the similarities between John's prologue and Philo's *De opificio* 16-19, in which his *logos* doctrine of creation is described, see C. H. Dodd, *The Interpretation of the Fourth Gospel* (Cambridge: Cambridge University Press, 1953), pp. 66-73, 276-77.

[5]R. N. Whybray comments, "It should be noted how the writer . . . was so insistent on pressing home the fact of Wisdom's unimaginable antiquity that he piled up every available synonym in a deluge of tautologies: *re'sît,* **beginning,** *qedem,* **the first,** *me'az,* **of old,** *me olam,* **ages ago,** *mero's,* **at the first** or 'from the beginning' (compare Isa. 40.21; 41.4, 26), *miqqad' me'ares,* **before the beginning of the earth:** the emphasis is not so much on the *mode* of Wisdom's coming into existence, . . . but on the *fact* of her antiquity" (R. N. Whybray, *Proverbs,* New Century Bible Commentary [Grand Rapids, Mich.: Eerdmans, 1994], pp. 131-32).

Otto Plöger comments that through God's creative work "the possibility of speaking of 'time' was first given; thus, before this time, right at the beginning, Wisdom came into existence through Yahweh [the LORD]."[6] The passage was so understood by other ancient writers. The Septuagint renders *me 'olam* in Proverbs 8:23 as *pro tou aionios* (before time), and Sirach 24:9 has Wisdom say, "Before the ages, in the beginning, he created me, and for all the ages I shall not cease to be" (cf. 16:26; 23:20).

Significantly, certain New Testament passages also seem to affirm a beginning of time. For example, the doxology in Jude 25 ascribes glory to God "before all time and now and forever" *(pro pantos tou aionos kai nun kai eis pantas tous aionas).* The passage contemplates an everlasting future duration but affirms a beginning to past time and thereby implies God's existence, using an almost inevitable *façon de parler,* "before" time began. Similar expressions are found in two intriguing passages in the Pastoral Epistles. In Titus 1:2-3, a passage laden with temporal language, we read of those chosen by God "in the hope of eternal life *[zoes aioniou]* that God, who never lies, promised before age-long time *[pro chronon aionion]* but manifested at the proper time *[kairois idiois]*." And in 2 Timothy 1:9 we read of God's "purpose and grace, which were given to us in Christ Jesus before age-long time *[pro chronon aionion],* but now *[nun]* manifested by the appearing of our Savior Christ Jesus." W. F. Arndt and F. W. Gingrich render *pro chronon aionion* as "before time began."[7] Similarly, in 1 Corinthians 2:7 Paul speaks of a secret, hidden wisdom of God "which God decreed before the ages *[pro ton aionon]* for our glory." Such expressions are in line with the Septuagint, which describes God as "the one who exists before the ages *[ho hyparchon pro ton aionon]*" (Ps 54:20 LXX [Ps 55:19]). That such *pro* constructions are to be taken seriously is confirmed by the many similar expressions concerning God and his decrees "before the foundation of the world *[pro kataboles kosmou]*" (Jn. 17:24; Eph 1:4; 1 Pet 1:20; cf. Rev 13:8). Evidently it was a common understanding of the

---

[6]Otto Plöger, *Sprüche Salomos,* Biblisches Kommentar altes Testaments 17 (Neukirchen-Vluyn, Germany: Neukirchner Verlag, 1984), p. 92. Cf. Arndt Meinhold's comment: "Its [time's] beginning is set at the first act of creation" (Arndt Meinhold, *Die Sprüche,* Zürcher Bibelkommentare [Zürich: Theologischer Verlag Zürich, 1991], 1:144).

[7]Walter Bauer, *A Greek-English Lexicon of the New Testament,* trans. and ed. W. F. Arndt and F. W. Gingrich (Chicago: University of Chicago Press, 1979), s.v. "aionios."

creation described in Genesis 1:1 that the beginning of the world was coincident with the beginning of time or the ages; but since God did not begin to exist at the moment of creation, it therefore followed that he existed "before" the beginning of time. God, at least "before" creation, must therefore be atemporal.

Thus, although scriptural authors speak of God as temporal and everlasting, there is some evidence, at least, that when God is considered in relation to creation he must be thought of as the transcendent Creator of time and the ages and therefore as existing beyond time. It may well be the case that in the context of the doctrine of creation the biblical writers were led to reflect on God's relationship to time and chose to affirm his transcendence. Still the evidence is not clear, and we seem forced to conclude with James Barr that "if such a thing as a Christian doctrine of time has to be developed, the work of discussing it and developing it must belong not to biblical but to philosophical theology."[8]

Divine Timelessness

"Whatever includes and possesses the whole fullness of interminable life at once and is such that nothing future is absent from it and nothing past has flowed away, this is rightly judged to be eternal," wrote the medieval theologian Boethius.[9] On such an understanding of divine eternity God transcends time altogether. But what reasons can be given for adopting such an understanding of God's eternity?

One of the most important arguments in favor of divine timelessness rests on the claim that the fleeting nature of temporal life is incompatible with the life of a most perfect being such as God is. For example, in his study of time and eternity, Brian Leftow draws upon Boethius's characterization of eternity in order to argue for the defectiveness of temporal existence.[10] Leftow points out that a temporal being is unable to enjoy what is past or future for it. The past is gone forever, and the future is yet to come. The passage of time thus renders it impossible for any temporal being to possess all its life at once. Even God, if he is temporal, cannot reclaim the past. Leftow emphasizes that even perfect memory

---

[8]James Barr, *Biblical Words for Time* (London: SCM Press, 1962), p. 149.
[9]Boethius *Consolation of Philosophy* 5.6.25-31.
[10]Brian Leftow, *Time and Eternity* (Ithaca, N.Y.: Cornell University Press, 1991), p. 278.

cannot substitute for reality: "the past itself is *lost,* and no memory, however complete, can take its place—for confirmation, ask a widower if his grief would be abated were his memory of his wife enhanced in vividness and detail."[11] By contrast a timeless God lives all his life at once because he literally has no past or future and so suffers no loss. Therefore since God is the most perfect being, he is timeless.

We can formulate this argument as follows:

1. God is the most perfect being.

2. The most perfect being has the most perfect mode of existence.

3. Temporal existence is a less perfect mode of existence than timeless existence.

4. Therefore God has the most perfect mode of existence.

5. Therefore God has a timeless mode of existence.

I think that we have here an argument for divine timelessness which is really promising. The premises of the argument rest on very powerful intuitions about the irretrievable loss that arises through the experience of temporal passage, a loss that intuitively should not characterize the experience of a most perfect being. Time has a savage way of gnawing away at life, leaving it transitory and incomplete, so that life in its fullness can never be enjoyed by any temporal being.[12] The claim that the life of a most perfect being must be an indivisible actuality has, I think, a good deal of plausibility.

Some philosophers might try to avert the force of this argument by adopting a view of time—of which I shall have more to say later—according to which things and events do not in fact come to be or pass away. According to this view of time, often called the "tenseless" or "static" view, the past and future are just as real as the present. The difference between past, present and future is usually explained as just a subjective illusion of human consciousness. For the people located in 1868, for example, the events of 1868 are present and we are future; by the same token, for the people living in 2050 we are past, and it is the

---

[11] Ibid.

[12] The force of these considerations is such that Stump and Kretzmann rest their case for God's atemporality solely on the shoulders of this argument (Eleonore Stump and Norman Kretzmann, "Prophecy, Past Truth and Eternity," *Philosophical Perspectives* 5 [1991]: 395; cf. Eleonore Stump and Norman Kretzmann, "Eternity, Awareness and Action," *Faith and Philosophy* 9 [1992]: 463).

events of 2050 that are present. Time is akin to a spatial line, and all the points of the line are equally real. On such a view of time, if something has a finite lifetime, it does not come into being at a certain point and go out of being at a later point. Rather it just exists at those two points and all the points in between. The longer a thing's temporal extension, the longer its lifetime. If the temporal extensions of two persons overlap, then they will regard themselves as both present during that period of overlap. If one has a longer time line than the other, then the person with the longer time line will regard the other as at some point no longer present; but, say the philosophers who hold this view, if that person is philosophically informed, he will not regard his fellow as nonexistent.

Albert Einstein, who came to adopt this view of time, took this idea so seriously that when his lifelong friend Michael Besso died he tried to comfort Besso's surviving son and sister by writing, "This signifies nothing. For us believing physicists the distinction between past, present, and future is only an illusion, even if a stubborn one."[13] On this view of time no temporal being ever really loses its past or has not yet acquired its future. Just as things are extended in space, so they are also extended in time. A temporal being has nothing to lose and nothing to gain; it just exists tenselessly at its temporal locations. Thus a temporal God would exist at all temporal locations without beginning or end to his temporal extension. On this view of time God does not lose or acquire portions of his life.

The problem with this escape route is that it fails to appreciate that the argument is based on the *experience* of temporal passage rather than on the objective reality of temporal passage itself. The flow of time is an ineradicable part of the experience of a temporal being. Even if the future never becomes and the past is never really lost, the fact remains that for a temporal being the past is lost *to him* and the future is not accessible *to him*. As H. G. Wells's celebrated Time Traveler, who believed that time was a fourth dimension of space, remarked, "Our mental existences, which are immaterial and have no dimensions, are passing along the Time-Dimension with a uniform velocity from the cra-

---

[13]Letter of Albert Einstein, March 21, 1955, quoted in Banesh Hoffmann with Helen Dukas, *Albert Einstein: Creator and Rebel* (London: Hart-Davis, MacGibbon, 1972), p. 258.

dle to the grave."[14] Even if the cradle and the grave are just as real as the present, we still find ourselves experientially at some point in between; events that are located at times earlier than that point are irretrievably lost to us, and events later than that point can only be anticipated. For this reason a tenseless or static theory of time does nothing to alleviate the loss occasioned by our experience of temporal becoming. I dare say that the bereaved find little comfort in the thought that a deceased loved one exists tenselessly at earlier temporal coordinates than those they occupy. Time's tooth gnaws away at our experience of life regardless of the tenseless existence of all events making up one's life. For this reason it would be futile to attempt to elude the force of this argument by postulating a temporal deity in a tenseless time.

Perhaps, however, the realization that the argument for divine timelessness from the incompleteness of temporal life is essentially experiential in character opens the door for a temporalist alternative. When we recall that God is perfectly omniscient and so forgets absolutely nothing of the past and knows everything about the future, time's tooth is considerably dulled for him. His past experiences do not fade as ours do, and he has perfect recall of what he has undergone. To be sure, the past itself is gone (given a tensed or dynamic view of time), but his experience of the past remains as vivid as ever. A fatal flaw in Leftow's analysis is his assumption that God, like the widower, has actually lost the persons he loves and remembers. According to Christian theism, this assumption is false. Those who perish physically live on in the afterlife, where they continue to be real and present to God. At worst, what are past are the experiences God has enjoyed of those persons, for example, Jones's coming to faith in Christ. But in the afterlife Jones lives on with God, and God can recall as though it were present his experience of Jones's conversion. So it is far from obvious that the experience of temporal passage is so melancholy an affair for an omniscient God as it is for us.

Moreover, it needs to be kept in mind that the life of a perfect person may have to be characterized by the incompleteness that would in other contexts be considered an imperfection. There is some evidence that con-

---

[14]H. G. Wells, *The Time Machine* (New York: Berkeley, 1957), p. 10. Of course the "passing along" must have reference to our *experience* of time's flow; contrary to Wells, psychological time passes at various rates.

sciousness of time's flow can actually be an enriching experience.[15] R. W. Hepburn cautions against downplaying the importance of the flow of consciousness in awareness of music, for example. Music appreciation is not merely a matter of apprehending tenselessly the succession of sounds. Quoting Charles Rosen to the effect that "the movement from past to future is more significant in music than the movement from left to right in a picture," Hepburn believes that the phenomenon of music calls into question any claim that a perfect mode of consciousness would be exclusively atemporal. All this goes to call into question premise 3 of the argument for divine timelessness from the incompleteness of temporal life. Timeless life may not be the most perfect mode of existence of a perfect person.

Still, I think we must admit that the argument has some force and could motivate justifiably a doctrine of divine timelessness in the absence of countermanding arguments. The question then will be whether the reasons for affirming divine temporality do not overwhelm this argument for divine timelessness.

Divine Temporality

Reacting to the Boethian view of divine eternity, the medieval Scottish theologian John Duns Scotus protested, "Eternity will not, by reason of its infinity, be present to any *non-existent* time. . . . If (assuming the impossible) the whole of time were *simultaneously* existent, the whole would be simultaneously present to eternity. . . . For the 'now' of eternity is formally infinite and therefore formally exceeds the 'now' of time. Nevertheless it does not co-exist with *another* 'now.'"[16] On Scotus's understanding of time and eternity, God coexists only with the present moment or "now." He is eternal in the sense that he endures forever. Again, we want to ask what reasons might be given for adopting this temporalist understanding of divine eternity. Of the various arguments on behalf of divine temporality, three stand out as especially significant.

The impossibility of atemporal personhood. Could God exist timelessly? Is there no logically conceivable world in which God exists and time does

---

[15]See the very interesting piece by R. W. Hepburn, "Time-Transcendence and Some Related Phenomena in the Arts," in *Contemporary British Philosophy,* 4th series, ed. H. D. Lewis, Muirhead Library of Philosophy (London: George Allen & Unwin, 1976), pp. 152-73.

[16]John Duns Scotus *Ordinatio* 1.38-39.9-10.

not? According to the Christian doctrine of creation, God's decision to create a universe was a freely willed decision from which God could have refrained. We can conceive, then, of a possible world in which God does refrain from creation, a world that is empty except for God. Would time exist in such a world? Certainly it would if God were changing, experiencing a stream of consciousness. But suppose God were altogether changeless. Suppose that he did not experience a succession of thoughts but grasped all truth in a single, changeless intuition. Would time exist?

An adherent of a relational view of time would say no, for there are no events to generate a relation of *earlier than* or *later than*. There is just a single, timeless state. Substantivalists of a Newtonian stripe would disagree, of course. For Newton timeless existence was a logical impossibility. But there is no reason why we should side with Newton on this score. In the utter absence of change it seems plausible to think that time would not exist. Why, then, should we think that God could not exist timelessly in such an empty world?

"Because God is personal!" is the answer given by certain advocates of divine temporality. They contend that the idea of a timeless person is incoherent and therefore God must be temporal. They argue that in order to be a person, one must possess certain properties that inherently involve time. Since God is essentially personal, he cannot be timeless.

We can formulate this argument as follows (using x, y, z to represent certain properties to be specified later):

1. Necessarily, if God is timeless, he does not have the properties x, y, z.

2. Necessarily, if God does not have the properties x, y, z, then God is not personal.

3. Necessarily, God is personal.

4. Therefore, necessarily, God is not timeless.

The argument, if successful, shows that timelessness and personhood are incompatible, and since God is essentially personal, it is timelessness that must be jettisoned.

The defender of divine timelessness may attempt to turn back this argument either by challenging the claim that the properties in question are necessary conditions of personhood or by showing that a timeless God could possess the relevant properties after all. So what are the properties x, y, z that the advocate of divine temporality is talking about?

The metaphysician Robert Coburn has argued that a timeless God cannot be a self-conscious, rational being because he could not exhibit certain forms of consciousness which we normally associate with personal beings (namely, ourselves). He writes:

> Surely it is a necessary condition of anything's being a person that it should be capable (logically) of, among other things, doing at least some of the following: remembering, anticipating, reflecting, deliberating, deciding, intending, and acting intentionally. To see that this is so one need but ask oneself whether anything which necessarily lacked all of the capacities noted would, under any conceivable circumstances, count as a person. But now an eternal being would necessarily lack all of these capacities in as much as their exercise by a being clearly requires that the being exist in time. After all, reflection and deliberation take time, deciding typically occurs at some time—and in any case it always makes sense to ask, "When did you (he, they, etc.) decide?"; remembering is impossible unless the being doing the remembering has a past; and so on. Hence, no eternal being, it would seem, could be a person.[17]

Now even if Coburn were correct that a personal being must be capable of exhibiting the forms of consciousness he lists, it does not follow that a timeless God cannot be personal. For God could be *capable* of exhibiting such forms of consciousness but be timeless just in case he does not *in fact* exhibit any of them. In other words, the hidden assumption behind Coburn's reasoning is that God's being timeless or temporal is an essential property of God, that either God is necessarily timeless or he is necessarily temporal. But that assumption seems to me dubious. Suppose, for the sake of argument, that God is in fact temporal. Since God's decision to create is free, we can conceive of possible worlds in which God alone exists. If he is unchanging in such a world, then God would be timeless, as we have seen. So just as my height is a contingent rather than essential property of mine, God's temporal status is plausibly a contingent rather than essential property of his. Apart from highly controversial claims on behalf of divine simplicity or immutability, I see no reason to think that God is either *essentially* temporal or *essentially* timeless.

---

[17]Robert C. Coburn, "Professor Malcolm on God," *Australasian Journal of Philosophy* 41 (1963): 155.

So if timelessness is a merely contingent property of God, he could be entirely capable of remembering, anticipating, reflecting and so on; only were he to do so, then he would not be timeless. So long as he freely refrains from such activities he is timeless, even though he has the *capacity* to engage in those activities. Thus by Coburn's own lights God must be regarded as personal.

At a more fundamental level, it is in any case pretty widely recognized that most of the forms of consciousness mentioned by Coburn are not essential to personhood—indeed not even the capacity for them is essential to personhood. Take remembering. Any temporal person who lacked memory would be mentally ill. But if an individual exists timelessly, then he has no past to remember. He thus never forgets anything! Given God's omniscience, there is just no reason to think that his personhood requires memory. Similarly with regard to anticipation: since a timeless God has no future, there just is nothing to anticipate. Only a temporal person needs to have beliefs about the past or future.

As for reflecting and deliberating, these are ruled out not so much by God's timelessness as by his omniscience. An omniscient being cannot reflect and deliberate, because he already knows the conclusions to be arrived at! Even if God is in time, he does not engage in reflection and deliberation. But he is surely not impersonal as a result.

What about deciding, intending and acting intentionally? I should say that all of these forms of consciousness are exhibited by a timeless God. With respect to deciding, again, omniscience alone precludes God's deciding in the sense of making up his mind after a period of indecision. Even a temporal God does not decide in that sense. But God does decide in the sense that his will intends toward one alternative rather than another and does so freely. It is up to God what he does; he could have willed otherwise. This is the strongest sense of libertarian freedom of the will. In God's case, because he is omniscient, his free decisions are either everlasting or timeless rather than preceded by a period of ignorance and indecision.

As for intending or acting intentionally, there is no reason to think that intentions are necessarily future-directed. One can direct one's intentions at one's present state. God, as the Good, can timelessly desire and will his own infinite goodness. Such a changeless intention can be as timeless as God's knowing his own essence. Moreover, in the empty world we have envisioned, God may timelessly will and intend to refrain from creating a universe. God's willing to refrain from creation should not be confused with the mere absence of the intention to create. A stone is characterized by the absence of any will to create but cannot be said to will to refrain from creating. In a world in which God freely refrains from creation, his abstaining from creating is a result of a free act of the will on his part. Hence it seems to me that God can timelessly intend, will and choose what he does.

In conclusion, then, the argument for divine temporality based on God's personhood cannot be deemed a success. Advocates of a temporal God have not been able to show that God cannot possess timelessly the properties essential to personhood. On the contrary, a timeless God can be plausibly said to fulfill the necessary and sufficient conditions of being a person. A timeless, divine person can be a self-conscious, rational individual endowed with freedom of the will.

Divine relations with the world. All this has been said, however, in abstraction from the reality of a temporal universe. Given that such a universe exists, it needs to be asked whether God can remain untouched by its temporality.

It is very difficult to see how he can. Imagine once more God's existing changelessly alone without creation, but with a changeless determination of his will to create a temporal world with a beginning. Since God is omnipotent, his will is done, and a temporal world comes into existence. Now this presents us with a dilemma: either God existed prior to creation or he did not. Suppose he did. In that case God is temporal, not timeless, since to exist *prior to* some event is to be in time. Suppose, then, that God did not exist prior to creation. In that case, without creation, he exists timelessly, since he obviously did not come into being along with the world at the moment of creation.

This second alternative presents us with a new dilemma: once time begins at the moment of creation, either God becomes temporal in virtue of his real relation to the temporal world, or else he exists just as timelessly with creation as he does without it. If we choose the first alternative, then once again God is temporal. But what about the second alternative? Can God remain untouched by the world's temporality? It seems not. For at the first moment of time, God stands in a new relation in which he did not stand before (since there was no "before"). Even if in creating the world God undergoes no *intrinsic* change, he at least undergoes an *extrinsic* change.[18] For at the moment of creation, God comes into the relation of *sustaining* the universe or, at the very least, of *coexisting with* the universe, relations in which he did not stand before. Since he is free to refrain from creation, God could have never stood in those relations, had he so willed. But by virtue of his creating a temporal world, God comes into a relation with that world the moment it springs into being. Thus even if it is not the case that God is temporal prior to his creation of the world, he undergoes an extrinsic change at the moment of creation which draws him into time in virtue of his real relation to the world.

The argument of the advocate of divine temporality can be summarized as follows:

1. God is creatively active in the temporal world.

2. If God is creatively active in the temporal world, God is really related to the temporal world.

3. If God is really related to the temporal world, God is temporal.

4. Therefore God is temporal.

This argument, if successful, does not prove that God is essentially temporal, but that if he is Creator of a temporal world—as he in fact is—then he is temporal.

One way to escape this argument is to deny premise 2. This was Thomas Aquinas's solution. But this does not appear to be a very promising strategy, since it seems obvious that God is related to his creatures insofar as he sustains them, knows them and loves them.[19] Recent defenders of timeless eternity have turned their guns on premise 3 instead. They have tried to craft theories of divine eternity which would permit God to be really related to the temporal world and yet to exist timelessly.

For example, Eleonore Stump and Norman Kretzmann attempt to formulate an eternal-temporal simultaneity relation (abbreviated as ET-simultaneity), which they believe will allow a timeless God to relate to

---

[18]It is disputed among philosophers of religion whether creating the world involves some intrinsic change on God's part (for example, an exercise of power). My argument does not presuppose an intrinsic change in God but is based on the inevitability of mere extrinsic change on God's part.

[19]See my discussion in William Lane Craig, "Timelessness, Creation, and God's Real Relation to the World," *Laval théologique et philosophique* (forthcoming).

his creation.[20] Appealing to the analogy of the Special Theory of Relativity (STR), Stump and Kretzmann propose to treat modes of existence as analogous to reference frames and to construct a definition of ET-simultaneity in terms of two reference frames (timelessness and temporality) and two observers (one in eternity and one in time). Their definition is very complicated in its wording, but the basic idea is as follows. Take some eternal being x and some temporal being y. These two are ET-simultaneous in the case that relative to some hypothetical observer in the eternal reference frame x is eternally present and y is observed as temporally present, and relative to some hypothetical observer in any temporal reference frame y is temporally present and x is observed as eternally present. On the basis of their definition of ET-simultaneity, Stump and Kretzmann believe themselves to have solved the problem of how a timeless being can be really related to a temporal world. For relative to the eternal reference frame, any temporal entity that exists at any time is observed to be present, and relative to any moment of time God is observed to be present.

Now the Stump-Kretzmann account is a veritable mare's nest of philosophical difficulties. But in the interest of brevity, let us pass them by and cut to the heart of the matter: their proffered definition of ET-simultaneity is explanatorily vacuous. As many critics have pointed out, the language of observation employed in the definition is wholly obscure.[21] In STR very specific physical content is given to the notion of observation through Einstein's operational definitions of distant simultaneity. But in the definition of ET-simultaneity no hint is given as to what is meant, for example, by x's being observed as eternally present relative to some moment of time. In the absence of any procedure for determining ET-simultaneity, the definition reduces to the assertion that relative to the reference frame of eternity x is eternally present and y is temporally present and that relative to some temporal reference frame y is tem-

───────────────────────────────

[20]Eleonore Stump and Norman Kretzmann, "Eternity," *Journal of Philosophy* 78 (1981): 429-58.

[21]Stephen T. Davis, *Logic and the Nature of God* (Grand Rapids, Mich.: Eerdmans, 1983), p. 20; Delmas Lewis, "Eternity Again: A Reply to Stump and Kretzmann," *International Journal for Philosophy of Religion* 15 (1984): 74-76; Helm, *Eternal God*, pp. 32-33; William Hasker, *God, Time and Knowledge* (Ithaca, N.Y.: Cornell University Press, 1989), pp. 164-66; John C. Yates, *The Timelessness of God* (Lanham, Md.: University Press of America, 1990), pp. 128-30; Leftow, *Time and Eternity*, pp. 170-72.

porally present and x is eternally present—which is only a restatement of the problem! Worse, if y is temporally present to God, then God and y are not ET-simultaneous at all but temporally simultaneous. Thus God would be temporally simultaneous with every temporal event, which is to sacrifice divine timelessness.

Paul Helm is not being uncharitable when he complains that Stump and Kretzmann's "'solution' to the problem is found simply by rewording the problem with the help of the device of ET-simultaneity. ET-simultaneity has no independent merit or use, nothing is illuminated or explained by it."[22]

Leftow has offered another, different account of divine eternity in order to refute premise 3.[23] It will be recalled that on the Stump-Kretzmann model, there is no common reference frame or mode of existence shared by timeless and temporal beings. As a result, Stump and Kretzmann were unable to explain how such beings could be causally related. The essence of Leftow's proposal is to remedy this defect by maintaining that temporal beings do exist in eternity; they share God's mode of existence and so can be causally related to God. But, he insists, this does not imply that time or temporal existence is illusory, for temporal beings also have a temporal mode of existence. Leftow's argument is based on three theses:

    I. The distance between God and every thing in space is zero.

    II. Spatial, material things do not change in any way unless there is a change of place (a motion involving a material thing).

    III. If something is in time, it is also in space.

On the basis of these theses Leftow argues as follows: There can be no change of place relative to God because the distance between God and everything in space is zero. But if there is no change of place relative to God, there can be no change of any sort on the part of spatial things rel-

---

[22]Helm, *Eternal God*, p. 33. To their credit, Stump and Kretzmann later revised their definition of ET-simultaneity so as to free it from observation language (Stump and Kretzmann, "Eternity, Awareness and Action," pp. 477-78). The fundamental problem with this new account of ET-simultaneity is that it is viciously circular (see Leftow, *Time and Eternity*, p. 173).

[23]Brian Leftow, "Eternity and Simultaneity," *Faith and Philosophy* 8 (1991): 148-79; cf. Leftow, *Time and Eternity*, chap. 10.

ative to God. Moreover, since anything that is temporal is also spatial, it follows that there are no temporal, nonspatial beings. The only temporal beings there are exist in space, and none of these change relative to God. Assuming, then, some relational view of time, according to which time cannot exist without change, it follows that all temporal beings exist timelessly relative to God. Thus, relative to God all things are timelessly present and so can be causally related to God.

The problem with this solution, as I have elsewhere tried to show, is that all three of its foundational theses seem false, some obviously so.[24] Take III, for example. We have already seen good reason to reject this radical thesis. Even in the absence of a physical universe, God could choose to entertain a succession of thoughts or to create an angelic being or an unembodied soul that experiences a stream of consciousness, and such a series of mental events alone is sufficient for such entities' being in time. Even if our *measures* of time and space are bound up together, that is no reason to think that time and space themselves cannot exist independently. Thus things can exist temporally without existing spatially. Since all of Leftow's key theses are at least dubious if not clearly false, we have little choice but to conclude that he has given no good grounds for thinking that temporal beings exist in timeless eternity.

Moreover, we must ask, is Leftow's theory even coherent? If all events exist timelessly in God's eternal reference frame, then none of them can exist *earlier than, simultaneous with* or *later than* another event, for these are temporal relations. Thus in God's reference frame, all he is confronted with is a chaos of point-events all temporally unrelated to one another. This not only seems incompatible with divine omniscience and providence but contradicts Leftow's own statements that in eternity God discerns the sequence in which events occur. Thus Leftow's theory proves no more successful than Stump and Kretzmann's in explaining how God can be timeless and yet causally related to the world.

In summary, it seems to me that we have here a powerful argument for divine temporality. Classical attempts like Aquinas's to deny that God is really related to the world and contemporary attempts like those of Stump, Kretzmann and Leftow to deny that God's real relation to the

---

[24]See William Lane Craig, "The Special Theory of Relativity," *Faith and Philosophy* 11 (1994): 19-37.

world involves him in time all appear in the end to be less plausible than the premises of the argument itself. It seems that in being related to the world God must undergo extrinsic change and so be temporal.

Divine knowledge of tensed facts. We have seen that God's real relation to the temporal world gives us good grounds for concluding God to be temporal in view of the extrinsic change he undergoes through his changing relations with the world. But the existence of a temporal world also seems to entail intrinsic change in God in view of his knowledge of what is happening in the temporal world. Defenders of divine temporality have argued that a timeless God cannot know certain tensed facts about the world—for example, what is happening now—and therefore, since God is omniscient, he must be temporal.

The key notion to be understood here is the idea of "tensed facts." First, I need to say a word about what we mean by "fact." A fact may be defined as the state of affairs described by a true declarative sentence.[25] Thus, for example, while "Snow is white" and "Der Schnee ist weiss" are two different sentences, they both describe the same fact, that snow is white.

Second, we need to define what we mean by a "tensed fact." We are all familiar with tense as it plays a role in language. The function of tense is to locate something in relation to the present. Although most of our ordinary language is tensed, there are occasions on which we employ sentences that are grammatically in the present tense to express what are really tenseless truths. For example, we say such things as "Lady Macbeth commits suicide in act V, scene v," "The glass breaks easily," "The area of a circle is πr^2," "Centaurs have the body of a horse and the torso of a man," and "The 1996 presidential election is earlier than the 2004 presidential election." Dates can be employed in conjunction with tenseless verbs to locate things tenselessly in time. For example, we can state, "In 1962 John Kennedy *pledges* to send a man to the moon before the end of the decade" (the italics being a stylistic convention to show that the verb is tenseless). This sentence expresses a tenseless fact and is therefore always true. Notice that even if one knew this truth, one would not know whether Kennedy has issued his pledge unless

---

[25]What I am calling a fact could be treated as a true proposition. Accordingly, what I call "factual content" is the same as "propositional content." I am trying my best to avoid technical jargon.

one also knew whether 1962 was past or future. By contrast, if we replaced the tenseless verb with the past-tensed verb "pledged," then we would know that the event referred to has happened. This tensed sentence would, however, not always be true: prior to 1962 it would be false. Prior to 1962 the tensed verb would have to be the future-tense "will pledge" if the sentence is to be true. In contrast to tenseless sentences, then, tensed sentences serve to locate things in time relative to the present and so may change their true value.

The salient point of all this is that in addition to tenseless facts, there also appear to be tensed facts. The information conveyed by a tensed sentence concerns not just tenseless facts but tensed facts as well, facts about how far from the present something is. Thus what is a fact at one moment may not be a fact at another moment. It is now a fact that I am writing this sentence; in a moment it will no longer be a fact. Thus the body of tensed facts is constantly changing.

The upshot is that a being that knew only tenseless facts about the world, including which events *occur* at any date and time, would still be completely in the dark about tensed facts. He would have no idea at all of what is now going on in the universe, of which events are past and which are future. On the other hand, any being that *does* know tensed facts cannot be timeless, for his knowledge must be in constant flux, as the tensed facts known by him change.

Thus we can formulate the following argument for divine temporality:

1. A temporal world exists.

2. God is omniscient.

3. If a temporal world exists, then if God is omniscient, God knows tensed facts.

4. If God is timeless, he does not know tensed facts.

5. Therefore God is not timeless.

Again, this argument does not prove that God is essentially temporal, but if successful, it does show that if a temporal world exists, then God is not timeless.

Defenders of divine timelessness have attempted to refute this argument either by arguing that, contrary to premise 4, a timeless God can know tensed facts, or by revising the definition of omniscience so that, contrary to premise 3, God may still qualify as omniscient even if he is ignorant of tensed facts.

Let us look first at the plausibility of denying premise 4. Can a time-less God know tensed facts? Jonathan Kvanvig contends that he can.[26] Kvanvig's defense of this point is based upon his analysis of beliefs in terms of a personal attitude, the factual content of a belief, and a partic-ular way of accessing or grasping that factual content. Take a sentence like "Today is June 1, 1999." Kvanvig contends that the same factual content is expressed by the sentence "Today is June 1, 1999," when that sentence is used on June 1, 1999, as is expressed by the sentence "Yes-terday was June 1, 1999," when that sentence is uttered on June 2, 1999. In his view temporal indexical words like *today* and *yesterday* express the individual essence of the moment they refer to (an essence being a set of properties that uniquely designate a thing). In this example, the words *today* and *yesterday,* by expressing the essence of the moment referred to, pick out the same time. A person will grasp this factual con-tent *directly* only if he grasps it at the very time referred to (in which case he will form a present-tense belief), and a person will grasp the same content *indirectly* if he does so not at that time (in which case a temporal person will form beliefs involving other tenses).

In God's case, then, if he is timeless, he grasps the factual content of tensed sentences indirectly and so does not form tensed beliefs as we do. Therefore, Kvanvig concludes, "one can affirm the doctrines of time-lessness, immutability and omniscience by affirming that God indirectly grasps every temporal moment, and directly grasps none of them."[27]

Does Kvanvig's theory succeed in giving an account of how a time-less God can know tensed facts? It seems not. For on Kvanvig's analysis the essences of the times picked out by temporal indexical words do not include the tense of those times (whether they are past, present or future). Otherwise a time would be, say, essentially past, in which case it is impossible for that time ever to have been present or future, which is absurd. Words like *today* and *yesterday* could not refer to the same day, since they, being different in tense, would express different essences. And God could not timelessly grasp the factual content involving such essences, since if he grasped a moment that is essentially present, he

[26]Jonathan L. Kvanvig, *The Possibility of an All-Knowing God* (New York: St. Martin's, 1986), pp. 150-65.
[27]Ibid., p. 159.

would exist at the time of that moment. Thus it is evident that the factual content expressed by tensed sentences is, on Kvanvig's analysis, tenseless. Tense is merely a feature of our mental state, the byproduct of how we grasp the tenseless factual content of tensed sentences. Kvanvig explicitly denies that there is any temporal element expressed by tensed sentences which is not part of their factual content. On Kvanvig's view, then, tense is merely linguistic: there are no tensed facts.

Thus Kvanvig's account backfires. Far from explaining how a timeless God can know tensed facts, on his analysis there are no tensed facts to be known. The factual content expressed by the sentence "Kvanvig now teaches at Texas A&M" is something like *Kvanvig teaches* (tenselessly) *at Texas A&M at time t.* God, grasping this factual content indirectly, has no idea where Kvanvig is now teaching or whether he has even been born or is long dead and buried.

A somewhat similar, but crucially modified, account of God's knowledge of tensed facts has been offered by Edward Wierenga in his philosophical analysis of the principal divine attributes.[28] On Wierenga's view the factual content of a present-tense sentence includes the tense expressed in the sentence. Like Kvanvig, he believes that moments of time have individual essences. Unlike Kvanvig, however, Wieringa seems to believe that the individual essence of a moment somehow involves the present tense. If the factual content of a sentence includes a moment's individual essence, then that content will involve presentness. Anyone who grasps that content at the time referred to will form a present-tense belief about what is "now" the case.

Wierenga contends that a timeless God is able to grasp the factual content of a tensed sentence but without forming a present-tense belief as we do. For one forms a present-tense belief only if one both exists at the time referred to in the factual content of a sentence and grasps that content at that time. God grasps this factual content timelessly and so forms no present-tense belief about what is "now" going on. Thus God knows tensed facts without having tensed beliefs.

Does Wierenga's account of God's knowledge of tensed facts fare any better than Kvanvig's analysis? The crucial difference between

---

[28]Edward R. Wierenga, *The Nature of God* (Ithaca, N.Y.: Cornell University Press, 1989), pp. 179-85.

them is that Wierenga makes presentness a feature of the individual essence of every moment of time. Wierenga's analysis thus entails the metaphysical doctrine of *presentism,* according to which the only time that exists is the present time. According to presentism, future times do not yet exist and past times no longer exist. Therefore there literally are no times that have the property of pastness or futurity. When a time becomes past, it does not exchange the property of presentness for the property of pastness; rather it just ceases to exist altogether. Times exist when and only when they are present. They come into existence successively and are present just as long as they exist. No time exists which is not present.

If the individual essence of every moment of time somehow involves presentness, then the question is whether a timeless God can grasp the factual content involving such an essence. It remains extraordinarily difficult to understand on Wierenga's account how God can grasp the essence of a time without that time's being present for him. If the individual essence of a time involves presentness, then in order to grasp the factual content of a sentence involving such an essence one would need to be present. If I say, "John left three hours ago," then there is no problem in a timeless God's grasping factual content involving the time *t* and the property *being such that John leaves three hours earlier than then,* which is ascribed to *t*—no problem, that is, so long as *t* is a tenseless date or clock-time. But if *t* involves presentness, then God, in grasping *t* as present, must be in the present, that is to say, must be temporal. Later at *t'* it will be true that "John left four hours ago," and God will no longer grasp the essence of *t,* but of *t',* for *t* is no longer present. It is always true that John *leaves* three hours earlier than *t,* and God immutably knows that fact. But if he is to know tensed facts, he must know that *t* is present. Thus his factual knowledge must be constantly changing, in which case God must be in time. Hence in making presentness part of the individual essence of every time, Wierenga only succeeds in temporalizing God.

Kvanvig's and Wierenga's accounts are the most sophisticated attempts to explain how God can be timeless and yet know tensed facts, yet they both fail. Thus premise 4 of the argument for divine temporality from God's knowledge of tensed facts seems secure.

The defender of divine timelessness has no recourse, then, but to deny premise 3. He must deny that omniscience entails a knowledge of tensed facts. According to the traditional definition of omniscience, a person is omniscient if and only if he knows every fact and does not also hold any false beliefs. The general problem with the strategy of revising the traditional definition of omniscience is that any adequate definition must be in line with our intuitive understanding of the concept. We are not free to "cook" the definition arbitrarily just to solve the problem under discussion. On the traditional definition, if there are tensed facts, an omniscient person must know them. What plausible alternative definition of omniscience might the defender of divine timelessness offer?

Wierenga, as a sort of second line of defense, offers a revised account of omniscience which would not require God to know tensed facts.[29] Some facts, he says, are facts only from a particular perspective. They must be known to an omniscient being only if he shares that particular perspective. Thus a person is omniscient if and only if, for every fact and every perspective, if something is a fact from a certain perspective, then that person knows that it is a fact from that perspective, and if that person shares that perspective, then he must know the fact in question. Wierenga treats moments of time as perspectives relative to which tensed facts exist. So while a temporal person existing on December 8, 1941, must (if he is omniscient) know the fact *Yesterday the Japanese attacked Pearl Harbor,* a timeless person must know only that from the perspective of December 8, 1941, it is a fact that *yesterday the Japanese attacked Pearl Harbor.* On this definition God's omniscience does not require that he know the tensed fact, but only the tenseless fact that from a certain perspective a certain tensed fact exists.

Wierenga's revised definition of omniscience seems to me to be unacceptably "cooked." It might be tempting to understand his definition as an attempt to eliminate tensed facts in favor of exclusively tenseless facts. For example, to say, "The Japanese attack is past relative to December 8, 1941," might sound like just a circumlocution for saying the attack is earlier than December 8, 1941, which is a tenseless fact. To say something is past, present or future relative to a time is just a misleading way of saying that it is earlier than, simultaneous with or later than that

---

[29]Ibid., p. 189.

time. One is not stating a tensed fact at all. If this were Wierenga's meaning, then he would simply be denying that there are tensed facts, and there would be no need to revise the definition of omniscience.

Rather Wierenga wants to allow that there really are tensed facts but to maintain that an omniscient being need not know them. This claim seems quite implausible. On Wierenga's view temporal persons like you and me know an incalculable multitude of facts of which God is ignorant. Temporal persons know that the Japanese attack on Pearl Harbor is over; God has no idea whether it has occurred or not. He knows merely that for people on December 8, 1941, and thereafter, it is a fact that the attack is over. Since he does not know what time it actually is, he does not know any tensed facts. This is an unacceptably limited field of knowledge to qualify as omniscience.

It seems to me, therefore, that no adequate grounds have been given for thinking that someone could be omniscient and yet not know tensed facts. The traditional definition of omniscience requires it, and we have no grounds that do not involve special pleading for revising the usual definition.

The attempt to deny premise 3 of the present argument thus seems to fare no better than the effort to refute premise 4. From the premises of the argument it follows that God is not timeless, which is to say, he is temporal. So in addition to the argument from God's real relation to the world, we now have a second powerful reason, based on God's changing knowledge of tensed facts, for thinking that God is in time.

A way out for advocates of divine timelessness? On the basis of the foregoing discussion, we have seen weak grounds for affirming divine timelessness but two powerful arguments in favor of divine temporality. It would seem, then, that we should conclude that God is temporal.

But there does remain one way of escape still open for defenders of divine timelessness. The argument based on God's real relation to the world assumes the objective reality of temporal becoming, and the argument based on God's knowledge of the temporal world assumes the objective reality of tensed facts. If one denies the objective reality of temporal becoming and tensed facts, then the arguments are undercut. In short, the defender of divine timelessness can escape the arguments by embracing the static or tenseless theory of time. Given a static view of time, it is easy to see why God never experiences extrinsic change in relation to temporal events. For nothing in the space-time block ever comes into or goes out of being, nor does the space-time block as a whole come into being or pass away. It simply exists timelessly along with God. Similarly, on the static theory of time there really are no tensed facts. The factual content of sentences containing tensed verbs and temporal indexicals includes only tenseless locations and tenseless relations of events. Linguistic tense is an egocentric feature of language users. It serves only to express the subjective perspective of the user. Thus there really are no tensed facts for God to know. In knowing all tenseless facts, God is truly and timelessly omniscient.

The defender of divine timelessness therefore has a way out: he can adopt a static theory of time and deny the reality of tensed facts and temporal becoming. But this represents a very unpalatable route of escape, for the static theory of time faces formidable philosophical and theological objections, not to mention the arguments that can be offered on behalf of a dynamic theory of time.[30] I therefore prefer to cast my lot with the dynamic theory. And it is noteworthy that almost no defender of divine timelessness has taken this route. Virtually the only person who appears to have done so is Paul Helm. On his view there is no ontological difference between the past, present and future: "Do the times which are at present future to us exist, or not? Answer: they exist for God . . . and they exist for those creatures contemporaneous with that future moment, for that moment is present to them, but it is not now present to us."[31] In the same way, "the past event . . . belongs in its own time, and is therefore real, belonging to the ordered series of times which comprise the creation and which are . . . eternally present to God."[32] Thus Paul affirms what he takes to be Augustine's view that "God created the temporal order, by an eternal act, as a B-series."[33] He explains, "In creation God brings into being (timelessly) the whole temporal matrix," and "God knows *at a glance* the whole of

[30]See William Lane Craig, *The Tenseless Theory of Time: A Critical Examination,* Synthese Library (Dordrecht, Netherlands: Kluwer Academic, 2000); and William Lane Craig, *The Tensed Theory of Time: A Critical Examination* (Dordrecht, Netherlands: Kluwer Academic, 2000).
[31]Paul Helm, "Eternal Creation: The Doctrine of the Two Standpoints," in *The Doctrine of Creation,* ed. Colin Gunton (Edinburgh: T & T Clark, 1997), p. 42.
[32]Ibid., p. 43.
[33]Ibid., p. 40.

his temporally ordered creation."[34] Similarly, tense is but an ephemeral feature of language; the truth conditions of tensed sentences are given by tenseless facts, facts that are known to God.[35] Paul thus appears to be the one advocate of divine timelessness who has seen and taken the way out. But it is a hard and lonely road.

Timelessness and Omnitemporality

Given a dynamic theory of time, it follows from God's creative activity in the temporal world and his complete knowledge of it that God is temporal. God quite literally exists now. Since God never begins to exist nor ever ceases to exist, it follows that God is omnitemporal. He exists at every time that ever exists.

This might seem to imply that God has existed for infinite time in the past and will exist for infinite time in the future. But what if the temporal world has not always existed? According to the Christian doctrine of creation, the world is not infinite in the past but was brought into being out of nothing a finite time ago. Did time itself also have a beginning? Did God exist literally before creation, or is he timeless without the world?

Why did God not create the world sooner? There is an old problem that bedevils proponents of an infinite, empty time prior to creation: why did God not create the world sooner? On a relational view of time, time does not exist in the total absence of events. Hence time may begin at the moment of creation, and it is simply maladroit to ask why God did not create the world sooner, since there is no "sooner" prior to the moment of creation. Time comes into existence with the universe, and so it makes no sense to ask why it did not come into being at an earlier moment. But if time never had a beginning, God has endured through an infinite period of creative idleness up until the moment of creation. Why did he wait so long?

This problem can be formulated as follows (letting t represent any time prior to creation and n represent some finite amount of time):

1. If the past is infinite, then at t God delayed creating until $t + n$.

2. If at t God delayed creating until $t + n$, then he must have had a good reason for doing so.

---

[34]Helm, *Eternal God*, pp. 27, 26.
[35]Ibid., pp. 25, 44, 47, 52, 79.

3. If the past is infinite, God cannot have had a good reason for delaying at *t* creating until *t* + *n*.

4. Therefore if the past is infinite, God must have had a good reason for delaying at *t* and God cannot have had a good reason for delaying at t.

5. Therefore the past is not infinite.

Premise 1 is obviously true, given a dynamic view of time. At *t* God could have created the world. But he did not. He deliberately waited until a later time. He self-consciously refrained from creating at *t* and delayed his action until *t* + *n*.

Premise 2 seems to be plausibly true. It does not depend for its truth on the validity of some broader principle of sufficient reason (a controversial principle defended by Leibniz to the effect that everything has a reason it is the way it is). Rather it states merely that in this specific case God, in deciding to delay creating the world until some later time, must have had some good reason for doing so. Notice also that premise 2 does not presuppose either the finitude or the infinitude of the past. It merely asserts that if at some moment prior to creation God deliberately defers creating until a later moment, then he must have a reason for doing so. A perfectly rational person does not delay some action that he wills to undertake unless he has a good reason for doing so. Since God is a supremely rational being, premise 2 strikes me as eminently plausible.

That brings us to premise 3, which again seems obviously true. As Leftow points out in his interesting analysis of this problem,[36] if God comes to acquire at some moment a reason to create the world, this reason must be due to some change either in God or in the world. The only change going on outside God is the lapse of absolute time itself. But since all moments of time are alike, there is nothing special about the moment of creation which would cause God to delay creating at *t* until *t* + *n* had arrived. After all, at *t* God has already waited for infinite time to create the world, so why wait any longer? There is nothing about *t* + *n* that makes it a more appropriate time to create than *t*. As for God himself, he has from time immemorial been perfectly good, omniscient and omnipotent, so that there

---

[36]Brian Leftow, "Why Didn't God Create the World Sooner?" *Religious Studies* 27 (1991): 157-72.

seems to be no change that could occur in him that would prompt him to create at some time rather than earlier. Thus it seems impossible that God should acquire some reason to create which he did not always have, nor by the same token does it seem possible for him to have always had a reason for singling out $t + n.$ as the moment to create.

Leftow tries to escape this reasoning by suggesting that God's reason for delaying creation is the joy of anticipation of creating. Just as we find joy in the anticipation of some great good, so God can enjoy the anticipation of creation. But why would God delay creating for *infinite* time? Having already at t anticipated for infinite time creating the world, why would he yet delay even longer until $t + n?$ Why did he quit anticipating at $t + n$, instead of earlier or later? Leftow answers that there comes a point at which the joy of anticipating begins to fade. So God will not want to delay creating beyond that point. He knows from all eternity precisely when his anticipation peaks and so will not delay beyond that point. Leftow imagines a sort of pleasure curve charting God's rising and falling anticipation of creation (see figure 1).

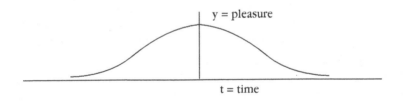

Figure 1. God's anticipatory pleasures rises from a low at $t=$ -∞ to a peak value before declining toward a low at $t=$ +∞.

God will create the world at the moment when his anticipatory pleasure peaks.

We might be skeptical of such a portrayal of God's anticipatory pleasure as grossly anthropomorphic; but never mind. The more serious problem is that Leftow's scheme does not explain anything. For we may still ask, why does God's anticipatory pleasure peak at $t + n$ instead of at $t?$ Leftow answers that since the curve displayed in figure 1 extends infinitely into the past and future, it cannot be "shifted" in either direction. It is fixed in time and so must peak when it does.

This answer fails to appreciate the paradoxical nature of the actual infinite. God's pleasure curve, though infinitely extended, can be shifted backward in time simply by dividing every value of the x-coordinate by two. Since the past is supposed to be actually infinite, there is no danger of "scrunching up" the earlier slope of the curve by such a backward shift. If such a shift seems impossible, this only calls into question the infinity of the past. But if the past is infinite, there is no problem. Therefore Leftow has not provided a good reason for why God at *t* should delay creating until *t* + *n*. After all, by *t* God has already had eternity to anticipate creating the world.

But if premises 1-3 are true, then 4 and 5 logically follow. We thus seem to have a good argument for denying the infinity of the past and holding to the beginning of time. It is plausible to believe that time began to exist and that therefore God has not existed for infinite time. But now we are confronted with an extremely bizarre situation. God exists in time. Time had a beginning. God did not have a beginning. How can these three statements be reconciled? If time began to exist—say, for simplicity's sake, at the big bang—then in some difficult to articulate sense God must exist beyond the big bang, alone without the universe. He must be changeless in such a state; otherwise time would exist. And yet this state, strictly speaking, cannot exist before the big bang in a temporal sense, since time had a beginning. God must be causally, but not temporally, prior to the big bang. With the creation of the universe, time began, and God entered into time at the moment of creation in virtue of his real relations with the created order. It follows that God must therefore be timeless without the universe and temporal with the universe.

Now this conclusion is startling and not a little odd. For on such a view there seem to be two phases of God's life, a timeless phase and a temporal phase, and the timeless phase seems to have existed earlier than the temporal phase. But this is logically incoherent, since to stand in a relation of *earlier than* is by all accounts to be temporal.[37]

---

[37]See Leftow's statement of the objection: Brian Leftow, "Eternity," in *A Companion to Philosophy of Religion,* ed. Philip L. Quinn and Charles Taliaferro, Blackwell's Companions to Philosophy (Oxford: Blackwell, 1997), 8:257-63.

Amorphous time. How are we to escape this apparent antinomy? One possibility is suggested by a reexamination of our argument for the finitude of the past. Strictly speaking, the argument did not reach the conclusion "Therefore time began to exist." Rather what it proved is that there cannot have been an infinite past, that is to say, a past that is composed of an infinite number of equal temporal intervals. But if we can conceive of a time that is not divisible into intervals, a sort of undifferentiated time, then the argument is compatible with the existence of that sort of time prior to creation. God existing alone without the universe would exist in an amorphous time before the beginning of divisible time as we know it. A number of philosophers associated with Oxford University have defended such a view of divine eternity, so that one could aptly speak of the Oxford school on this issue.[38]

Members of the Oxford school tend to embrace the doctrine of *metric conventionalism* with respect to time. The metric of time has to do with the measure of time, that is, with whether two separate intervals of time can be said to be equal or unequal in extent. Conventionalism is the view that there is no objective fact about this matter. There is no objective fact that two separate temporal intervals are equal; it all depends on our stipulation. Thus in the absence of any measures, there is no objective fact that one interval is longer or shorter than another distinct interval. Prior to creation it is impossible to differentiate between a tenth of a second and ten trillion years. There is no moment, say, one hour before creation. Time literally lacks any intrinsic metric.

Such an understanding of God's time prior to creation seems quite attractive. It enables us to speak literally of God's existing before creation. And yet we avoid the problematic claim that God has endured through infinite time prior to creating the universe.

Nevertheless, a close inspection of the view reveals difficulties. Metric conventionalism is the view that there is no objective fact of the matter concerning the comparative lengths of separate temporal intervals. But metric conventionalism does not hold that there really are no intervals of

---

[38]John Lucas, *A Treatise on Time and Space* (London: Methuen, 1973), pp. 311-12; Padgett, *God, Eternity,* pp. 122-46; Richard Swinburne, "God and Time," in *Reasoned Faith,* ed. Eleonore Stump (Ithaca, N.Y.: Cornell University Press, 1993), pp. 204-22.

time or that no intervals can be objectively compared with respect to length. Thus even in a metrically amorphous time there are objective factual differences of length for certain temporal intervals (see figure 2).

Figure 2. Intervals in a metrically amorphous time prior to the moment of creation t = 0

According to metric conventionalism there is no fact of the matter concerning the comparative lengths *dc* and *cb* or *db* and *ca*. But there is an objective difference in length between *da* and *ca* or *cb* and *ca*, namely *da* >*ca* and *cb* <*ca*. For in the case of intervals that are proper parts of other intervals, the proper parts are factually shorter than their encompassing parts.

But this implies that prior to creation God has endured through a beginningless series of longer and longer intervals. In fact we can even say that such a time must be infinite. For the past is finite if and only if there is a first interval of time. (An interval is first if there exists no interval earlier than it, or no interval greater than it but having the same end point.) The metrically amorphous past is clearly not finite. But is it infinite? The past is infinite if and only if there is no first interval of time and time is not circular. Thus the amorphous time prior to creation would be infinite, even though we cannot compare the lengths of separate intervals within it. And all the difficulties of an infinite past return to haunt us.

The shortcoming of the Oxford school is that it has not been radical enough. It proposes to dispense with the metric of time while still retaining the geometry of time as a line. Since on a geometrical line intervals can be objectively distinguished and, when included in one another, compared in length, time is not sufficiently undifferentiated to avoid the problems attending an infinite past. What must be done is to dissolve the geometrical structure of time as a line. One must maintain that prior to creation there literally are no intervals of time at all. In such a time there would be no earlier and later, no enduring through successive intervals and hence no waiting, no temporal becoming, nothing but the eternal "now." This state would pass away as a whole, not successively, at the moment of creation, when time begins. It would be an undifferentiated "before," followed by a differentiated "after."

The problem is that such a changeless, undifferentiated state looks suspiciously like a state of timelessness! It seems to have the topology of a point, the traditional representation of timeless eternity. The only sense in which such a state can be said to be temporal is that it exists literally before God's creation of the world and the beginning of differentiated time.

Timeless without creation. Perhaps this realization ought to prompt us to reconsider the alternative that God is simply timeless without creation and temporal subsequent to creation. Detractors of this position simply assume that if God's life lacks earlier and later parts, then it has no phases. But why could there not be two phases of God's life, one timeless and one temporal, which are not related to each other as earlier and later? Critics have perhaps too quickly assumed that if any phase of God's life is timeless, the whole must be timeless.

We have already seen that a state of undifferentiated time looks very much like timelessness. This impression is reinforced by recalling the dynamic theory of time. On a static theory of time, it is very tempting to picture the two phases of God's life as equally existent, bounded by the moment of creation, the one earlier and the other later. But given a dynamic theory of time, this picture is a misrepresentation. In reality God existing without creation is changelessly alone, and no event disturbs this complete tranquillity. There is no before, no after, no temporal passage, no future phase of his life. The only possible reason we could have for calling such a state temporal is that temporal states of affairs come after it. But insofar as God exists without creation, there are, of course, no temporal states—not in eternity and not later either! There is just God.

To claim that time would exist without the universe in virtue of the beginning of the world seems to postulate a sort of backward causation: the occurrence of the first event causes time to exist not only with the event but also before it. But on a dynamic theory of time, such retrocausation is metaphysically impossible, for it amounts to something's being caused by nothing, since at the time of the effect the retro-cause in no sense exists.[39]

Perhaps an analogy from physical time will be illuminating. The initial big bang singularity is not considered to be part of time but to constitute a boundary to time. Nevertheless, it is causally connected to the universe. In an analogous way, perhaps we could say that God's timeless eternity is, as it were, a boundary of time that is causally, but not temporally, prior to the origin of the universe.

It seems to me, therefore, that it is not only coherent but also plausible that God existing changelessly alone without creation is timeless and that he enters time at the moment of creation in virtue of his real relation to the temporal universe. The image of God existing idly before creation is just that: a figment of the imagination. Given that time began to exist, the most plausible view of God's relationship to time is that he is timeless without creation and temporal subsequent to creation.

---

[39]For discussion see William Lane Craig, *Divine Foreknowledge and Human Freedom,* Brill's Studies in Intellectual History 19 (Leiden, Netherlands: E. J. Brill, 1991), pp. 150-56.

RESPONSE TO
WILLIAM LANE CRAIG

PAUL HELM

*B*ill's basic positive thoughts are that God cannot be untouched by the temporality of the universe that he creates, and that although God is timeless before he creates the universe, he is temporal afterward. He spends a good deal of time articulating the sense in which God is not in time before the creation. I shall say something about each of these points.

Bill also spends a good deal of his time effectively attacking the views of eternalists such as Stump and Kretzmann, and Leftow, Kvanvig and Wierenga, particularly their attempt to combine divine eternalism with the temporal becoming of the creation. But I see no need to come to their aid on this issue, for the project of combining eternalism and temporalism in the ways criticized by Bill is in my view doomed. As Bill shows, many of those who attempt to deny the proposition "If God is really related to the temporal world, God is temporal" understand "temporal world" in a tensed fashion. And their efforts to combine eternalism in God with temporalism in his relation to his temporal creation do not seem very convincing. But for a consistent B-theorist this project need not be undertaken in the first place; indeed it ought to be studiously avoided. For such a person, God is really related to the universe by virtue of freely creating and sustaining it. But God is not thereby rendered temporal. The question is whether Bill's own particular variant of this proposal fares any better. I fear that it does not.

I'll first say something about whether being Creator of a temporal universe means that God is himself temporal (in, presumably, the A-series sense). A mere extrinsic relation is not sufficient to do the trick. God certainly has a relation to the creation which he would not have had had there been no creation, but what does this show? It certainly does not show that God must be temporal any more than if I think about the number seven for five minutes then the number seven is temporal.

On the question whether God undergoes intrinsic change in creating and sustaining the universe, given that he needs to maintain his omniscience, there is need to reflect on the idea of omniscience (understood as the knowledge of every fact and the possession of no false beliefs) a little. To start with, perhaps God's omniscience is not captured by that definition, because perhaps God does not have beliefs. Perhaps God's timeless knowledge of the universe involves him in being aware of states of affairs that he could not be aware of if he were temporal, aware of the universe "all at once," say. If so, then if an eternal God cannot be omniscient because he does not know tensed facts, so a temporal God is not omniscient because he cannot know the universe all at once.

But apart from this, one might assimilate the problem raised by indexicals and timeless omniscience to a familiar problem about omnipotence, a notion that, it is widely agreed, presents general difficulties of analysis. It might be argued that the failure of a timeless God to "know" tensed facts is not a failure of knowledge-that but of know-how, of divine power, just as a failure to smell the characteristic smell of Marmite while knowing its chemical composition is not a case of ignorance but a lack of know-how, the ability to discriminate immediately the smell of Marmite from, say, the smell of honey. God, aside from the possibilities raised by the incarnation, which would require independent discussion, lacks this know-how, lacks the power necessary to smell Marmite because he does not have the necessary olfactory apparatus. Does this mean that he does not know what Marmite is? In a similar way, being timeless he cannot use a knowledge of temporal indexicals to help his agency in time because he is timelessly eternal and so unable to do what is in any case unnecessary for him. So on either view about God there are problems with omniscience; or if, as I would prefer, we wish to construe these problems as problems about power, there are problems over what omnipotence involves. But the existence of such problems is not news to anyone.

I must say that I find Bill's own positive views of God's relation to time somewhat obscure, and I'll end these remarks by saying why. In thinking of God's relation to time before the creation we must dissolve, he says, the geometrical structure of time as a line. I'm not convinced that he does this successfully. A member of the "Oxford school" such as Richard Swinburne may make the counterclaim that there is no objective difference in lengths in a metrically amorphous time, since in such time no intervals are proper parts of other intervals. Thus Swinburne claims that "in the absence of laws of nature, there will be no temporal distances."[1] And it seems reasonable to say that if there are no temporal distances there are no temporal intervals and a fortiori no intervals within intervals. But let us suppose that Bill is correct on this point, and the "Oxford school" wrong. The problem is not (as Bill avers) that the result of dissolving the geometrical structure of time as a line makes pre-creation time look like timelessness, but that if, as Bill says, there is time but it cannot be divided into intervals, then we seem driven to the conclusion that the whole of time before the creation must be one indivisible interval, earlier than the time of the creation. So I do not think that this helps with Bill's divine timelessness before creation idea.

Pursuing this idea, Bill says, "In reality God existing without creation is changelessly alone, and no event disturbs this complete tranquillity. There is no before, no after, no temporal passage, no future phase of his life." Bill says the only possible reason we could have for calling such a state temporal is that temporal affairs come after it. But surely this is an excellent reason for calling this state temporal. I cannot see that in so saying we are committed to backwards causation; it is simply that if someone exists either timelessly or in time, and exists before some temporal states of affairs, then this is a good, indeed a pretty conclusive reason for saying that that individual is also in time.

---

[1]Richard Swinburne, *The Christian God* (Oxford: Clarendon, 1994), p.79.

Bill appears, not surprisingly, to want to have his cake and to eat it too! In the time before the creation, there would be no earlier and later, no waiting, no temporal becoming. So he wishes to say that before creation God exists in a timeless instant. God before the creation occupies an indivisible moment of timeless existence and then becomes temporal. Bill says this, but does it make sense?

The difficulty of combining divine timelessness before the creation with temporality after the creation is compounded by the fact that God's alleged timelessness (if I understand Bill correctly) must be understood in A-series terms despite his saying that "there is no before, no after, no temporal passage, no future phase of his life." For Bill appears to have a priori objections to the very idea of a B-series view of time's being the fundamental view of what time is. He says that the static view of time "faces formidable philosophical and theological objections, not to mention the arguments that can be offered on behalf of a dynamic theory of time." I take it that Bill thinks that these difficulties effectively demote the B-series from providing us with the basic view of time. Bill also rejects the idea that there might be two phases of God's life, a timeless phase and a temporal phase, as logically incoherent. But how can God exist timelessly (but not statically), occupying (until the creation) a timeless point of an A-series, existing "literally before God's creation of the world and the beginning of differentiated time"?

Apart from the intrinsic oddity of the view, does not the old problem of timelessness and the knowledge of indexicals come back to haunt Bill at this point? Does God, existing in his A-series timeless moment of time before the creation, know what is future to him? If he does, then surely he is, contra Bill, in time. And if he does not, then he is not omniscient on Bill's own understanding of what omniscience is. So Bill's efforts to distinguish clearly a point of dynamic timelessness (possessing the topology of a point) after which there are dynamic temporal states appear to stall. The position that he advocates looks unstable, and he may be forced to choose either the eternalist or the temporalist option.

RESPONSE TO
WILLIAM LANE CRAIG

ALAN G. PADGETT

*T*he chapter by William Lane Craig contains much that I am in agreement with. Bill was able in a few pages, under the section "Divine Relations with the World," to encapsulate the main problem I have with the traditional theory of divine eternity. The nature of this kind of dialogue, however, requires us to focus on our (few) disagreements. So we must now turn to these.

I am happy to represent what Bill calls the "Oxford school" on the nature of divine eternity. In fact, we have already debated in print on this topic, in the pages of *Religious Studies*.[1] Bill correctly notes that the debate between us turns on the idea of metric conventionalism. Since he does not spell this out very much, I will do so here.

Any area of natural science establishes certain units of measure for its work. Some of these are natural or intrinsic to the object of study, for

---

[1]See Alan G. Padgett, "God and Time: Toward a New Doctrine of Divine Timeless Eternity" *Religious Studies* 25 (1989): 209-15; William Lane Craig, "God and Real Time," *Religious Studies* 26 (1990): 335-47; and Alan G. Padgett, "Can History Measure Eternity? A Reply to William Craig" *Religious Studies* 27 (1991): 333-35.

example, the mass of a material object. Some physical properties, however, are extrinsic, relative to the situation in which the measure is taking place. The weight of an object is like this. The same object weighs much less on the moon than it does on the earth—and even less in outer space. Now which kind of measure is *time* for physical objects? Strange as it may seem, contemporary physics has taught us that the measure or metric of time is not intrinsic or absolute. There is no objective fact of the matter concerning some temporal interval between two events, as to how long it is. The measurement of temporal intervals depends on the choice of a clock and the inertial frame of reference in which the "clock" and the events are placed. Even observers using the same clock will measure the same temporal interval differently, if they are moving at great speeds relative to each other (or if one of them is in a very strong gravity field). Metric conventionalism with respect to temporal measure is a fact of our universe. God has created the world that way.

Although I believe there is a sense in which God is temporal, I also hold that God is "relatively timeless." By this I mean: not being in measured time, not in our space-time, not in physical time. God is timeless *relative* to our space-time universe, that is, relative to physical time. On the other hand, along with Bill, I believe that God has real relations with the world and undergoes change in his activity (and therefore is temporal) in relation to a dynamic universe. Thinking both of these ideas together is what I mean by "relative timelessness."

But prior to the creation of the universe, was God still temporal in some sense? Bill has correctly pointed out that at some remote, distant moment, prior to the creation and to any change in God, there may well have been an infinite, changeless eternity that was "timeless." We are, of course, far beyond what is revealed about God through Jesus Christ and Holy Scripture. This kind of speculation is always done with a grain of salt! Still, the creation of a coherent theology is a worthy goal for the church, and there are bound to be some more speculative elements in that larger theological vision. Even if there might have been other universes before ours, at some time in the far and nearly infinite past, there must have been a time when God alone, the Blessed Trinity, dwelt in perfect harmony. There would then have been no need for change or exchange between the perfect, infinite Mind of Love. Let us call this period the time B.F.C., "before the First Change" in God's eternity (whenever that was).

Bill is critical of this viewpoint, in which God is changeless and relatively timeless B.F.C. without being fully timeless. His criticism, however, contains a contradiction. At the beginning of his section "Amorphous Time" he correctly notes that "we can conceive of a time that is not divisible into intervals." Yet his criticism insists that such a precreation eternity is divisible into intervals. The chart (figure 2) that he creates as an illustration divides God's time B.F.C. into such intervals—yet he clearly understands that according to metric conventionalism there simply cannot be any such "intervals of time" B.F.C.

Bill needs to grasp more fully the point that in such an unchanging, perfect eternity B.F.C. *there cannot be temporal intervals.* So his criticism is wide of the mark. He goes on to state that "the past is infinite if and only if there is no first interval of time and time is not circular." Yet this proposition is true only if all prior time is capable of being divided into intervals—which I deny. There is, let us say, an unending, nonfinite and immeasurable "time" B.F.C. If you want to call this an "interval," fine, but it is a very odd one! Any division into subintervals is wholly arbitrary: in fact there are no "divisions" in this temporal interval B.F.C. Instead of thinking of this "precreation" peaceful eternity as an *infinite amount of time* (since infinity has mathematical properties), we are better off thinking of it as a *nonfinite eternity.* In other words, time before all thought of creation is without end or limit (nonfinite) without being infinite in a mathematical sense (i.e., an infinite *amount* of something). So I would change Bill's proposition to this: the past is infinite if and only if (a) time is not circular and (b) either there is no first interval of time or the first "interval" of time is a nonfinite, eternal duration.

I will be the first to admit that all such speculation is just that: speculation. Yet the mind is restless until it comes to some kind of coherent understanding of even such remote issues in the relationship between God and the world. The proposal of a nonfinite, eternal and changeless duration B.F.C. is one that satisfies the mind. I find rest in the thought of infinite rest, infinite bliss and unchanging eternity. But is it right to call this existence "temporal"? That depends on one's definition of time. I have defined time as the dimension of the possibility of change.

With Bill and a number of philosophers, I reject the idea that change *must* (logically must) happen in order for duration to occur. I use *duration* to stand for an interval of time. Duration can occur without change. But what, then, is the relationship between time and change? I created the following argument some ten years ago, and I still can find no flaws in it now (perhaps due to creeping senility?).[2]

1. Necessarily, if no duration occurs then no change occurs.

In other words, if you imagine a timeless "slice" out of the history of the world, no change would take place in that timeless instant. Changes take time in order to happen. This does not just happen to be true but is true of necessity. So it follows that:

2. Necessarily, if a change occurs then duration occurs.

Now I want to introduce a proposition that I will in fact argue must be false. This is an important step in many arguments.

3. If a duration occurs, then it must be the case that a change does not occur (at that time).

This (false) proposition states that if some amount of time goes by, then it must be the case that no change happened during that time. This proposition seems false on the face of it. But it can be shown to contradict 2, that is, shown to be false. If a change occurs, according to 2, then a duration occurs. But if a change occurs, according to 3 and the laws of logic *(modus tollens)*, then a duration does not occur. Both 2 and 3 cannot be true in any world where at least one change occurs (like ours). So therefore 3 must be false for all worlds where at least one change happens. Logically, the fact that 3 is false can be expressed in positive form. It follows from David Lewis's definition of an "if . . . then it might be . . ." conditional sentence that the falsehood of 3 is equivalent to[3]

4. If a duration occurs, then it might be the case that a change occurs.

In other words, time is the dimension of the *possibility* of change. Change does not have to occur in order for time to occur, but the possibility of change follows from the reality of time.

How does this bear on our discussion with Bill? Even prior to the First Change, if it is *possible* for God to change, then God must in some weak

---

[2]See Alan G. Padgett, *God, Eternity and the Nature of Time* (London: Macmillan, 1992), pp. 15-16, 147 n. 9.

[3]David Lewis, *Counterfactuals* (Oxford: Blackwell, 1973), pp. 1-4. My argument is based on his counterfactual semantics for conditional sentences of a certain type. I am translating these symbols here as "if . . . then it must be the case that . . ." and "if . . . then it might be the case that . . ."

sense be temporal. In reply to Bill, I have created the following argument, which parallels 1-4:

5. If no duration occurs, then it is not possible for a change to occur.

This is a slightly different version of 1 but is still true. If no duration occurs, then it is impossible for change to occur. Another way of putting this same point would be: there is no possible world that both is fully timeless and in which change occurs. Yet from 5 we derive

6. If possibly a change occurs, then duration occurs.

Putting 4 and 6 together yields my basic point: time is the dimension of the possibility of change. So it is not coherent for Bill to claim that in the nonfinite eternity before the First Change, God was fully timeless. This is because, for Bill, change was possible for God. If change was not possible, God could never create the world! There could be no First Change for a God who was fully timeless. So even before the First Change, it was *possible* for God to change. And so even before the First Change, God was temporal in some (rather weak) sense. Of course this turns on the idea, which I share with Nick, Paul and Bill, that bringing about a dynamic universe requires a change in God's power—that is, a real relation.

RESPONSE TO WILLIAM LANE CRAIG

NICHOLAS WOLTERSTORFF

*T*here's not much that I disagree with in Bill Craig's discussion—mainly because, on the issues that I articulate and defend, Bill and I pretty much agree, whereas he, like Alan Padgett, goes beyond this and commits himself on an issue on which I have no settled view. He holds that God's existence alone without creation was most likely timeless, Alan holds that it was most likely temporal, whereas I find the considerations either way indecisive. All three of us agree, however, that God's existence *with creation* is temporal.

A significant issue that Bill raises early in his discussion is whether there isn't something inherently defective about temporal existence and thus incompatible with divine perfection. Bill himself does not regard this consideration as decisive, since he holds that God's existence is temporal; nonetheless he thinks the argument does have considerable weight.

"Life in its fullness," he says, "can never be enjoyed by any temporal being." True enough. But what exactly is the alternative to our present mode of existence that we are being invited to consider? Obviously I can't experience all at once everything that I have experienced: youth, adulthood, getting married, having five children, beginning to teach, traveling in Europe and so forth. These can't all be jammed into one static momentary slice. So apparently what I'm being asked to imagine is that all I would ever experience would be just one momentary slice out of my present life. My experience of listening to music would be the experience of listening eternally to one chord, my experience of reading would be the experience of gazing eternally on just one eye-full of letters, and so forth. All the other experiences that I've had, and that I *could* have because my life has been stretched out over time, would be lost to me.

I must say that it seems to me just mad to suppose that such a life would be preferable to my actual life. When one's children grow up, their childhood is "lost" to one. But why would anybody want their children to remain forever children? I think time is not something we should long to escape from, as something bad or deficient, but something we should give thanks to God for. So far as I can see, the loss that people experience is not the "loss" inherent in present events' becoming past events but a loss that occurs *within* time, the loss of things we treasure—our health, our child, our reputation, whatever.

I agree with Bill that the arguments of those of us who hold that God is temporal boil down to two: we hold that a proper understanding of God's action vis-à-vis the creation implies that God is temporal, and we hold that a proper understanding of God's knowledge implies that God is temporal. In fact I think God's temporality is also implied by the fact that God exists now, and existed yesterday, and will exist tomorrow; but in my experience, defenders of divine timelessness are not impressed with this argument—though why not has never been clear to me. In any case, the arguments that seem to have most polemical force are of the two sorts mentioned.

Bill considers attempts by Stump and Kretzmann, and by Leftow, to "deny that God's real relation to the world involves him in time," and concludes that they all fail. I agree with this assessment; my own objections to their positions are pretty much the same as those Bill offers. I do think, however, that Aquinas's "way out," which I discuss in my article, has rather more force than Bill seems to allow. Upon deciding to create, God considers all the alternatives, including all the things that human beings would freely do in different situations; then God creates the initial temporal slice of creation and stands back, as it were. The causal powers that God places in things in that initial slice then play themselves out as long as creation endures. (Of course it couldn't really be the case that first God considers the alternatives and *then* creates!)

If one were willing to adopt an entirely noninterventionist understanding of God's action vis-à-vis creation, then this account would explain how God could act on creation while nonetheless remaining untainted by temporality. Such an understanding seems to me distinctly unacceptable, however. To mention just two considerations: it implies that God does not respond to what transpires in creation, and it implies a heterodox view of the incarnation. On this view, the only way God could act in Jesus' life, death and resurrection is the same way God acts in any event: that is, God intended that event to happen, and God created the contents of the initial slice of creation's history with just exactly the right causal powers to ensure that eventually, as the scroll unrolls, it will happen.

To Bill's discussion of various attempts on the part of timelessness advocates to evade the argument for God's temporality from God's knowledge of tensed facts I also have nothing substantial to add; what he says in response to Kvanvig and Wierenga seems to me correct. So let me, in closing, say a few things about some of the points he makes in defense of his conclusion that it's plausible to hold that, apart from creation, God is timeless.

For one thing, he is impressed with the old argument that if there were time before creation, God would have to have some reason for deciding to create, and then creating exactly when he did rather than at some other time, yet it doesn't seem that there could be any such reason. But I must say that for quite some time now I have not found this argument persuasive. At a certain moment I decide to get out of bed in the morning. No doubt I have a reason for deciding to get out of bed; but do I also have a reason for deciding to get out *at just that moment,* rather than earlier or later? Or if at 6:15 I decide to get out at precisely 6:26 on my clock, do I have a reason for making the decision at 6:15 rather than earlier or later? So far as I can tell, I have no such reason; at a certain moment I just decide to get up. You ask me why not a second earlier, or a second later. I have no reason—just as I also often have no reason for walking to the right around some puddle rather than to the left, or vice versa.

Second, I'm not persuaded by the conclusions Bill derives from his reflections on a metric for time. In the first place, having a metric for time is clearly not essential to temporal experience. In fact no human being has ever lacked a metric for time—not for long anyway. Though most human beings have lacked clocks of any sort whatsoever, always there was the rising and setting of the sun to mark off days. One can imagine, however, that the movement of the earth relative to the sun might have been such that at certain places on the earth's surface the sun would not rise or set; people living there, if they didn't have clocks, would then have no metric—as indeed those do not who, for purposes of experiment or punishment, live in total darkness for a time. Nonetheless, such people would still have temporal experience and would be able to make judgments about it. If two tones began to sound simultaneously, and then one ceased while the other continued, they would judge the duration of the latter to be longer than that of the former. Or if one tone were sounded by itself for five seconds, and then another were sounded for a minute, they would judge the latter to be longer in duration than the former. They would even be able to make some judgments as to when one tone endured twice as long as another, and so forth.

The view of the "Oxford school," as Bill calls it, seems to be that God's experience apart from creation is temporal, even though, in the absence of creation, there are no cyclical processes whereby a metric for time could be instituted. Bill disagrees with the Oxford school. What he says is this: "The shortcoming of the Oxford school is that it has not been radical enough. It proposes to dispense with the metric of time while still retaining the geometry of time as a line. Since on a geometrical line intervals can be objectively distinguished and, when included in one another, compared in length, time is not sufficiently undifferentiated to avoid the problems attending an infinite past."

I do not understand this. Apparently Bill agrees that there's no problem in the suggestion as such that in God's life apart from creation there are discriminable temporal intervals even though the cyclical processes necessary for a metric for time are lacking. The difficulty he sees is that God's time will not be "sufficiently undifferentiated to avoid the problems attending an infinite past." I do not know what Bill is referring to here. What is this problem of an infinite past, such that only if intervals in God's life are relatively undifferentiated can that problem be avoided?

It is for these reasons that I am unable to join Bill in his conclusion that "God existing without creation is changelessly alone, and no event disturbs this complete tranquillity. There is no before, no after, no temporal passage, no future phase." This may be true; then again, the alternative view, defended by Alan Padgett, may be true; I fail to see decisive considerations in either direction.

RESPONSE TO CRITICS

WILLIAM LANE CRAIG

*R*ather than respond to my colleagues sequentially, I prefer in this counterresponse to review the positive case advanced in my essay and to consider their queries and objections as they apply to the positions that I advocated.

Biblical Data on Divine Eternity
I argued that the biblical data concerning divine timelessness/temporality are mixed. Usually the Bible speaks of God in temporal terms; but in contemplating God's creation of the world, the biblical authors do state that time had a beginning and thereby imply that God without the universe is timeless. In my response to Nick, I also charged that he adopts a hermeneutically naive approach to biblical descriptions about God as temporal and overlooks those passages dealing with the beginning of the world.

None of my colleagues elected to respond to this portion of my essay, and I do not yet know how Nick will respond to the charge I made in my response to his essay. So I take it that Scripture is open on the issue of the nature of divine eternity.

Divine Timelessness: The Incompleteness of Temporal Life

I presented an argument for divine timelessness based on the imperfection entailed by temporal existence and concluded that, while powerful, its force is mitigated in the case of an omniscient being and that, moreover, the incompleteness of temporal life may not be an imperfection with regard to personal existence.

Paul is oddly silent on this argument in his response, but Nick has a good deal to say. He asks, "What exactly is the alternative to our present mode of existence that we are being invited to consider?" He answers, "What I'm being asked to imagine is that all I would ever experience would be just one momentary slice out of my present life"—a response that draws his exclamation, "It seems to me just mad to suppose that such a life would be preferable to my actual life."

But Nick has erected a straw man. First, the contrast to my temporal life is God's atemporal life. Even if my life is better temporal than atemporal, that is irrelevant to whether God's life is better temporal than atemporal. Even if creaturely life is better temporal than atemporal, that says nothing about the life of an infinite, uncreated being. Second, in any case the relevant scenario for my atemporal existence is not one slice out of my temporal life but rather a wholly different kind of life. For example, it might be an unembodied existence consisting of the contemplation of God or of the beatific vision of Christ. Such an enraptured, changeless state would be a state of supreme blessedness and so hardly inferior to our transitory, temporal existence and the finite goods made available through it. So I think the argument from the incompleteness of temporal life has a good deal going for it—though in the end I think it inconclusive.

Divine Temporality

The impossibility of atemporal personhood. In this section I presented and rejected an argument for the incompatibility of personhood and atemporality. Perhaps my most significant contention here is that God's temporality/atemporality is a contingent property of God.

Again, none of my interlocutors disagreed with what I said on this. I take it, then, that there is a possible world in which God exists timelessly. This will be important when we come to consider God's temporal status sans creation.

Divine relations with the world. I argued that if a dynamic theory of time is correct, then in virtue of God's real relation to the temporal world, God is temporal. On this issue, significantly, all four contributors to this volume are one. Paul simply denies the assumption that a dynamic theory of time is correct, thereby undercutting the argument. The "consistent B-theorist," he says, should avoid any attempt to relate divine atemporality to a temporal, tensed creation. So when Paul says that "a mere extrinsic relation" to the world is not sufficient to render God temporal, he is presupposing a static view of time, according to which God's extrinsic relations do not change, that is, come to be and pass away. On a dynamic view of time, God's changing extrinsically in his relations to creatures would suffice to temporalize God.

Nick does muster some defense of what he takes to be Aquinas's "way out" of this problem, that God acts once to produce effects that will appear at their appointed times in history. I maintain that Aquinas's concern in the relevant passage is to explain how God can immutably will a temporal world without that world's always existing, that is, without its having an infinite past. Even if successful, Aquinas's argument at best shows that God's efficacious will remains changeless as the world comes to be and as events successively occur and pass away. He says nothing in this context (nor was it his intention) to show how the origin and unfolding of a temporal world would not taint the eternal God with temporality in virtue of his real relation to the temporal sequence of events changelessly willed by him. However we take Aquinas's affirmation that "God's action existed from all eternity, whereas its effect . . . existed at that time when, from all eternity, He ordained it,"[1] it seems to me that Nick's defense of divine timelessness fails: (1) If Aquinas is thinking here of a sempiternal deity who acts from eternity past to produce effects at their appointed times, then God is temporal, not timeless. (2) If we

---

[1]Thomas Aquinas *Summa Contra Gentiles* 2.35.3.

take Aquinas to be speaking of God's acting "from eternity" in the sense of "out of eternity," that is, out of his timeless state into time, then what we have, as Aquinas elsewhere makes clear, is the real presence of all events in the time line to God in eternity, which I can only understand as an implicit affirmation of the static theory of time.[2] In such a case God does not, as Nick puts it, "create the initial temporal slice of creation and stand back, as it were." Rather he creates or sustains the whole spatiotemporal block timelessly, with all the events at their appointed times. Nick's interpretation that God creates the initial slice and stands back turns Aquinas into a deist, which is absurd. What Nick also fails to reckon with is that if time is not static but dynamic, then even God's creation of the initial slice of the temporal world will suffice, in virtue of God's real relation with the world, to draw God into time at that point. The only way to avert that conclusion is to deny that God's causal relation to the world is a real relation, which is fantastic.

Divine knowledge of tensed facts. I explained that if a dynamic theory of time is correct, then God, in virtue of his omniscience, must know tensed facts. Since tensed facts can be known only by a temporal being, God must be temporal.

It is a little odd that Paul does not simply dismiss this argument as he did the foregoing one on the grounds that, given a static theory of time, there simply are no tensed facts. Instead he seems to want to deny premise 3:

3. If a temporal world exists, then if God is omniscient, God knows tensed facts.

First, he suggests, perhaps God has no beliefs—that is to say, the objects of his knowledge are not facts as such. But even if we adopt such a nonfactual account of God's knowledge, in virtue of his maximal cognitive excellence God cannot be ignorant of what we finite knowers apprehend as tensed facts. A temporal deity could be aware of all tenseless facts (or what we express as tenseless facts) about the universe and so know everything a timeless deity knows, plus an infinitude of (what we express as) tensed facts as well. Thus time-

---

[2]William Lane Craig, "Was Thomas Aquinas a B-theorist of Time?" *New Scholasticism* 59 (1985): 473-83.

lessness compromises omniscience in a way that temporality does not.

Paul also suggests that we assimilate God's knowledge-that to knowledge-how. Since omniscience does not require God to have all knowledge-how (for example, knowing how it feels to be oneself a sinner), God's ignorance of tensed facts would not count against his omniscience. But this escape, I think, is a desperate expedient, since knowing that, say, Abraham Lincoln was assassinated is just not at all a case of knowledge-how. Even if God need not know how it feels to be shot, as an omniscient being he must know that Lincoln was shot, which is a tensed fact.

Thus Paul would have more plausibly stuck with the static theory of time and boldly affirmed that there simply are no tensed facts for an omniscient being to know.

A way out for advocates of divine timelessness? The issue, then, boils down to whether a static or dynamic theory of time is correct. I present here a summary of the reasons for which I accept a dynamic theory of time:

I. Arguments for a Dynamic Theory of Time
  A. Tensed sentences, which can neither be translated into synonymous tenseless sentences nor be given tenseless, token-reflexive truth conditions, correspond, if true, to tensed facts.
  B. The experience of temporal becoming, like our experience of the external world, is properly regarded as veridical.
II. Refutation of Arguments Against a Dynamic Theory of Time
  A. McTaggart's celebrated paradox is based on the misguided marriage of a tenseless ontology of events or things with objective temporal becoming, as well as the unjustified assumption that there should exist a unique, complete description of reality.
  B. The passage of time is not a myth but a metaphor for objective temporal becoming, a notion that can be consistently explicated on a presentist metaphysic.
III. Refutation of Arguments for a Static Theory of Time
  A. Temporal becoming is compatible with relativity theory if we reject space-time realism in favor of a neo-Lorentzian interpretation of the formalism of the theory.

B. Time as it plays a role in physics is a pale abstraction of a richer metaphysical reality, omitting indexical elements such as the "here" and the "now" in the interest of universalizing the formulations of natural laws.

IV. Arguments Against a Static Theory of Time

    A. In the absence of objective distinctions between past, present and future, the relations ordering events on the static theory are only gratuitously regarded as genuinely temporal relations of *earlier/later than*.

    B. The claim that temporal becoming is mind-dependent is self-defeating, since the subjective illusion of becoming involves itself an objective becoming in the contents of consciousness.

    C. The static theory entails perdurantism, the doctrine that objects have spatiotemporal parts, a view that is metaphysically counterintuitive, is incompatible with moral accountability and entails the bizarre counterpart doctrine of transworld identity.

    D. The tenseless theory is theologically objectionable, since its claim that God and the universe coexist tenselessly is incompatible with a robust doctrine of *creatio ex nihilo*.

In his responses to Alan and Nick, Paul does attempt to defend the static view against certain of these arguments (which they raise), and I trust that they in their final counterresponses will explain why Paul's defense is not satisfactory.

Timelessness and Omnitemporality

In this section I raise the question of God's temporal status sans creation. This issue serves to differentiate my view from Alan's and Nick's. I was somewhat amused to find Alan protesting that we are here involved in speculation "far beyond what is revealed about God through Jesus Christ and Holy Scripture" and therefore to be taken "with a grain of salt." This from a person who espouses the recondite doctrine of "relative timelessness"! In talking about the nature of divine eternity at all we have already moved, as we all recognize, far beyond biblical revelation. If we are to craft a tenable doctrine of divine eternity, we cannot pull back at this point. For in the first place, a robust doctrine of *creatio ex nihilo* demands that we address the question of

God's temporal status sans creation. A biblical doctrine of *creatio ex nihilo* involves the dual affirmation that God brought the universe into being out of nothing at some moment in the finite past and that he thereafter sustains it in being moment by moment.[3] God's temporal status sans creation cannot therefore be a matter of indifference to the Christian theologian—indeed, if time did not begin at creation, then God has existed for infinitely longer without the world than with it! If one tries to avoid this conclusion by dissolving time's metric prior to creation, then one has already launched his bark onto the metaphysical deep.

In the second place, an intellectually relevant theology cannot avoid the question before us, because it lies at the heart of contemporary cosmology. According to the standard big bang theory, not only all matter and energy but physical space and time themselves originated in the initial cosmological singularity. Is this prediction of the standard model correct? If so, then profound metaphysical questions arise, such as why the universe exists rather than nothing. If not, then what is the correct physical theory of the pre-big bang universe? According to Charles Misner, Kip Thorne and John Archibald Wheeler in their classic text, "No problem of cosmology digs more deeply into the foundations of physics than the question of what 'preceded' the 'initial state' of infinite (or near infinite) density, pressure, and temperature."[4] If God is in time insofar as he coexists with the world, then Christian theologians cannot in light of contemporary cosmology shrug off the question of God's temporal status without the world.

Why did God not create the world sooner? I presented a five-step argument for the finitude of the past arising out of the ancient puzzle of why God did not create the world sooner. As Leibniz saw, this question poses a truly serious problem for Newtonian views of God enduring through infinite time prior to creation.

Now obviously the most controversial premise in the argument is

2. If at *t* God delayed creating until *t* + *n*, then he must have had a good reason for doing so.

---

[3]See William Lane Craig, "Creation and Conservation Once More," *Religious Studies* 34 (1998): 177-88.
[4]C. Misner, K. Thorne and J. A. Wheeler, *Gravitation* (San Francisco: W. H. Freeman, 1973), p. 769.

Not unexpectedly, this is the premise Nick denies. He appeals to the illustration of getting out of bed in the morning: "No doubt I have a reason for deciding to get out of bed; but do I also have a reason for deciding to get out *at just that moment,* rather than earlier or later?" Now this analogy is misconstructed in perhaps important ways. For 2 does not speak of God's deciding at t to create at $t + n$ but of his delaying at t to create until $t + n$. An omniscient God does not make decisions at certain times, because he already foreknows such decisions. Hence either God does not make decisions at all (in the sense of moving from indecision to decision) or else he makes decisions eternally (in the sense of having a free, unchanging intention to execute some action). Thus God has intended from eternity to create the world. But on the Newtonian view he has again and again and again delayed carrying out that intention. Premise 2 states that he must have had a good reason for so desisting from carrying out his intention. The proper analogy for this, therefore, would be my lying in bed, intending to get up, but continually delaying getting up until finally at some moment I do get up. But in this scenario is it so obvious, as Nick claims, that I have no reason for my delaying at each moment getting up? It seems to me that I do have a reason. I'm tired, I don't feel like getting up, I can still make it to work if I wait a little longer. When those reasons no longer hold—when time is pressing, I'm no longer sleepy, I'm feeling guilty for being so lazy—then I no longer delay, and I get up. Similarly, if God delays creating the world, which he has eternally willed to create, then he must have some good reason for so delaying. In any case, Nick's human analogies are flawed because I, unlike God, am not a supremely rational agent. As a supremely rational being, God surely would not delay carrying out what he intends to do unless he has a good reason for doing so. The implication is that past is not infinite but had a beginning.

Amorphous time. In this section I examine the Oxford school's doctrine of an amorphous time prior to creation. My fundamental criticism is that the Oxford thinkers have not been radical enough: they deny an objective metric to time prior to creation but retain its topological isomorphism to a line. They cannot therefore evade the conundrum of why God did not create the world sooner.

There seems to be considerable confusion among my coauthors concerning the metric of time.[5] As I explain in my essay and my response to Alan, the question whether time has an objective metric is a question about whether there is an objective fact about the comparative lengths of nonnested temporal intervals. This is a question of chronometry (the temporal equivalent of geometry). Questions about time's structural properties that remain unchanged under arbitrary but continuous distortions, like separation, neighborhood, boundary and enclosure, are matters of the topology of time. So long as time has the topology of a line, then distinct temporal intervals can be identified within it even if it is metrically amorphous. For a line is a one-dimensional manifold of specifiable points ordered by a relation of betweenness: if x, y and z are three points on a line, then one of the points (say y) is between the other two. Therefore distinct intervals $x\,y$ and $y\,z$ exist as part of the line, even if there is no objective matter of fact concerning the comparative lengths of $x\,y$ and $y\,z$. Moreover, even on metric conventionalism $x\,z > y\,z$, since the latter is a proper part of the former. The points, or instants, of time are ordered by unique *earlier than/later than* relations. If time did not begin to exist, then there are instants $w, v, u, \ldots$ earlier than x on the timeline. Therefore there is a beginningless series of longer and longer temporal intervals prior to any instant z: yz, xz, wz, $\ldots$, even granted metric conventionalism.

With this understanding in mind, we see that many of my colleagues' responses to my critique are simply misconceived. For example, Nick's reflections on our perception of the comparative lengths of temporal intervals concern *psychological* time, or our experience of time, not time

---

[5] I think Alan has clearly confounded metric conventionalism with time dilation. Alan correctly notes that on the customary interpretation of relativity theory, measurements of the time interval between two events are relative to reference frames. Relative to one frame the temporal interval between two events will be measured to be one hour, while relative to another frame that same interval will be measured to be two hours. This is called time dilation. But metric conventionalism holds that *within a single reference frame* there is no objective fact about the comparative lengths of two nonoverlapping temporal intervals. For example, Henri Poincaré, who was a metric conventionalist about space and time, boldly asserted that there is no factual difference about the comparative distances from New York to Paris and from Paris to London! If, as most philosophers think, Poincaré was wrong about this, then relativity will do nothing to rescue metric conventionalism. For in every frame of reference the distance from New York to Paris will be greater than from Paris to London, even if the distance measurements themselves are different from frame to frame. The same holds for temporal distances.

itself. Everyone recognizes that intervals in psychological time between events are not isochronic, even if the corresponding intervals in time itself are ("time flies when you're having fun!"). Thus, contrary to Nick, the question is not one of divine psychology or of God's experience of time without creation. Rather the problem is God's idly enduring through a infinite series of temporal intervals, repeatedly delaying without reason his creation of the world until a later time. Thus Nick has misunderstood me when he asserts that I myself see "no problem in the suggestion as such that in God's life apart from creation there are discriminable temporal intervals." On the contrary, that is precisely the problem.

Paul and Alan recognize the problem but cling to the view that metric conventionalism can avoid it. Quoting Swinburne to the effect that "in the absence of laws of nature, there will be no temporal distances," Paul claims, "it seems reasonable to say that if there are no temporal distances there are no temporal intervals and a fortiori no intervals within intervals." This inference is mistaken. Distance concerns the measure of time, not its topological structure. On metric conventionalism, there are objective intervals, as we have seen, but no objective distances. Thus even if there are no factual temporal distances in precreation time (such as one hour before creation), still there is a beginningless series of progressively longer temporal intervals prior to creation. Similarly, Alan asserts, "in such an unchanging, perfect eternity B.F.C. *there cannot be temporal intervals.*" I agree that this is the solution to the problem if such a time is conceivable, but my point is that metric conventionalism will not get you there. What Alan must do is to deny that precreation time is topologically linear, and in his response Alan is quite evidently ready to make this move.

Such an undifferentiated precreation time seems, as I say, to be topologically pointlike. But then I wonder whether it really deserves the name *time*. It has no past, present or future within it nor any instants or intervals earlier or later than one another. It looks like a state of timelessness to me!

Now Alan offers a proof of such a state's temporality. But while his premise

1. Necessarily, if no duration occurs, then no change occurs

is true, his premise

5. If no duration occurs, then it is not possible for a change to occur is false. For imagine a possible world in which God refrains from creation (as he is free to do) and just exists changelessly alone. Such a world is, plausibly, timeless. Hence there is no duration in such a world. Nevertheless, it is still possible in such a world for God to will differently and to create a temporal universe. Thus it is possible in such a world for a change to occur, even though it never in fact does. Alan has apparently confused his false 5 with the true statement

5'. It is not possible that no duration occurs and that change occurs.

The composite impossibility expressed in 5' does not imply the impossibility of the consequent of 5 given the truth of its antecedent. Therefore, contrary to Alan, the mere possibility of change does not imply the existence of time.

So why think that such a changeless, undifferentiated state is temporal? As I said, about the only reason an Oxford scholar could offer would be that temporal states come after it. Paul responds that this seems like a pretty good reason! Indeed, were it true; but the question is: Is it true? Paul evidently thinks that I mean to affirm that temporal states do come chronologically after God's changeless state, when in fact my model denies this. I argue that on a dynamic theory of time Paul's envisioned scenario presupposes backward causation: it is implied that because God acts to create the world, the production of the first event not only causes time to come into being coincident with the first event but retroactively causes time to have existed before the first event—which seems metaphysically impossible. Paul denies the necessity of backward causation, asserting, "It is simply that if someone who exists either timelessly or in time, and exists before some temporal states of affairs, then this is . . . conclusive reason for saying that that individual is also in time." But this argument is question-begging, for the question we are asking is precisely whether someone does exist "before some temporal state of affairs." My claim is that the affirmation that God sans creation exists literally before creation seems to presuppose an impossible retrocausation, and therefore God does *not* exist temporally before creation. Paul never explains how the occurrence of a first event serves to produce time *before* the event occurs. Paul has clearly misunderstood me to be affirming that temporal states come after God's changeless state, for he says, "Bill . . . wishes to say that before creation God exists in a timeless instant." But I deny this self-contradictory statement. God is causally, but not temporally, prior to creation; therefore I speak of God's existing timelessly *sans* creation, not *before* it. God's timeless state is not temporally before creation, nor is the creation temporally after God's timeless state. Thus the position Paul says makes no sense—that God exists timelessly, occupying a timeless point of an A-series existing literally before God's creation of the world—is not my position but is closer to Alan's, which I mean to reject. My position is that God is timeless sans creation and temporal since creation.

Finally, Paul raises an interesting objection based on divine omniscience: "Does God, existing . . . before the creation, know what is future to him? If he does, then surely he is . . . in time. And if he does not, then he is not omniscient." This objection is based again on the erroneous assumption that on my view God exists "before the creation." Nevertheless, it serves to bring out an interesting feature of my view. For God existing alone without creation there is no literal future, since time does not exist. Therefore any future-tense propositions that exist must be uniformly false. Is God sans creation therefore ignorant of what happens once he creates the world? No, for he knows all tenselessly true propositions sans creation (for example, *In A.D. 1969, United States astronauts land on the moon*). At the moment of creation myriad future-tense propositions suddenly switch truth-values, and God believes only and all those that are true. Thus his foreknowledge, strictly speaking, begins at the moment of creation, for without creation there is no time, and without time there are no future-tensed truths, and without future-tensed truths there is no literal foreknowledge.

I should be the first to admit that my hybrid view of divine eternity is certainly curious. But curiosity is not incoherence, and I think that the view that God is timeless sans creation and temporal since creation, once properly understood, is the most plausible doctrine of divine eternity.

5

UNQUALIFIED DIVINE TEMPORALITY

NICHOLAS WOLTERSTORFF

*G*od is represented in Scripture as One who has a history of acting and responding. Recall Exodus 3—4: when Moses was tending the flocks of his father-in-law in the wilderness, his curiosity was piqued one day by a bush engulfed in flames but not consumed. He walked over; and as he approached, God addressed him out of the bush: "Moses, Moses!" It's the narrator who tells us that it was God addressing him; Moses didn't yet know what to make of what was happening. Moses responded, "Here I am," whereupon God said, "Come no closer! Remove the sandals from your feet, for the place on which you're standing is holy ground." Then the speaker in the bush identified himself: "I am the God of your father, the God of Abraham, the God of Isaac, and the God of Jacob." Moses was gripped by fear and, no longer daring to look, covered his face.

God then told Moses that he had seen the affliction of his people, had heard their cry of suffering, and had "come down" to bring them out of servitude into a land where they could flourish. "So come," said God, "I will send you to Pharaoh to bring my people, the Israelites out of Egypt."

188 ─── GOD & TIME

What then follows is a series of protests by Moses. *Who am I that I should go to Pharaoh and lead my people out?* I'll be with you, says God. *But if I tell my people that the God of their fathers has sent me to lead them out, they'll want to know your name.* Tell them that I AM WHO I AM, says God. *But they won't believe me when I tell them that you appeared and spoke to me.* I'll enable you to perform a couple of wonders as signs, says God. *But I'm a poor speaker.* I'll give you the right words when they're needed, says God. *But I don't want to do it; pick somebody else,* No, says God, exasperated now, you're the one. I'll appoint your brother Aaron to speak for you in public; but you are to be the leader.

Is God Timeless?

This episode stands out as one of the great numinous episodes of the biblical narrative. But its representation of God as having a history, which then can be narrated, is not exceptional but typical of Scripture's representation of God: God responds to what transpires in human affairs by performing a succession of actions, including actions of speaking. An implication of this representation of God is that there's change in God's life; if a person does one thing at one time and a different thing at a later time, then there's change in that person's life. Behind the change in action there is, in turn, a change in knowledge: God's successive responses to Moses were motivated by God's knowledge, each time, of Moses' new protest; the changes in God's knowledge tracked the changes in Moses' protest. These, I say, are implications of how Scripture represents God: God has a history, and in this history there are changes in God's actions, responses and knowledge. The God of Scripture is One of whom a narrative can be told; we know that not because Scripture tells us that but because it offers such a narrative. I hold that an implication of this is that God is in time. If something has a history, then perforce that being is in time.

And now let me articulate a methodological principle that on this occasion I will affirm without defending: an implication of one's accepting Scripture as canonical is that one will affirm as literally true Scripture's representation of God unless one has good reason not to do so.

This principle, when conjoined with the points made above, has the consequence that, for Christians, the burden of proof is on those who hold that God is outside of time—on those who hold that God is timeless, eternal. Until the past century the Christian theological tradition has so massively affirmed the eternity of God that we tend to think otherwise; but the burden of proof lies on those who hold that the biblical representation of God, as One who has a history that can be narrated is not to be taken as the literal truth of the matter.

It's appropriate to ask whether the massiveness of that theological tradition has not shifted the burden of proof, so that now it lies on those who hold that God, though everlasting, is not eternal. No it has not shifted the burden of proof. What it has done is place on those of us who disagree with the theological tradition a weighty obligation. We are obligated to understand as deeply and sympathetically as we can the considerations offered by our predecessors in favor of God's eternity. The burden of proof remains on them, however. They are claiming that we should not accept as literally true this aspect of the biblical representation of God; for that we need cogent arguments. Otherwise what's left of the church's confession that Scripture, for it, is canonical?

We cannot dismiss in advance the possibility of such cogent arguments. Concerning some of Scripture's representations of God, all Christians believe that we do have good reason not to affirm those representations as literally true. On occasion Scripture represents God as having wings; no Christian affirms that representation as literally true. The representation *points* to something true, no doubt; but God is not among the winged things of reality.

Am I not being tendentiously selective? Granted that Scripture represents God as having a narratable history of acting and responding; are there not also scriptural passages that tell us that God is immutable and timeless? I think not—with one possible exception. Of course if there were such passages we would then be faced with the question whether or not to take *these* passages as literally true; it wouldn't just automatically follow from the presence of such passages that the all-pervasive biblical picture of God as having a history of acting and responding has to be interpreted as figurative. But I think that there are no such passages—with, as I say, one possible exception.

Let's begin with those that have traditionally been cited in support of God's timelessness—all together an exceedingly small number, I might add; and rather than making a complete survey, let's confine our attention to those that the people who cite these passages would regard as the weightiest. One is Psalm 90:

> Lord, you have been our dwelling place
>   in all generations.
> Before the mountains were brought forth,
>   or ever you had formed the earth and the world,
> from everlasting to everlasting you are God.
>
> You turn us back to dust,
>   and say, "Turn back, you mortals."
> For a thousand years in your sight
>   are like yesterday when it is past,
>   or like a watch in the night. (Ps 90:1-4)

One is amazed that this passage would ever have been cited in support of divine timelessness. What it says on the face of it is not that God is timeless but that God existed *before* creation, indeed from everlasting to everlasting. How could God exist *before* creation and yet be timeless? The writer adds that, as God sees things, a long time is in retrospect like a day, or like a night watch. Rather than supporting divine timelessness this seems, if anything, to do the opposite. When God looks back over a thousand years they seem, to God, to have lasted no longer than a day or a night: Evidently to God's experience there is a felt temporality.

We find a variant on this last point in the New Testament passage "With the Lord one day is like a thousand years, and a thousand years are like one day" (2 Pet 3:8). Given the use of temporal language to describe God's experience, it again amazes one that this passage should ever have been cited in support of eternity. What it says, on the face of it, is that with God experiential duration does not match up with clock time.

Lastly, consider Jesus' declaration in John 8:58, "Before Abraham was, I am." Jesus is here taking onto himself God's self-given name, "I AM"; but rather than affirming thereby that God is outside of time, he tacitly does the opposite. If I AM existed *before* Abraham, how could I AM be timeless?

The conclusion is inescapable: the scriptural passages traditionally cited as supporting divine timelessness provide no such support whatsoever.

Is God Ontologically Immutable?

The three passages traditionally cited in support of God's immutability have more going for them, on the face of it, than those traditionally cited in favor of God's timelessness. When one considers what the writers were likely to have been saying with their words, however, at least two of them prove quite obviously not to be affirming ontological immutability.

Begin with Malachi 3:6: "For I the LORD do not change." To discern what the writer would have been saying we do not, in this case, have to go outside the text of Malachi into the ambient culture; all we need do is consider the passage in context. The prophet has just been saying to his listeners that God is wearied by all their talk. Nonetheless God, after sending a messenger to prepare the way before him, will himself purify and refine his people, like a refiner and purifier of silver. When that has been accomplished, the offerings of Judah and Jerusalem will once again be pleasing to the Lord, as they were in the days of old. Then comes this wonderful assurance: "For I the LORD do not change; therefore you, O children of Jacob, have not perished. Ever since the days of your ancestors you have turned aside from my statutes and have not kept them. Return to me, and I will return to you" (vv. 6-7). Surely the prophet is not here affirming God's ontological immutability but instead saying that God's fidelity to the covenant he has made with his people remains unalterable. The passage affirms covenantal fidelity, not ontological immutability.

Consider next the affirmation of the psalmist, addressed to God in Psalm 102:27, that "you are the same." Again, rather than taking this passage in isolation and then allowing it to stimulate our ontological imaginations, let's try to discern what the writer was saying. For this it will once again be sufficient to consider the context. Let's have before us some of the preceding verses, along with the one following:

> He has broken my strength in midcourse;
>   he has shortened my days.
> "O my God," I say, "do not take me away
>   at the midpoint of my life,
> you whose years endure
>   throughout all generations."

> Long ago you laid the foundation of the earth,
>   and the heavens are the work of your hands.
> They will perish, but you endure;
>   they will all wear out like a garment.
> You change them like clothing, and they pass away;
>   but you are the same, and your years have no end.
> The children of your servants shall live secure;
>   their offspring shall be established in your presence. (Ps 102:23-28)

The writer is indeed making an ontological—or perhaps better, a cosmological—point; but that point is not ontological immutability. Whereas God's creation is transitory, God abides. For God, unlike the creature, does not wear out; God's years are without end. What the writer says is not that God is ontologically immutable but that God is everlasting; God endures. God has years, indeed, but to those years there is no end.

The passage most plausibly cited in support of God's ontological immutability is no doubt James 1:17, in which it is said that with God "there is no variation or shadow due to change." Let's have before us the preceding verse along with the verse following:

> Do not be deceived, my beloved. Every generous act of giving, with every perfect gift, is from above, coming down from the Father of lights, with whom there is no variation or shadow due to change. In fulfillment of his own purpose he gave us birth by the word of truth, so that we would become a kind of first fruits of his creatures. (Jas 1:16-18)

In place of "no variation or shadow due to change" some ancient manuscripts say, "no variation due to a shadow of turning." Probably that doesn't make any difference. The writer appears to be working with the image of a beam of light shining on a rotating object, different parts of the object falling into shadow as the object rotates. God, he says, is not like such an object; God is like the light. The writer has just told his readers that when they are tempted to do evil, they must not ascribe that temptation to God; "God cannot be tempted by evil and he himself tempts no one" (Jas 1:13). God is the source only of what is good—God is the sole source of good. In that respect God is like a source of light in which there is "no variation or shadow due to change."

Is the writer of James here affirming God's ontological immutability? I think the most we can say is that though it's possible he's doing that, it's not likely. It's likely that what he's saying is that God is unchangeable in that God is never the source of evil, only and always of good—which falls far short of affirming ontological immutability. Yet the context does not entitle one to dismiss entirely the possibility that the writer was alluding to God's ontological immutability. That would go beyond what his argument required, yet he might nonetheless have been alluding to it as grounding his argument. But if these considerations are correct—though it's not likely that the writer was alluding to ontological immutability, the possibility that he was doing so cannot be decisively dismissed—then obviously this passage cannot be used as a proof text for ontological immutability.

I conclude that the situation for God's ontological immutability is like that for God's timelessness: there are no passages in Scripture which can be cited as supporting the doctrine.

On the Nature of Time

Whether or not we should take Scripture as literally true in its representation of God as having a narratable history depends, I said, on whether we have good reasons for not so taking it; the burden of proof, for Christians, lies on those who think it should not be so taken. We will want to take note of the reasons that have been offered. But I propose spending the bulk of my time developing some arguments of my own in support of the view that God does have a history, and that God accordingly is not timeless—everlasting, and necessarily so, but not eternal. If these arguments are cogent, the effect will be that we will know in advance that the burden of proof will be impossible to bear—or to speak more modestly, that it will be extremely difficult to bear.

My strategy will be first to offer some reflections on the nature of time, then to move on to consider what it would be for something to be outside of time; and then finally to use the results of these inquiries to show why God cannot be outside of time.

It will be asked where I propose to get the knowledge of God to which I'll be appealing at that last point of the argument. My answer is: I'll be getting it from Scripture; I'll be appealing to what we learn about God from Scripture. I make no pretense of constructing a piece of natural theology.

But then what's the point? We have already learned that Scripture represents God as having a history, from which it is to be concluded that God is not timeless. Why plunge into philosophical reflections on time to establish that God is not timeless when the understanding of God that will be employed in the argument is the understanding presented to us in Scripture? The only thing relevant is a scrutiny of the arguments of those who claim to be able to bear the burden of proof against taking as literally true Scripture's representation of God as having a history.

Let me say again that the reflections on time that follow will not be used to construct an argument independent of Scripture for the conclusion that God is everlasting but not eternal. Their relevance is rather that we will emerge with a deeper understanding of the implications of the biblical representation of God as having a history. Or to put it the other way round: We will emerge with a deeper understanding of how much of the biblical representation of God has to be given up if one holds that God is timeless. The discussion will be a specimen of the Anselmian project of faith seeking understanding: the believer seeking to understand something of the "why" of what already he or she believes.

Early in the twentieth century the English philosopher J. M. E. McTaggart made an important advance in our understanding of time by explicitly distinguishing two different ways in which events are ordered within time.[1] Everybody—nonphilosophers and philosophers alike—operated with these two systems of ordering before McTaggart came along; however, it is generally agreed that to McTaggart belongs the honor of first having explicitly and emphatically distinguished them.

All events are ordered in terms of some happening now, some having happened in the more or less distant past, and some going to happen in the more or less distant future; likewise all pairs of events are ordered in terms of either member of the pair's preceding the other or being simultaneous with it. McTaggart called these two orderings the *A-series* and the *B-series,* respectively. Of course there are overlaps in both series: a given event may be partly over, partly happening right now and partly still to come; and one event may partly precede another and partly be simultaneous with it. Such overlaps won't make any difference to the truth of what I want to say in the following; accordingly, I'll make things

[1]J. M. E. McTaggart, *The Nature of Existence,* vol. 2 (Cambridge: Cambridge University Press, 1927).

easier for ourselves by talking as if there were none. Taking explicit account of the overlaps would require needless complications in formulation.

McTaggart himself believed that time was not real; the A-series and the B-series alike are nothing more than features of the merely apparent temporality of reality. Few have followed McTaggart on this point; on this occasion I'll have to forgo scrutinizing his argument and showing why I too do not regard it as cogent. The discussion in recent years has focused instead on whether the A-series is an objective feature of time. No one disputes that the ordering of events in the B-series is objectively real; the issue under discussion is whether the distinction between past, present and future marks a difference in ontological status of events.

What would be the alternative? Well, consider the spatial concepts of *here* and *there.* Nobody supposes that these mark a distinction in objective space; nobody supposes that some areas of space have hereness and the others have thereness. The fact that for each of us, at any time, some areas of space are *here* and the others are *there* is merely a consequence of the fact that each of us has a location in space, by virtue of having bodies. Here is simply where I am. For bodiless angels there's no here and no there.

Perhaps past, present, and future are like that. Just as each of us has a location in space, by virtue of each having a body and those bodies having a location, so also each of our actions and responses has a location in time—that is, in the B-series. Perhaps the present is simply the location in time of my act of writing down these words, and of whatever else is simultaneous with that. The past would then be whatever precedes that, and the future whatever succeeds it. It's only because there are selves having bodies with spatial locations that the concepts of *here* and *there* have applicability; perhaps it's only because there are agents whose actions and reactions have locations in the B-series that the concepts *of past, present, and future* have applicability.

The thesis that the A-series is not objectively real has come to be called the *tenseless* theory of time; the view that it is objectively real is called the *tense* theory. I am an adherent to the tense theory. Let me give some of my reasons.

To get going, let's have before us the outlines of the two very different pictures of time which the theorists of these two views embrace.

Start with the tense theory. The account sometimes given of the tense theory—usually by those who do not hold it is that the past, the present and the future are properties that events possess for a while and then lack. Every event that appears in the B-series is such that for a certain stretch of time in that series it has the property of being future while lacking those of being present and of being past; then at a certain time in the B-series it loses the property of being future and gains that of being present while continuing to lack the property of being past; then it loses that property and ever after has the property of being past while lacking that of being present or being future.

What's wrong with this picture, as the tense theorist sees things, is that it treats past, present and future as properties of events and regards the three properties as equal in status. In fact the present is basic, in the following way. What's fundamental in time is the *occurrence* of events—this for the most part having nothing to do with your and my temporal relationship to those events. When an event occurs, that's when it's present; being present at *t* and occurring at *t* come to the same thing. It's only because an event occurs—and it can't occur without occurring at some time—that it has a location anywhere in the B-series. If it's now past, that's because its occurring is now sometime in the past. There's no other way for it to get into the past than that way. Its occurring is now over. What remains now is the *fact that it did occur*. But the *fact that it did occur* is very different from *its occurring*. The distinction between present, past and future marks a difference in the ontological status of events; and of these, the status of the present is basic.

Does an event that occurred still exist when it *is* past? That depends on what one means by the question. If one means, Does that event continue to occur? the answer is of course no; its occurring is over. If one means, Can that event be a component of various facts—preeminently of the fact that it is past—and can we refer to it? the answer is yes. If one chooses to use *exist* so that a sufficient condition of something's now existing is that it is now a component of facts and can be referred to, then past events exist.

What about the future? Are future events likewise components of facts, and can we refer to them? Tense theorists divide on this point. My own view, which I won't here defend since it won't make any difference in what follows, is that only when an event is occurring or has occurred can it be a component of facts and can it be referred to. There are lots of general facts about the future, but no facts having particular events as constituents.

Now for the picture with which the tenseless theorist operates. Things and events are spread throughout B-series time as they are throughout space, and no event in the series differs from another in ontological status, nor does any event ever change its ontological status. Those whose date is 2099 have exactly the same status as those whose date is 1899 and as those whose date is 1999 (this last being when this present essay is being written); and of no event is it the case that at a certain time it has the ontological status of occurring and then at a later time the different ontological status of having occurred—after having been nowhere present in the B-series before it occurred.

Past, present and future enter the picture when agents who do things at times (in the B-series) enter the picture. We all use two distinct ways of specifying the positions of events in the B-series. One consists of picking out some event and then specifying the temporal position of everything else by reference to that event: *the letter arrived a week after he mailed it*. In addition to ad hoc employments of this strategy, we now have a universal system, consisting in part of taking the birth of Christ as the universal reference point and locating all other events by reference to that one; as in, for example, *the stock market crashed in A.D. 1929*. The other is the indexical strategy. We specify the location of events in terms of their relation to the location of what's now; for example, *the stock market crashed seventy years ago*. The distinction between past, present and future has no ontological significance. When I say, "The kettle is whistling now," I am making no claim concerning the ontological status of the kettle's whistling; I am simply relating the kettle's whistling to my act of *saying* that it's whistling. What I say is true if the kettle's whistling is simultaneous with my act of saying that it's whistling—if it occurs at the same date. Correspondingly, its whistling is in the past if it precedes my act of saying, and it's in the future if it follows my act of saying.

Now some of my reasons for holding that the tenseless theory is untenable. Most of the discussion of these matters over the past fifty years or so has been conducted in terms of language, propositions, speech acts, truth and meaning. Early on it was the contention of the tenseless theorists that any proposition asserted by assertively uttering a tensed sentence on some date could equally well be asserted with a tenseless sentence in which one specified that date. For example, the proposition I assert by assertively uttering in 1999 the tensed sentence "The stock market crashed seventy years ago" could equally well have been asserted by uttering the dated tenseless sentence "The stock market crashes seventy years before 1999."

Suppose this claim were true; it's not obvious what ontological conclusion should be drawn. The proposition asserted can be expressed with either a tensed date-free sentence or a tenseless dated sentence; how do we get from that to the conclusion of the tenseless theorist that the only *facts* are *tenseless* facts—B-series facts? Be that as it may, however, I argued in an earlier essay on these matters that the claim is mistaken.[2] The proposition asserted in the one case is not identical with that asserted in the other; they have different entailments. What I say in assertively uttering "The stock market crashed seventy years ago" entails nothing at all about the date of the crash; what I say in assertively uttering "The stock market crashes in 1929" entails nothing at all about how long ago that was.

The tenseless theorist D. H. Mellor in effect concedes this point[3]—*in effect,* since he conducts his discussion in terms of the meaning of sentences rather than the identity of propositions: he concedes that a date-free tensed sentence does not mean the same as any dated tense-free sentence. To this he adds the important point that tensed sentences are indispensable in human affairs. Having conceded that no dated tense-free sentence is identical in meaning with a date-free tensed sentence, some tenseless theorist might think to handle the problem in procrustean fashion by proposing abolishing sentences of the latter sort; since they cannot be "reduced" to tenseless sentences, get rid of them. We cannot, Mellor argues; for we cannot do without that indexical system of temporal reference. The alternative nonindexical system is not sufficient.

This leads Mellor to propose, in place of the claim by earlier tenseless theorists about identity of meaning of sentences, a claim about *truth*

---

[2]Nicholas Wolterstorff, "God Everlasting," in *God and the Good: Essays in Honor of Henry Stob,* ed. Clifton Orlebeke and Lewis B. Smedes (Grand Rapids, Mich.: Eerdmans, 1975).
[3]D. H. Mellor, *Real Time* (Cambridge: Cambridge University Press, 1981).

conditions for tensed sentences. To understand his claim, we must have in hand the distinction between a sentence, on the one hand, and utterances and inscriptions of that sentence, on the other. Mellor marks the distinction with the now-familiar terminology first introduced by C. S. Peirce, "type" and "token." The sentence as such is a *type;* utterances and inscriptions of the type are *tokens.* The account of the truth conditions for tense which Mellor offers is a thesis concerning the truth conditions of *tokens* of tensed sentences. More specifically, since the statement of conditions mentions the token, it is a *token-reflexive* account. More specifically yet, it is, as one would expect, a *tenseless token-reflexive* account. For tokens of present-tense sentences, the account goes as follows:

> Any token T of "E is occurring now" is true if and only if E occurs simultaneously with T.

The thought is this: from the set of all sentence-tokens that ever exist and which are of the form, "E is occurring now" (where E stands in for a designation of some event), pick any one you wish; that token will be true just in case the event designated occurs simultaneously with—at the same time in the B-series as—the token. ("Occurs" is to be understood as *tenseless.)* The reader can easily figure out for herself the corresponding truth conditions for tokens of past tense and of future tense sentences.

The criterion offered seems to me definitely correct; let's not spend time worrying the matter. The question to consider is what significance that has. There is an a priori reason for expecting that it won't have much. Sentences of vastly distinct meaning, and propositions of vastly distinct content, often have the same truth conditions. Take the proposition *It's an animal if a cat,* and the proposition *2+3=5;* their truth conditions are exactly the same: they're both true in all possible worlds. Hence the sentence "It's an animal if a cat" is true if and only if *2+3=5.*

But let's go beyond a priori considerations to look at the case before us. Notice, in the first place, that the criterion for the truth of the token entails the existence of the token; the token T cannot occur simultaneously with the event E unless T exists. That the criterion should have this entailment seems correct. Mellor takes sentence-tokens to be the bearers of truth and falsehood; and a condition of some bearer of truth and falsehood's being true is that the bearer exist. In this regard, the criterion proposed by Mellor is a definite improvement over one proposed at around the same time by J. J. C. Smart.[4] Smart's account has come to be called the "tenseless date theory" (compared to Mellor's "tenseless token-reflexive theory"). For present-tense tokens, Smart's account goes like this:

> Any token *T* of "*E* is occurring now," uttered or inscribed at time *t*, is true if and only if *E* occurs at *t*.

Smart's criterion is not sufficient for the truth of the token; what's needed is not just that the event referred to occur at the time the token was uttered or inscribed, but that there *be* that token at that time.

Back then to Mellor's proposal. Notice that the very thing that makes it satisfactory as a necessary and sufficient condition for the truth of a tensed sentence-token—that it entails the existence of the token—makes it unsatisfactory as a specification of the *meaning* of the sentence, and unsatisfactory as a specification of the content of the proposition asserted by the assertive utterance of the sentence. When I assertively utter a sentence of the form "*E* is occurring now," I am making no claim whatsoever about my act of assertively uttering the sentence, nor about the sentence-token I have thereby produced. Suppose I assertively utter, "The twentieth century is about to end." In doing so I make no claim whatsoever about my act of utterance nor about the token produced. The truth of *what I say* is independent of the existence of my act of utterance and of the token I produce—this in spite of the fact *a condition of that token's being true* is that there be that token. But surely what we require from the tenseless theorist is some account of *what we're saying* when we use the language of tense—a *tenseless* account! Truth conditions do not give us that account.

There's an additional difficulty that is more indicative of what is wrong with the tenseless theory. The situation considered thus far involves picking out some token of a tensed sentence and determining whether its truth condition is satisfied. Consider rather the circumstance of deciding to do something when some time or event comes around.

---

[4]J. J. C. Smart, "Time and Becoming," in *Time and Cause: Essays Presented to Richard Taylor*, ed. Peter van Inwagen (Dordrecht, Netherlands: D. Reidel, 1980), pp. 3-15.

One of Mellor's examples will do nicely: deciding to turn on the radio to hear the one o'clock news. To enact this decision I must turn on the radio when I believe that it is *now* one o'clock. How do I determine that, on the tenseless account? Well, says the tenseless theorist, see to it that your act of turning it on is simultaneous with the event of its becoming one o'clock. Well, Yes. But twice a day every day it becomes one o'clock; with which of that multitude of events am I to make my act of turning on the radio simultaneous? And come to think of it, there are also many acts of my turning on this radio, spread out across time. If I somehow come to know which of all those events of its becoming one o'clock is of concern to me, then I still have to know which of all my acts of turning on this radio I am to make simultaneous with that event of its becoming one o'clock.

Of course the answer is that it's this *present* event of its becoming one o'clock that is of concern to me, and this *present* act of my turning on the radio. To operate the indexical system of temporal reference I have to be able to determine which date is now—or which events are happening now. All the references that the system enables are ultimately related to that. The tenseless theorist, for whom all dates and events have exactly the same ontological status, has no way of accounting for how we make that determination. If all events of its becoming one o'clock, and all acts of my turning on this radio, have exactly the same ontological status, how do I get started in implementing my decision that my *present* act of turning on this radio shall coincide with this *present* event of its becoming one o'clock (alternatively: with this present event of the beginning of the one o'clock news)?

Mellor rightly recognizes that the acceptability of his tenseless token-reflexive account of the truth conditions for tensed sentence-tokens does not, by itself, imply that the A-series is not an objective dimension of time; accordingly, after articulating his account of truth conditions he goes on to offer an argument for the nonobjectivity of tense by adapting McTaggart's argument for the nonreality of time in general. The argument seems to me fallacious. I judge that on this occasion I can forgo showing that, however, since we already have good reason for concluding that the basic thesis of the tenseless theorist, that tense supervenes on our operation of the indexical system for specifying temporal location, cannot be sustained. Rather than tense supervening on our operation of the system, we cannot operate the system without being able to pick out those events and dates that have the unique ontological status of occurring *now*. Knowing which events occur simultaneously with which falls short of knowing which ones *are occurring now*.

Outside of Time?

What would it be for something to be outside of time—timeless, eternal? Best to begin with what it is for something to be within time. Events are obviously within time. They are that by virtue of occurring within a period (or moment) of time, hence of beginning at a time and of ending at a time; if they endure, they are also within time by virtue of being half over at a certain time, a quarter over, and so forth. And if there are changes within the event, then the event is also within time by virtue of the lapse of time between the two termini of the change.

The situation for things other than events—substances, such as human beings, animals and plants; properties, such as being quizzical and being smart; numbers; and so on—is different. Such entities, though many of them have spatial parts, do not have temporal parts. Only a small part of that rather long event that is Bill Clinton's occupancy of the office of U.S. president is occurring today; by contrast, our fourteen-year-old cat is all here right now; he's not mostly over, not more than half gone.

In many cases the significance of this difference between events and nonevents is considerably diminished by virtue of the fact that for many nonevents there is the *history* or *biography* of that entity; and the history or biography of an entity is a complex event. Our cat has a history. That history began at a certain time; so too it will end at a certain time; and since fourteen is already rather old for a cat, his history is by now well more than half over. Furthermore, over the years there have been a lot of new developments in that history. In short, a story could be told about our cat; a narrative of its history could be composed.

But there's no story to be told about numbers, no narrative to be composed. That's because numbers have no history. They neither come into existence nor go out; nor do they change. For some numbers it happens that they are discovered at a certain time; but the event of a number's discovery is an item in the history of its discoverer, not in the history of the number. Its discovery makes no difference to the number; it represents no change in it.

When it comes to nonevents I propose that we take whether or not something has a history as the determinant of whether or not it is in time. What brings it about that you and I are in time? The fact that we each have a history; about each of us there's a story that can be told, a narrative that can be composed. What brings it about that numbers are not in time—that they are timeless? The fact that none has a history.[5]

Does God Have a History?
So our main question is this: Does God have a history? Is there a story to be told about God, a narrative to be composed? There's nothing to be narrated about God's coming into or going out of existence, since, as we all agree, God doesn't come into or go out of existence, necessarily so. The question comes down to whether there's a history of God's actions and responses, and of the knowledge that lies behind those. Is there a story to be told about God's actions, about God's responses to what transpires in God's creation, and about the flow of God's knowledge which lies behind those?

Scripture offers us such a narrative. I took note of a small bit of it at the beginning of our discussion: after hearing the Hebrews' cry of suffering, God addressed Moses out of an unburnt flaming bush and, upon being asked for his name, told Moses that he was to be called I AM.

Those who hold that God is timeless agree, of course, that Scripture offers us this narrative. They deny, nevertheless, that God has a history. Not only does God not come into or go out of existence, there are also

---

[5]One might hold that something is (or was or will be) in time if it's ever true to say of it that it now exists. Then the theist will perforce be committed to the view that God is in time. For the theist holds that God exists. And by *exists* I don't see that one ever has any option but to mean "presently exists," or "did and does and will exist," or "does or did or will exist." In general, our verbs have no truly tenseless sense. The so-called tenseless sense is really the disjunctive sense: *does* or *did* or *will*.

My reason for not using the criterion cited just above for determining whether God is in time has to do with the central reason that the tradition offered for holding that God is timeless. That reason was that God must be understood as changeless. It was God's ontological immutability that was of central concern. It appears to me that Anselm did interpret God's timelessness so rigorously that one cannot even say, "God presently exists." But I fail to see that he offers any other reason for concluding that God is timeless than that God does not in any way change; and surely it would be a mistake to conclude that numbers, for example, change just because we can say of some number that it presently exists, and did and will exist.

no changes in God: no alterations in action, response or knowledge. The biblical narrative is not to be interpreted as presenting items in God's history; it's to be interpreted as presenting items in human history. The analogue to numbers is helpful: what appears at first sight to be a history of numbers is in fact a history of human beings dealing with numbers.

Everybody in the orthodox Christian tradition would agree, however, that for the purposes at hand there are some absolutely decisive differences between God and numbers. For our purposes the most important differences to note are that whereas God acts, numbers do not; and whereas God has knowledge, numbers do not.

If one concedes that God acts, how can one nevertheless hold that God has no history, and that the narrative of God's actions presented to us in Scripture cannot be interpreted as a narrative of God's history? The classic solution to this puzzle was articulated by Thomas Aquinas in the following passage:

> Nor, if the action of the first agent is eternal, does it follow that His effect is eternal. . . . God acts voluntarily in the production of things. . . . God's act of understanding and willing is, necessarily, His act of making. Now, an effect follows from the intellect and the will according to the determination of the intellect and the command of the will. Moreover, just as the intellect determines every other condition of the thing made, so does it prescribe the time of its making; for art determines not only that this thing is to be such and such, but that it is to be at this particular time, even as a physician determines that a dose of medicine is to be drunk at such and such a particular time, so that, if his act of will were of itself sufficient to produce the effect, the effect would follow anew from his previous decision, without any new action on his part. Nothing, therefore, prevents our saying that God's action existed from all eternity, whereas its effect was not present from eternity, but existed at that time when, from all eternity, He ordained it.[6]

The core of the point Aquinas is making is that one must distinguish between (a) the time at which one enacts one's decision to do what's necessary to make something happen and (b) the time at which, so one has decided, it shall happen. I think there are better analogies to illus-

---

[6]Thomas Aquinas *Summa Contra Gentiles* 2.35; cf. 2.36a.

trate the point than the one Aquinas offers. Most of us will remember those toys from childhood in which one releases a marble at the top of the toy and the marble then descends through a series of loops, springs, trapdoors and the like, until thirty seconds or so later it emerges at the bottom. Perhaps I am especially fond of that sequence in which the marble opens the trapdoor, falls through it, hits the spring and is tossed up into the air. In order that that may happen, I, at a certain moment, release the marble at the top; no more decisions are necessary on my part. Nonetheless, it's not until fifteen seconds after I released the marble that it opens the trapdoor, and not until three seconds later is it tossed up into the air. Perhaps I also decide that it shall be tossed up into the air at the very moment that the clock in the hall begins to strike noon. Then I release the marble precisely eighteen seconds before the time at which, so I calculate, the clock will begin to strike. And that's all I do; in particular, I don't do anything in addition at noon.

It's along these lines, so Aquinas suggests, that we should think of God's action. From the fact that God decided to bring about a sequence of two events it doesn't follow that God first enacted the decision to bring about the earlier event and then enacted the decision to bring about the later. For any pair of events that God decided to bring about, no matter how separated in time those events may be, God's enactment of the decision to bring about one of them is simultaneous with his enactment of the decision to bring about the other. The temporal sequence is entirely in the events, not at all in God.

To which the only thing to be added is that there's no such thing as the time before God made the decision and no such thing as the time after God made the decision; were that the case, God would after all have a history. What separates the position of traditional orthodox Christianity theology from deism is the insistence, on the part of the former, that there's no time at which God is not yet enacting the decision, nor any at which God is no longer enacting it. The deist holds that God made the decision *and ever since then* has watched it play out.

An implication of the traditional orthodox position is that none of God's actions is a response to what we human beings do; indeed, not only is none of God's *actions* a response to what we do, but nothing at all in God's life is a response to what occurs among God's creatures.

Why is that? The traditional theologians had a number of reasons for holding that there is nothing in God that is a response, chief among them their conviction that responsiveness on God's part would compromise God's aseity, God's unconditionedness. For our purposes there's another reason that's more relevant, however. Responsiveness would require tensed knowledge on God's part; and were God to have tensed knowledge of what happens in human affairs, God would perforce have a history.

One responds to something upon knowing that it is happening, or has happened or is about to happen. I hold my excitement over its turning a new millennium until I see that it *is* turning a new millennium; I'm saddened by my mother's death upon learning that it *has* happened. If all I know about the time of my mother's death is tenseless facts—B-series facts—then I don't grieve, because I don't know whether her death has yet happened. Likewise if all I know about the event of its turning a new millennium is tenseless facts, then I don't cheer, because again I don't know whether the event has yet happened. Earlier we saw that enacting the decision to act when it becomes a certain time, or when a certain event happens, requires knowledge (or belief) of tensed facts. In their relationship to time, there's a deep similarity between response and such action.

But if God has no history, then God lacks tensed knowledge. For one can know that something is presently happening only when it is; the knowledge that some event is occurring can occur only when that event itself is occurring. The endurance of the knowledge exactly tracks the endurance of the event. So if God has knowledge of present-tensed facts, then there's change in God's knowledge—as indeed there is if God has knowledge of past-tensed facts and future-tensed facts. Since those facts come and go, God's knowledge of them comes and goes. That's why, if God has knowledge of tensed facts, God has a history; there's a story to be told about God's knowledge.

Let me place in center stage the implication just noticed of the claim that God has no history and is accordingly out of time, timeless, eternal: Were God eternal, God's knowledge would be extremely constricted in scope. Of no tensed fact would God have any knowledge; God would not have knowledge of any A-series facts, only of B-series facts. As a consequence, God could neither respond to what transpires in the world nor enact the decision to act at a certain time. If God were eternal, God's action would have to be entirely noninterventionist.

Contrast this with how Scripture represents God. When Moses asks to be given God's name, God knows that Moses is doing so—knows not just the tenseless fact that Moses at some time or other asks for the name, but the tensed fact that Moses is *presently* asking for the name. Hence it is that God can now respond, and does now respond, by now giving the name; God intervenes. If all God knew was the tenseless fact that Moses at some time or other asks for the name, then God wouldn't know when to offer the name.

In place of this biblical representation of God as responding and intervening, those who hold that God is eternal think of God as considering in advance all the possibilities and acting accordingly—all of this being timeless. A variation on the child's toy I asked us to imagine earlier may be helpful. Suppose there are various paths that the marble can take, depending on where exactly I release it. The possibility of monitoring the progress of the marble and then, depending on what I think about it, intervening at certain points—opening or not opening a trapdoor at a certain bend—is not open to me. So what do I do in forming my decision as to where to release the marble? Let's add—this is important—that neither I nor anyone else has ever yet released a marble in this apparatus, or any like it. Well, what I do is figure out which path the marble *would* follow for each position of release, and then evaluate those paths. That is, I figure out the relevant counterfactuals, and I make my appraisals. If I released the marble here it would follow path A; and though that has a stretch that would be glorious, it also has a stretch that would be pretty dull. If on the other hand I released the marble there, it would follow path B; and though on B there would be nothing so glorious as that stretch in path A, there would also be nothing as dull. In the light of my discovery of these counterfactuals and my appraisal, I make my decision. I make my decision in the light of the various possibilities and their relative excellences; I don't mindlessly plunge ahead. So there's something like responsiveness in my process of decision: responsiveness to the possibilities. But having chosen one of the options, I don't respond to the actual progress of the marble, and I don't intervene.

Something like that is how the defender of divine eternity thinks of God's action—with the following important addition: If you and I are free agents, then God must also know what you and I would freely do. The toy through which the marble descends is entirely mechanical—no free action there. But human beings are central to God's decisions; and if we are capable of free action, then there must be facts of the matter as to what we would do in various situations, and God must know those facts. There must be "counterfactuals of freedom." For suppose we were capable of free action, but there were no facts as to what we would freely do in all the various situations in which we would find ourselves. Then God would simply have to take a risk. Hence it is that those who hold to God's eternity either deny human freedom or embrace the thesis that there are counterfactuals of freedom.

Time but No Space?
Rather often it is objected to those who hold that God's actions have temporal locations that, given the similarities between time and space, they must also hold that God has a spatial location; if one holds that God has a history, then consistency requires that God has a location. I hold that God does not have a spatial location; so what do I say in answer to the charge of inconsistency?

In advance the charge would seem to have very little going for it. An agent has a spatial location on account of having a body; the location of the agent's body being the location of the agent. When the agent speaks of something as *here,* "here" refers to the region of space in which his or her body happens to be located at that time. By contrast, if there's some variation in the acts that an agent performs, then the agent has a history; then it is "in" time. But if one doesn't hold that agents are necessarily embodied, then why shouldn't it be the case that certain agents—God, angels, and so forth—have a history without occupying a place?

In his book *Eternal God,*[7] Paul Helm offers a more specific version of the objection. He insists that to my argument, in "God Everlasting," that if God were timelessly eternal there would be temporal matters that God could never know, a precisely parallel argument can be constructed for the conclusion that if God has no spatial location, then there would be spatial matters that God could never know. God must have spatial location if God's actions have temporal location; if one wishes to hold that

---

[7]Paul Helm, *Eternal God* (Oxford: Clarendon, 1988), pp. 42-46.

God lacks spatial location, then one must also hold that God is timeless.

Now if one combined the claim that there would be temporal matters God could never know if God were timelessly eternal, with the claim that the A-series is not a feature of objective time, only the B-series, then it's likely that an argument along these lines would work. But of course that's not what I have done. I have argued that the A-series is a feature of objective time; the temporal matters that God could never know if God were eternal are all the *tensed facts*. To the A-series there is no counterpart in space. Correspondingly, I have argued that in speaking of some event as happening *now*, I am not just making a claim about the event's relation to my act of speaking—namely, that the two are simultaneous; I am saying that the event has the ontological status of *presently happening*. By contrast, when I say that something is here, I am doing no more than making a claim concerning its relation to where my body is (presently).

I have a body, God does not; does that imply that there are some facts I can know that God cannot? I know that the kettle is now boiling here; do I thereby know some fact that God cannot know? Definitely not. God knows that the kettle is boiling, and knows where I am, thereby knowing what region of space is here for me. There's nothing more God has to know than that the kettle is boiling here.

Divine Action

As we have seen, God's action, on the view of the eternalist, consists of timelessly bringing about events, the events brought about often having a location in time. God's speaking to Moses consists of timelessly bringing about the event consisting of those sounds emerging at that precise time from the unburned flaming bush.

The most important question for the Christian to consider, in reflecting on this understanding of divine action, is whether it is compatible with an orthodox understanding of what happens in the incarnation. So far as I can see, it is not; whatever we may think in general about Aquinas's strategy, at this point it fails. The actions of Jesus were not simply human actions brought about by God, plus human actions freely performed by Jesus in situations brought about by God; they were God's actions. In the life and deeds of Jesus it was God who dwelt among us. The narrative of the history of Jesus is not just a narrative concerning events in the history of the relationship of a human being to God; it's a narrative about God. God does have a history; the doctrine of the incarnation implies that the history of Jesus is the history of God.

Does God Change?

In the preceding discussion we have seen that holding that God has no history, and is on that account timeless, requires not only that one depart a long way from Scripture's narrative representation of God but that one depart, at various points, from the orthodox theological tradition as well. Accordingly, we will need powerful reasons for holding that God is timeless. In principle there might be such reasons. As I remarked earlier, we all do at certain points depart from Scripture's representation of God. My example was Scripture's occasional representation of God as having wings: none of us believes that God literally has wings; we all take Scripture's language on this point to be metaphorical. So we ought to be open to considering reasons for concluding that Scripture's narrative concerning God is not to be interpreted as a narrative of the history of God but only as a narrative of the history of human beings.

It will have been evident from remarks I have made along the way that I do not judge the reasons that the tradition has offered in favor of divine timelessness to be adequate to the task at hand; those who hold that God has no history have not succeeded in bearing the burden of proof. On this occasion I will not be able to show that; doing so would require another essay of at least the length of this present one. I will have to content myself with displaying where the issues lie and then leaving it there for the present.

It is not infrequently said, by those who oppose the doctrine of God's timelessness, that in embracing this doctrine the church fathers were succumbing to the power of Greek philosophical thought and that later theologians, on account of the prestige of tradition, then followed in the footsteps of their predecessors. From this claim I insist on dissociating myself, and that for a number of reasons.[8]

For one thing, not everything the Greek philosophers said was false;

---

[8]I am here to some extent disagreeing with things I said on this matter in my "God Everlasting."

to observe that some Greek philosopher held that the divine is timeless leaves open the question whether he was right about that. More important, the objection distorts what happened in the formation of Christian theology; it represents it as having simply been a matter of resisting or succumbing to cultural power.

No doubt all of us are subject to some degree to the formative power of our ambient culture. What impresses one about the church fathers, however, is how weak had become the cultural power of Greek philosophical thought over their thinking. Rather than simply giving voice to a supposed indoctrination into Greek philosophical thought, they had arguments for their theological convictions concerning God. Some of those arguments were no doubt first formulated by one or another Greek philosopher. But it's obvious to anybody who looks that the church fathers were already sufficiently removed from the cultural power of Greek philosophical thought to be eminently capable of sifting through that part of their inheritance, agreeing with what they judged themselves to have good reason to accept and rejecting the rest.

It is to their arguments, then, that we must attend; we cannot content ourselves with announcing that their loyalty to Scripture was subverted by the cultural power over them of Greek philosophical thought. Naturally some premises in their arguments which seemed plausible to them may not seem at all plausible to us; when we probe what accounts for that, we may sometimes conclude that they were at this point reflecting the mentality of the society in which they were reared. Nonetheless, since they gave reasons, it is to those reasons that we must attend; there's no shortcut around that.

I have suggested that the fundamental issue at stake, in the discussion concerning the relation of God to time, is whether God has a history; the defenders of eternalism hold that God has no history, those like myself who instead defend God's everlastingness hold that God does. And I argued that whether or not God has a history depends, in turn, on whether there is in any way change in God. Change in God is what is really at issue. On this issue I am in full agreement with my fellow discussant in this volume.[9]

What reasons have the theologians and philosophers of the Christian

---

[9]Helm, *Eternal God*, p. 20.

tradition offered for their claim that God is ontologically immutable? So far as I can determine, the arguments come down to three: mutability is incompatible with God's simplicity, simplicity in turn being grounded in aseity; mutability is incompatible with God's supreme excellence; and to suppose that God changes would blur the distinction between Creator and creature. All three of these reasons are developed, and sometimes blended together, in what is perhaps the most rigorous and sustained defense of God's timelessness in the Christian theological tradition: chapters 17-25 of Anselm's *Monologium.*

Here's how the first line of reasoning goes. God is not in any way composite. "For everything that is composite requires for its subsistence the things of which it is compounded, and, indeed, owes to them the fact of its existence, because, whatever it is, it is through these things; and they are not what they are through it, and therefore it is not at all supreme" (Anselm *Monologium* 17). In fact, though, everything derives its existence from God (5). It follows that God is simple—that is, not in any way composite. But now suppose that God had a history. Then God would be one thing, at one time, and another, at another"; God would have "parts distributed according to times" (21). Given simplicity, that is impossible.

In the following passage this reason is hinted at, and blended with, the other two reasons: that whereas God is supremely excellent, mutable things lack a certain excellence, and that the lack of mutability in God is one of the fundamental differences between Creator and creature:

> What . . . has no place or time is doubtless by no means compelled to submit to the law of place or time. No law of place or time . . . in any way governs any nature which no place or time limits by some kind of restraint. But what rational consideration can by any course of reasoning fail to reach the conclusion, that the Substance which creates and is supreme among all beings, which must be alien to, and free from, the nature and law of all things which itself created from nothing, is limited by no restraint of space or time. . . . The supreme Substance . . . is encompassed by no restraint of place or time, is bound by none of their laws. (22)

Unlike the creature, no part of God's eternity has "vanished from the present, . . . which no longer is; nor does it pass with the present, which is for an instant" (22). God does not "exist in terms of this fleeting present, in terms of which we live, nor has [God] existed, nor will [God] exist, in terms of past or future, since these are restricted to things finite and mutable, which [God] is not" (22).

I think Anselm is right in his contention that if God has a history, then God is not unconditioned *in the way he understands God to be conditioned,* and right in his contention that God lacks something *that he regards as an excellence;* likewise he is right in his contention that if God has a history, then the distinction between Creator and creature is not *grounded in the way he thinks it is grounded.* So obviously the questions to consider are whether Anselm's understanding of God's aseity and excellence is compelling, and whether the person who holds that God has a history is inevitably left without an adequate way of marking the distinction between Creator and creature. I hold that the answer to both questions is no. But it would be a disservice to the issues at stake, and a dishonoring of Anselm, to discuss them quickly and superficially. What one says about God's relation to time involves a very great deal of the rest of one's theology.

RESPONSE TO
NICHOLAS WOLTERSTORFF

PAUL HELM

*N*ick's paper is characteristically clear and interesting. His chief claim is that God has a history. As part of this he denies that God is what he calls "ontologically immutable," immutable in his very being or nature, but rather immutable in his resolve. But is this sufficiently strong to ground, say, the modalities of Hebrews 6:13-16? Is it impossible for God to lie simply because he has resolved not to? Might not something come up to make him change his mind? After all, Scripture says that he does change his mind.

Nick offers a methodological principle to the effect that one will affirm as literally true Scripture's representation of God unless one has good reason not to. How would Nick approach the representation of God as being surprised? Perhaps he would say that the Scriptures teach that God is omniscient. But is God ontologically omniscient? Perhaps God, as it happens, knows a very great deal, but not so much that he is never surprised. It is easy to see how someone might, by applying Nick's principle, be inclined to be an ontological minimalist in respect of the divine nature.

At the heart of the theological differences between the Christian eternalist and temporalist is a different estimate of what constitutes such a good reason not to take some scriptural representations of God literally. Nick thinks we have such a good reason in the case of anthropomorphisms but not in respect of scriptural representations of God's relation to time. He returns to this point at the end of his paper, strengthening his principle somewhat. In recounting Anselm's appeal to God's aseity and excellence, he does not think that Anselm's understanding of these features of God is compelling, and so he rejects them. So the reason not to take the scriptural representations of God literally has not simply to be a good reason but to be compelling. I cannot say that I know what an argument would look like that would force one to reject Anselm's understanding of the divine excellence and to accept Nick's.

Moves and countermoves over the tenseless theory of time have been well rehearsed, and so I do not propose to make any general comment on what Nick says on this, except to say something on the ineliminabilty of tensed beliefs and on the relation between time and space. As part of his critique of Hugh Mellor, Nick holds that tensed facts are ineliminable, and then argues later on for the eliminability of what we might call spatially indexed statements, holding that there is no spatial counterpart of the A-series. I think he's mistaken in this, for the following reasons.

Suppose, with Nick, that I know everything that there is to know concerning the sequence of temporal events; then I'll know that (say) a certain temporal event is now. One of the temporal facts that I'll know is that I'm aware on November 24 that the date is November 24, and this is sufficient to know that November 24 is now. How do I know when to turn on the radio for the one o'clock news? When I know on November 24 that it's one o'clock on November 24. The rules governing the uses of "here" are parallel. Just as I use utterances of "now" to refer to times temporally present to my utterances, so I use "here" to refer to places spatially present to the place where I make my utterance. If, while in the Strand, I use the word *here* to refer to the Old Kent Road, then I misuse the word, just as I do when on November 19 I say "now" to refer to November 18. Just as time presents us with an A-series and a B-series, so does space, though most of us believe that unlike space, time is unidirectional; that is, that in any two correct uses of *now* the second use must be at a time later than the first use.

Nick denies that in order for God to know that the kettle is boiling here there's nothing more that God has to know than to know where I am, so knowing which regions of space are here for me. But the temporal situation is parallel. All that God needs to know in order to know that the kettle is boiling now is that the kettle is boiling on some date and for him to know that that date is now for me. God knows it's now for me because he knows (for instance) that that time is the time immediately after the last of those times that it is logically possible for me to have memories of. If 1:00 p.m. is the time immediately after those times that I can have memories of, then God knows that 1:00 p.m. is now for me, and if the kettle is boiling at 1:00 p.m. then he knows that the kettle is boiling now (for me).

So while a proponent of tensed facts such as Nick may use an appeal to the ineliminability of tensed beliefs to establish the existence of tensed facts, he will also, in consistency, have to allow for the ineliminability of spatial indexical beliefs and the existence of spatial indexical facts, a result that would, I think, be unwelcome to Nick.

In his comments on Aquinas on God speaking, Nick uses the analogy of the marble slide. Consider an alternative model; one that is truer, I believe, to the case. Suppose I record a series of questions for anyone telephoning my business, directing them to the department relevant to their needs. When the machine is in use, is it not me speaking? And if I make a hash of things, directing people to the wrong department, am I not the one to blame? The eternalist position is not deistic because of course on Aquinas's scheme (the general outlines of which an eternalist will endorse) God eternally upholds the entire cosmos and intervenes miraculously, and (the Christian eternalist will say) he intervenes in the incarnation. But he does not intervene by forming the will to do so in time.

I think Nick is more or less correct in delineating some of the consequences of God's not being in time and so not having a history. But I'll say a word or two about God's responding. While it is true that there is a kind of responsiveness that requires tensed knowledge, an eternal God could eternally decree a response to what he knows will happen at a given time. Timelessly knowing that Hezekiah will plead at t_1 for a longer life, God timelessly determines his response at t_2 to that plea. So that it is not accurate to say that if God were eternal then God's action would be entirely noninterventionist. And even if God knows only tenseless facts then he certainly does know when to respond—simultaneously with or shortly after the time of the fact in question, say. When, in time, Moses asks God for his name, God timelessly knows when (in the temporal series) that is, and timelessly responds. So there is something like responsiveness in that God responds to various possibilities by actualizing one of them; he responds by timelessly willing to act in time. And in any case, given a temporal God's complete foreknowledge of the future, his responsiveness to a human cry will occur under very different epistemic conditions than a human being's responsiveness, and the meaning of *response* in such a situation may for that reason be said to be like, but not precisely the same, as its meaning in cases of human responsiveness.

For the Christian eternalist the incarnation, is, of course, the paradigm divine response, thus understood. Nick says the actions of Jesus were God's actions; more exactly, they were the actions of the God-man. And the eternalist Christian will hold that what happened in the incarnation is that the eternal Son of God united with human nature in the person of Jesus in such a way as to preserve his deity unchanged, uniting so closely as to form one person. As all Christians, eternalist or not, will agree that in the incarnation the Son of God did not cease to have the property of immensity (say)—he did not become wholly localized in Palestine—so the eternalist claims that in the incarnation the Son of God did not cease to be timelessly eternal.

Finally, and incidentally, a comment on Nick's view of how we are to understand the future. He says that "only when an event is occurring or has occurred can it be a component of facts and can it be referred to." Nick does not defend this view in his paper, and so I won't query it here. But such a view does have an interesting consequence for someone who believes, as Nick does, that God is in time. It is this. If the future is general and so cannot be referred to, how can it be that in the counterfactuals of freedom, which Nick appears to endorse, there are facts of the matter known to God as to what we would do in various situations? Either the descriptions that form these counterfactuals stop short at some point within them at which the present becomes the future, or they do not. If they do, how can God clearly distinguish one counterfactual of freedom from another, since all such counterfactuals will have components of a wholly general character? If they do not, how can they be counterfactuals of freedom? Put differently, if God is in time and for him the future is not general, and we are in time but for us the future is general, is there not a sense in which our being in time differs significantly from God's being in time?

RESPONSE TO
NICHOLAS WOLTERSTORFF

ALAN G. PADGETT

I am in fundamental agreement with everything that Nicholas Wolterstorff has to say in his chapter. As a theologian and philosopher, I agree with his point about accepting the priority of Scripture in our understanding of God, and I agree with his reading of Scripture. The biblical God has a history, and this means that God is temporal. Like Nick, I have also considered and rejected D. H. Mellor's theory of truth-conditions for tensed sentences.[1] I suppose I could go on listing areas of agreement. But one is forced to highlight differences in replies like this one. So I now turn to those.

There is only one difference I find of any importance between Nick and myself with respect to divine eternity. Nick is quite happy with a God who is fully temporal, who in no sense is "outside" of time. I believe, however, that some weight should be given to the intuition that time is created and finite, not a part of the divine Being. This is why I

---

[1] Alan G. Padgett, *God, Eternity and the Nature of Time* (1992; reprint Wipf & Stock, 2000), pp. 100-110.

have developed a notion of divine eternity as "relative timelessness."

Time and history are not identical. Anything that has a history is temporal, true. But what Nick does not consider is that not everything that is temporal has a history. A much more precise definition of *timeless* was once given by Nelson Pike: something is timeless if it is not located at any time and has no extension in time.[2] A unique and almost instantaneous event would have a date but not a history. Nevertheless, it would be temporal just because it has a date. Our system of clocks, calendars, dates and days is just as important to our notion of time as are history and narrative.

The metric and dating system of our physical, measured time is an important part of temporality *as we know it.* While I agree with Nick that God has a history, I deny that God's time can be measured by our space-time. Instead space-time is created by God. This implies that God is beyond the space-time of our universe. So Nick is wrong to suggest that theologians are interested in a timeless God simply because they believe God cannot change in any way. Just as important, I believe, is the idea of *time as a created category of existence.* I am seeking here to honor the intuition, shared by many if not most traditional theologians over the centuries, that God must in some sense transcend time since he created time.

My view is that God is beyond space-time, beyond time as we know it. There are a number of important ways in which God's experience of time is quite unlike ours, which I detail in my chapter. This allows me to argue that God is the Lord of Time. Why is this important? Why should Christian theologians go beyond the clear witness of Scripture to affirm that God transcends time? I believe one argument comes from God's transcendence and immanence. My own view is that God is both transcendent relative to time and immanent within time. God both transcends history, providing the very possibility of historical existence; and is within history, especially but not only in the incarnation of the Word.

I have tried to develop a notion of "relative timelessness" which allows us to coherently affirm both that God transcends time and that he is in some ways temporal. Such a seeming paradox is much more in keeping with what Christian theology generally wants to say about the

---

[2]Nelson Pike, *God and Timelessness* (London: Routledge, 1970), p. 7.

Blessed Trinity. God is beyond our knowledge and yet revealed. God is beyond space yet enters into the virgin's womb. These kinds of affirmations are typical of Christian thought. On these grounds, then, I would insist that Nick has grasped only one-half of the truth about the infinite-personal Lord of Time.

Response to
Nicholas Wolterstorff

William Lane Craig

*S*ince I believe that God is (present tense) in time, I largely agree with everything Nick Wolterstorff has to say in his essay. I was heartily cheered as well by his endorsement of a dynamic or tensed theory of time and his advocacy of a metaphysic of presentism, the view that the only temporal entities that exist are those that presently exist. It is precisely this metaphysic that makes it so hard to maintain that God exists timelessly.

I do have some quibbles. For example, I think it naive to take Scripture's representation of God as literally true unless one has good reason not to. By "good reason not to" Nick apparently means, judged by his method, some teaching in Scripture to the opposite effect. For example, we should not think that God has wings, because Scripture elsewhere affirms the incorporeality and omnipresence of God. Finding no convincing proof texts of divine atemporality, Nick concludes that we should take the temporal descriptions of God literally. But this hermeneutic is insensitive to the genre(s) of Scripture. A piece of literature belonging to a genre that is not intended to convey the literal truth about some subject ought not to be taken literally in that respect even if in the piece of literature itself there are no indications of the correct picture. Aesop's fables should not be interpreted as teaching that animals can talk, even though there are no indications to the contrary in the fables themselves.

Now when it comes to Scripture, the literature contained therein is definitely not of the genre of philosophy of religion like Philo's *On the Creation of the Cosmos* or Aristotle's *Metaphysics,* though metaphysical truths are certainly found therein. Rather much of the Scripture, especially the Old Testament, is, very broadly speaking, in the genre of *narrative.* Israel told stories about the saving acts of God in calling and redeeming his people. These stories display the vividness and drama that are part and parcel of the storyteller's art. It is hard to exaggerate how thoroughly anthropomorphic they are in their portrayal of God, not just in the obvious ways in speaking of God's face and eyes and ears and arm but also in the subtle and doubtless unconscious ways in which they speak of God as hearing, seeing, turning, coming and so on. There is just no reason to invest such portrayals with metaphysical significance. These stories describe God from our perspective, as he is related to us. If the static theory of time were in fact correct and reality were a four-dimensional, tenselessly existing, space-time manifold that God transcends and in which he timelessly produces effects at times t_0, t_1, t_2, would Israel's storytellers have told their stories any differently?

Moreover, Nick ignores those portions of Scripture in which the authors do reflect theologically on the beginning of the world and its creation by God. How are we to understand those didactic portions of Scripture which imply a beginning of time and God's existence "before" it?[1]

Without wanting to lose the focus of our discussion, I wish also merely to register my considered view that, whether or not there are facts having future events as constituents, there is no good reason to deny and good reason to affirm that future-tense propositions are bivalent, that is, are either true or false, and must therefore come

---

[1]See my essay for several passages.

within the purview of divine omniscience.[2]

I should also like to say that I think that Nick misunderstands the passage he quotes from Aquinas's *Summa Contra Gentiles* as describing how a timeless God might produce serial effects in time without acting at those times. A careful reading of the text, which is often misunderstood, will show that Aquinas is speaking here of a sempiternal deity who exists from eternity past. His more studied view is that the entire temporal series is present or real to God (as Paul Helm holds), and therefore every member of that series is available to be causally dependent on him. Thus the analogy of the marble rolling down the chute is completely misleading; a more apt analogy would be two-dimensional flatlanders' presence to a person in an embedding three-dimensional space. (Of course this analogy treats time like a spatial dimension, as the static theory of time must.)

But the above are mere quibbles. The really important shortcoming in Nick's essay lies not what he says but in what he leaves out: the implications of the doctrine of *creatio ex nihilo* for God's relationship to time. The Fourth Lateran Council (1215) codified the Christian doctrine of creation by declaring God to be "Creator of all things, visible and invisible, . . . who, by His almighty power, from the beginning of time has created both orders in the same way out of nothing." This remarkable statement affirms not only *creatio ex nihilo* in a temporal sense but even a beginning of time itself. What is Nick's view of the matter? Were there events prior to the moment of creation? If not, did time exist in the absence of any events? Could time have had a beginning? If it did, then how should we construe divine eternity and God's relationship to time? I invite Nick to reflect further for us on these questions.

---

[2]See William Lane Craig, *The Only Wise God: The Compatibility of Divine Foreknowledge and Human Freedom* (1987; reprint, Eugene, Ore.: Wipf and Stock, 2000).

RESPONSE TO CRITICS

NICHOLAS WOLTERSTORFF

*R*ather than discussing the responses to my contribution individually, I'll collect from them the points raised and arrange my discussion of them into an orderly sequence.

Hermeneutics

Let me begin with a hermeneutical principle that I proposed of which both Paul and Bill take explicit note, and against which Bill goes on to lodge some criticisms. The principle, quoting from my original paper, is this: "An implication of one's accepting Scripture as canonical is that one will affirm as literally true Scripture's representation of God unless one has good reason not to do so."

Paul correctly observes that, given this principle, "at the heart of the theological differences between the Christian eternalist and temporalist is a different estimate of what constitutes such a good reason not to take some scriptural representations of God literally." He poses a rhetorical question, "How would Nick approach the representation of God as being surprised?" and drops the matter with the comment that "it is easy to see how someone might, by applying Nick's principle, be inclined to be an ontological minimalist in respect of the divine nature."

Why he makes that last comment is not clear to me. I take it that he means by an "ontological minimalist" one who is willing to say very little, if anything, about the divine nature. I don't think accepting my hermeneutical principle produces in one an inclination to be that sort of person; and so of course I don't think it's *easy to see* how it produces that inclination! I myself, for example, accept the hermeneutical principle while at the same time being far from an ontological minimalist concerning the divine nature. I do, admittedly, think that some people claim to know a lot more about God than they, or anybody else, actually know; but I'm far from being an extreme minimalist. And I don't see any inconsistency in myself here.

Bill, as I said, doesn't just take note of my principle but goes after it. He says it's "naive to take Scripture's representation of God as literally true unless one has good reason not to." He takes me to have in mind by "good reason" "some teaching in Scripture to the opposite effect." And then he objects that "this hermeneutic is insensitive to the genre(s) of Scripture. A piece of literature belonging to a genre that is not intended to convey the literal truth about some subject ought not to be taken literally in that respect even if in the piece of literature itself there are no indications of the correct picture."

The criticism is based on a misunderstanding. I don't regard the good reasons in question as confined to reasons to be found in the text itself. Truth is, I don't think that *texts all by themselves* have any fixed sense, and so I don't think that they ever *all by themselves* provide good reason for not taking some sentence in the text literally. More radically: I don't think that they ever all by themselves provide either good or bad reasons for anything at all! (See chapters eight through eleven of my *Divine Discourse* for the argumentation.)[1]

I emphatically agree with Bill that sometimes a reason for not construing some sentence in a text literally is that doing so goes contrary to the intended genre—notice, *intended* genre. I don't think Bill's example of the Aesop fables is a felicitous example of the point, however. Typi-

---

[1]Nicholas Wolterstorff, *Divine Discourse: Philosophical Reflections on the Claim That God Speaks* (Cambridge: Cambridge University Press, 1995).

cally most of the language in an Aesop fable (in distinction from the appended moral) is used literally. What goes to make it a fable is that the illocutionary stance is fictional rather than assertoric. While telling a piece of fiction, one may use all one's words literally.

Let me be more forthcoming than I was in my original article as to why I hold the hermeneutic principle in question. I have two reasons. In the first place, I hold that the fundamental principle with which we all operate in our interpretation of all discourse is that the discourser is to be taken as speaking literally unless we have good reason, in a given case, to think she is not doing so. To speak literally is to say what one's sentence means in the language. Taking the discourser as speaking literally is the ground option; the alternative, that she is not speaking literally, has to bear the burden of proof if it is to be accepted. If she says, "It's late," then I interpret her as speaking literally saying what the sentence means in the language, that it's late—unless I have good reason to think that she was not on this occasion speaking literally. If it were always completely up for grabs as to whether a person was speaking literally, metaphorically, ironically and so forth, I don't see how one's interpretation of one's fellows could ever get off the ground.

My second consideration pertains specifically to scriptural interpretation. In a well-known passage in *De Doctrina Christiana,* Augustine remarked that "we must show the way to find out whether a phrase is literal or figurative. And the way is certainly as follows: Whatever there is in the word of God that cannot, when taken literally, be referred either to purity of life or soundness of doctrine, you may set down as figurative. Purity of life has reference to the love of God and one's neighbor; soundness of doctrine to the knowledge of God and one's neighbor" (111.10.14).

It seems to me that Augustine is clearly taking the literal interpretation to be what I called, above, "the ground option," and saying that when it comes to interpreting what Scripture says about God, we are to interpret the words literally unless doing so cannot "be referred either to purity of life or soundness of doctrine." If the literal interpretation conflicts with "purity of life or soundness of doctrine," then that's a good reason for not interpreting literally.

In offering my hermeneutical principle concerning biblical interpretation I did not say what sorts of reasons I regard as good reasons for not construing some biblical representation (or description) of God literally. That's because I don't have, and don't want, any a priori typology. I'm open to considering on its merits each reason offered—though it is my view that Augustine's two principles, if not exhaustive, are at least fundamental.

It's my impression that Bill does not disagree with my hermeneutical principle, thus explained. Whether he accepts it I don't know; but he doesn't seem to be explicitly disagreeing. Should he be inclined not to accept it, here's the question I would put to him: If we don't take Scripture as speaking literally about God unless we have good reason in a given case to conclude otherwise—whatever be that good reason—how then do we go about interpreting? To me it appears that it is this principle that prevents everything from being up for grabs in interpretation, a consequence of which would be that Scripture loses all authoritative function. Bill speaks of the "didactic portions of Scripture." If we don't accept some such principle as the one I have proposed, then why not interpret the didactic parts as figurative—or ironic, or whatever? Some people do!

Rather than explicitly disagreeing with my principle, I think, Bill is actually offering a very general reason for not interpreting anything in the biblical *narratives* about God both literally and assertorically. His eye is on the narratives. He says that "there is just no reason to invest such portrayals with metaphysical significance. These stories describe God from our perspective, as he is related to us." I take the import of the remark that the stories describe God only from our perspective, only as he is related to us, to be that they don't tell us what God is like as such but only how God is related to us. That leaves open the possibility that they speak literally of this relationship. But it appears to me that Bill thinks they don't even do this. They tell us how God is related to us in exclusively figurative language. My guess is that, for example, Bill thinks it's not literally true that God gets angry with us—though the biblical narratives certainly represent God as related to us that way.

In short, rather than explicitly disagreeing with my general principle, what Bill does is follow the very pattern of thought that my principle recommends: he offers what he regards as a good reason for departing totally from the literal in our interpretation of the biblical narratives about God. The issue between us is thus whether the reason he offers is in fact a good one. I judge that it is not. The reason, so far as I can see, is that "it is hard to exaggerate how thoroughly anthropomorphic [these narratives are] in their portrayal of God." But that's not a *reason* for adopting a radically nonliteral interpretation of the narratives; it's just a *declaration* that that's what we should do. These narratives are indeed highly anthropomorphic. But their being *highly* anthropomorphic is not a reason for concluding that *everything* in them is *purely* anthropomorphic. In particular, it's not a reason for treating as purely anthropomorphic their presentation of God as having a history of action, knowledge and response.

Time, Tense and Space

I'm sure there's nothing I can say in short compass—nor in long—that will bring Paul around to the tensed view of time! Nonetheless, I want to say a few things about his response on these matters to my argument, in my original paper, that (in his words) "tensed facts are ineliminable" and to my argument that space offers no counterpart to such facts.

Concerning the first point, he says that if "I know everything that there is to know concerning the sequence of temporal events; then I'll know that (say) a certain temporal event is now." His argument for this claim is couched in the form of an example: one of the temporal facts that he'll know, if he knows everything there is to know concerning the sequence of temporal events, is that he's aware on November 24 that the date is November 24; and knowing that, he says, is sufficient for him to know that November 24 is now. (I assume that Paul was writing these words on November 24, 1999!)

It seems clear to me that this is mistaken. In Paul's example there are two items of knowledge, one embedded within the other: his knowing on November 24 that the date is November 24, and his knowing that he knows this. Let's consider both items. Start with the embedding case of knowing—his knowing that on November 24 he knows that the date is November 24. I fail to see how knowing this is sufficient for him to know that November 24 is *now*. For on the supposition that he (always) knows everything there is to know about the temporal sequence of events, he also knows now that he knows on November 24 that the date is then November 24. But now is not November 24, 1999; it's June 29, 2000.

So take the other case of knowing, the embedded case: his knowing on November 24 that the date is November 24. Was that knowledge sufficient for his then knowing that November 24 is now? Well, yes. Or more precisely: it's not *sufficient* for his knowing it; it *just is* his knowing it. For what did he know when he knew that the date is November 24? He knew that the date is *presently* November 24. But the fact then looks for all the world like an objective tensed fact. What he knew was not the tenseless fact that it is or it was or it will be November 24, 1999; neither was it the tenseless fact that it is or was or will be the case that his believing that it is November 24 occurs simultaneously with its being November 24. He knew, to say it again, that *it is presently* November 24, 1999.

Consider also Paul's response to my example about the one o'clock news. He says, "How do I know when to turn on the radio for the one o'clock news? When I know on November 24 that it's one o'clock on November 24." Yes indeed. And when does he know on November 24 that it is one o'clock on November 24? When and only when it *is* one o'clock on that day—that is to say, when and only when it is *presently* one o'clock. And that, once again, looks for all the world like an objective tensed fact. If all he knew was the tenseless fact that it is or was or will be one o'clock on November 24, 1999, then he doesn't know when to turn on the radio for the one o'clock news. (Incidentally, Paul says that the rule for using *now* is that one uses it to refer to times "temporally present" to one's utterance; but he can't mean that, since on his view there is no objective phenomenon of *the present*.)

Second, a few remarks on Paul's response to my claim that, on account of there being objective tensed facts, temporal indexicals function in a fundamentally different way from spatial indexicals. I argued, in Paul's words, that in order "for God to know that the kettle is boiling here there's nothing more that God has to know than to know where I am" in space. Paul agrees but claims that "the temporal situation is parallel." "All that God needs to know in order to know that the kettle is boiling now is that the kettle is boiling on some date and for him to know that that date is now for me." The crucial question, of course, is what it is for God to know "that that date is now for me." Paul's answer is that "God knows it's now for me because he knows (for instance) that that time is the time immediately after the last of those times that it is logically possible for me to have memories of." But again, that can't be right. If it ever happens that the kettle boils simultaneously with Paul's having memories, then there will be a time such that both the kettle boils at that time and it's the time immediately after those times that it is logically possible for Paul to have memories of. Surveying the temporal spread, God will discern a lot of times like that. But if that's all God knows about the matter, God doesn't know which if any of those times is *now*. I continue to believe that there is a fundamental dissimilarity between time and space.

God and Time

Having a history. Enough of this! Let's move on to God and time. Alan doesn't much like the criterion I propose for saying that something is "in" time: that it has a history. He says that "a much more precise definition of *timeless* was once given by Nelson Pike: something is timeless if it is not located at any time and has no extension in time." Naturally I don't much like having it said of my definition that somebody else "gave a much more precise definition"; who would like that said of some definition he had crafted!

As a matter of fact I worked with that alternative definition which Alan describes as a "much more precise definition" in my essay of twenty-five years ago, "God Everlasting." And in a footnote to my present essay I considered the option of working with the first of Alan's two clauses. I said this: "One might hold that something is (or was or will be) in time if it's ever true to say of it that it now exists."

The reason I did not work with that definition is not that I thought it appropriate on this occasion to be a bit more sloppy! I don't think that precision—or as I would prefer to put it, *correctness*—is what is here at stake. It's not that there is some clear concept of timelessness that we all have in mind and concerning which the philosopher's formulations can be right or wrong, precise or imprecise. The philosopher has to craft a definition of *timelessness;* and his crafting of a definition has to be done in the light of his purposes. What I said on the matter, in my footnote, was that "the central reason that the tradition offered for holding that God is timeless . . . was that God must be understood as changeless." Now one has a history only if one changes in some way or other; hence it is that I used having a history as my criterion for being in time. It's entirely compatible with God's being immutable, and having no history, that God exists *now*. Numbers are like that. Defining atemporality in terms of lack of location is useless in getting at the issues that have vexed the theologians of the tradition.

God's response. In my essay I argued that, on the eternalist position, "none of God's actions is a response to what we human beings do; indeed, not only is none of God's *actions* a response to what we do, but nothing at all in God's life is a response to what occurs among God's creatures." In response, Paul concedes that "there is a kind of responsiveness that requires tensed knowledge," but he goes on to argue that the eternalist can nonetheless hold that God does genuinely respond to what human beings do. Again, I'm not convinced.

Here's Paul's case: "Timelessly knowing that Hezekiah will plead at t_1 for a longer life, God timelessly determines his response at t_2 to that plea." But on the view of the eternalist there is no such thing as God's action at t_1, God's action at t_2 and so forth. All there is is God's timeless determination to bring it about that one event occurs at t_1, another at t_2 and so forth. God can timelessly determine to bring it about that Hezekiah's continued life will ensue upon Hezekiah's plea. But Hezekiah's continued life is not an action on God's part; though brought about by God, it is itself not a divine action. God brings it about that the event of Israel's traversing the Red Sea occurs after the event of Moses' hearing a voice in the burning bush occurs; but God doesn't perform the action of leading Israel through the Red Sea after performing the action of speaking to Moses in the burning bush. Always the eternalist analyzes the events of history into two parts: the events proper, which have dates and stand in temporal relations to each other, and God's bringing about of those events, which happens timelessly.

It's for that reason that there's nothing that constitutes genuine response on God's part. If I respond to what someone does, then I do something later than, and on account of, another person's having done something. But on the eternalist view God doesn't perform the action of granting Hezekiah continued life in response to, and subsequent upon, Hezekiah's performing the action of pleading with God; rather, God eternally brings it about that the event of Hezekiah's continued life ensues upon the event of Hezekiah's pleading. Such divine responsiveness as there is on the eternalist view is located entirely in God's planning of all that happens, and in God's implementation of the plan by eternally bringing about our actual temporal order (that is, eternally bringing about the B-series); no divine responsiveness is to be located in the actual fabric of history.

Perhaps Bill Craig is correct in his suggestion that Aquinas was tacitly holding a tenseless view of time in developing these thoughts. I don't myself find that "a careful reading" of the passage I quoted leads quite as ineluctably to this conclusion as Bill thinks it does. Nonetheless, it's a suggestion definitely worth considering; I'm inclined to think that it's the only way to make sense of Aquinas's line of thought, that God timelessly determines the occurrence of events at different times.

The incarnation. I remarked that the eternalist strategy for avoiding saying that God does things in history—the strategy of distinguishing the events of history from God's bringing about of those events—runs afoul of the incarnation. Here we can no longer analyze the deeds of Jesus into the historical actions of a human being, on the one hand, and God's eternally bringing about those actions, on the other. Eternalism founders on the orthodox understanding of the incarnation. Paul is the only one of my fellow discussants who takes any note of this argument; I fail to see, though, that even he genuinely *deals* with it.

Is time God's creation? I have saved for last the point on which Alan and Bill both press me hardest: does God create time or is time an inherent feature of God's own life? Each wants me to take his side in their dispute with each other. I made clear in my responses to their initial contributions that on this issue I'm inclined to be an ontological minimalist—to use Paul's phrase—and to plead, "I don't know." But they have prodded me into coming out of my shell just a bit. The disadvantage of doing so now is that they won't have an opportunity to tell me if I have misunderstood them, or to correct me if my criticisms lack cogency. But as I say, they have prodded me!

Let me start with Alan. Alan's view appears to be that there are two times: our time and God's time. I don't understand this. I can understand, in a formal way, what it would be for there to be two times. It would be for there to be two sets of events such that each member within one set bore temporal relations to every member in that set, but no member of one set bore any temporal relation to any member of the other set.

But that's not how Alan is thinking. His thought, rather, is this: "We can and should distinguish between time as a pure duration, which can flow without any changes taking place in the world, and time understood as the measure of change. Aristotle, for example, defined time as 'the numbering of change according to before and after.' This is the time of ordinary life, the time of clocks and calendars, the time we know through physical science. Let us call the first kind of time 'pure duration' and the second kind 'measured time.'" Alan's claim, then, is that God's time is the time of pure duration whereas our time is the time of measured change. The latter sort of time is created by God, whereas the former is an intrinsic feature of God's own life.

As I say, there's much about this that I don't understand. I too am of the view that there can be time in the absence of cyclic processes that enable us to measure time; but I completely fail to understand why the absence or presence of cyclic processes making possible the measurement of time determines two different kinds of time, the time of pure duration and the time of measured change. Why would the absence or presence of such processes make for two different kinds of time? Why doesn't the absence or presence simply make for the impossibility and possibility of measuring time—with time being what it is either way? Alan gives no argument on the matter; for the life of me, I can't think of any.[2]

Furthermore, if there were these two times we would want to know how they are related; but on this topic, too, Alan says nothing to help us think about the matter. What he says is that "our time, created time, exists within the pure duration of God's time which is relatively timeless." I don't know what that means—that is, I don't know what it means to say that one time, our measured time, exists within another time, pure duration, while yet, presumably, remaining distinct.

Alan apparently holds that God's time remains pure duration; and that too I don't understand. Alan appears to me to hold that God acts

---

[2]There's a hint in what he says that Alan regards relativity theory as forcing on us the conclusion that our time is genuinely distinct from God's time. I am myself skeptical, however, that relativity theory as such has the ontological implications that are often assigned to it; but this is a matter that I have neither the time to investigate here nor the competence to investigate anywhere. In any case, it remains only a hint in Alan's paper, not an argument.

within our time—not acts in the attenuated way in which the eternalist thinks God acts, by eternally bringing about temporal events, but in the full-blooded way of performing actions at specific times. He says that "God really does change in order to sustain a dynamic, changing world." But if so, then we can measure the time between two divine actions; and that would seem to imply that God's time has been altered into our measured time. Alan said at the beginning that what makes our time distinct is that it can be measured. Well then, given that God's actions in history are also subject to measurement, God no longer has the time of pure duration but only measured time.

Not being able to make out this notion of two different sorts of time, I conclude that if time is an intrinsic feature of God's own life, then the thing to say is not that God created time but that God created the cyclic processes that enable us to measure time—along, indeed, with everything else that is a creature of God.

The reason Alan backs away from saying this is that he thinks it compromises the Christian confession that God transcends and is Lord of all. He broadly hints—indeed, *asserts*—that what he dislikes about my view, as he understands it, is that I compromise this confession. In his response to my original contribution he says that "Nick is quite happy with a God who is fully temporal, who in no sense is 'outside' of time." He adds that "Nick is wrong to suggest that theologians are interested in a timeless God simply because they believe God cannot change in any way. Just as important, I believe, is the idea of *time as a created category of existence.* I am seeking here to honor the intuition, shared by many if not most traditional theologians over the centuries, that God must in some sense transcend time since he created time."

But notice how thin is the way in which, on Alan's view, God transcends time and is the Lord of time (which is perhaps why he is so emphatic on the matter). Temporal duration is a dimension of God's own life; in that absolutely fundamental way God is not "outside" of time. God nonetheless "transcends" time in the sense that God created those cyclic processes that make possible the measurement of time, and in the sense that temporal duration is a dimension of God's life rather than God's life being somehow a dimension of time.

Setting off to the side for a moment the assumption that temporal duration is indeed a dimension of God's own life, I agree with all this.

There's no disagreement whatsoever between Alan and me on these matters. In the sense in which Alan construes the word *transcends,* when he says that God transcends time, I agree that God transcends time *in at least those ways.* Even if temporal duration is a dimension of the divine existence, God nonetheless creates the cyclic processes that make possible the measurement of time, and temporal duration is nonetheless not itself the divine substance but "merely" a dimension of the divine life.

In his original contribution Alan says, with his eye on such as me, that "the main problem with the everlasting model is not logical consistency but theological inadequacy. Given our notion of God as an infinite, personal Creator, we would expect God to transcend time in some way." I agree that God transcends time *in at least the ways* that Alan says God does. Possibly it was a mistake on my part not to have been emphatic on this in the first place. But it never occurred to me to make a point of saying that God created the cyclic processes that we find in our world; I took it for granted. Neither did it occur to me to make a point of saying that if temporal duration is an inherent dimension of the divine life, then it is no more than that: only a *dimension* of what is more basic, namely, the divine life. This too, I took for granted.

I have concentrated on what Alan means by saying that God transcends time and have neglected what he says on the topic of God as Lord of time. On that latter I also agree with him. Here's his full statement:

> The fact that God is the Lord of time I have interpreted to mean that he has a plan or design for history, that nothing takes place outside of the divine will; that he is not limited or changed in any fundamental way by the passage of time, and that God is a metaphysically necessary Being who lives forever and ever. To this I would add the metaphysical properties of relative timelessness. By "relative timelessness" I mean that God is the Creator of our (physical, measured) time; that in contrast to our time, God's eternity is infinite and immeasurable; and finally that God's time is dependent on God's Being, not the other way around.

Intrinsic to God? The question remains: Is time an intrinsic feature of the divine life or is it not? Alan says yes, Bill says no. The reason I've remained an ontological minimalist on the matter is that I have never seen any good reason for preferring one position to the other. I have already said that I discern no reason that Alan offers for his position. What then are Bill's reasons for the view, to quote from the conclusion of his original contribution, "that it is not only coherent but also plausible that God existing changelessly alone without creation is timeless and that he enters time at the moment of creation in virtue of his real relation to the temporal universe"?

I must say, in all candor, that I don't know what his reasons are. Bill gives good arguments for the conclusion, which I also defended, that God is now "in time"; likewise he gives what I judge to be good arguments for the intelligibility of the view that there was a first moment of time, that that first moment and all subsequent moments were brought about by God, but that the existence of time is not a condition of God's existence. But I fail to discern any substantive arguments for the conclusion that time is not an intrinsic feature of the divine life. Perhaps I'm missing something.

Bill rightly observes that the biblical writers sometimes talk as if time had a beginning—though the fact that many of the relevant passages use the language of "before all time," "before the ages" and so forth leads me at least to refrain from drawing decisive ontological lessons from these passages. If God existed *before* time and issued his decrees *before* the ages, then it appears that the writers were thinking of God as temporally preceding this present age, or something like that. But Bill observes that other biblical writers straightforwardly speak of God in language of everlastingness rather than of (timeless) eternity. So I agree with his summary, in his original contribution, that "the evidence is not clear, and we seem forced to conclude with James Barr that 'if such a thing as a Christian doctrine of time has to be developed, the work of discussing it and developing it must belong not to biblical but to philosophical theology.'"

In his response to me Bill cites the declaration of the Fourth Lateran Council, that God is "Creator of all things, visible and invisible, . . . who, by His almighty power, from the beginning of time has created both orders in the same way out of nothing." But it appears to me that Bill is citing this not so much as an infallible declaration as to press me to say what I think about it.

Let me parenthetically raise one question that has often been posed to those who, like Alan, hold that time is an intrinsic feature of the life of God—an objection that Bill discusses in his original contribution. If time is an inherent dimension of the divine life, then why did God decide to create when he did?

I have never been able to see any force in this objection, and nothing Bill says in his discussion helps me. Why *must* there be such a reason? When I reflect on my getting out of bed in the morning, I find that after lying awake for a while I just, at a certain moment, decide to get up. I don't have a reason for deciding to get up precisely when I do; I just do at a certain moment decide to get up. No doubt I do have reasons for getting up; but I don't have reasons, not usually anyway, for getting up precisely when I do. Why does it have to be different for God?

In short, I don't know whether or not temporality is an intrinsic feature of God's life. I see neither any cogent objection to either position nor any cogent reason for either position. That being the case, I can do naught else than say, "I don't know." I would like to know; but as things stand now, I don't. I am incapable of adjudicating the dispute between Alan and Bill.

Select Bibliography

Of the many books and articles our authors have published, only a few of the related ones are cited here. They are listed in chronological order so that the development of each writer's thought may be followed.

William Lane Craig
"God, Time and Eternity." *Religious Studies* 14 (1979): 497-503.
"God and Real Time." *Religious Studies* 26 (1990): 335-47.
"The Special Theory of Relativity." *Faith and Philosophy* 11 (1994): 19-37.
"Timelessness and Creation." *Australasian Journal of Philosophy* 74 (1996): 646-56.
"On the Argument for Divine Timelessness and Necessary Existence." *International Philosophical Quarterly* 37 (1997): 217-24.
"The Tensed vs. Tenseless Theory of Time: A Watershed for the Conception of Divine Eternity." In *Questions of Time and Tense,* edited by Robin Le Poidevin, pp. 221-50. Oxford: Clarendon, 1998.
The Tensed Theory of Time: A Critical Examination. Synthese Library. Dordrecht, Netherlands: Kluwer Academic, 2000.
The Tenseless Theory of Time: A Critical Examination. Synthese Library. Dordrecht, Netherlands: Kluwer Academic, 2000.

Gregory E. Ganssle
"Atemporality and the Mode of Divine Knowledge." *International Journal for the Philosophy of Religion* 34 (1993): 171-80.
"Leftow on Direct Awareness and Atemporality." *Sophia* 34, no. 2 (1995): 30-37.
"Does the B-Theory of Time Entail Fatalism? A Reply to Hasker." *International Philosophical Quarterly.* 35, no. 2 (1995): 217-18.
Edited with David M. Woodruff. *God and Time: Essays on the Divine Nature.* New York: Oxford University Press, 2001.
"Direct Awareness and God's Experience of a Temporal Now." In *God and Time: Essays on the Divine Nature.* New York: Oxford University Press, 2001.

Paul Helm
"Timelessness and Foreknowledge." *Mind* 84 (1975): 516-27.
"Omnipotence and Change." *Philosophy* 51 (1976): 454-61.
"God and Spacelessness." *Philosophy* 55 (1980). Reprinted in *Contemporary Philosophy of Religion,* edited by Steven M. Cahn and David Shatz, pp. 99-110. New York: Oxford University Press, 1982.
"Time and Place for God." *Sophia* 24 (1985): 53-55.
Eternal God: A Study of God Without Time. Oxford: Clarendon, 1988.
"Omniscience and Eternity." *Proceedings of the Aristotelean Society* Supplement 63 (1989): 75-87.

Alan G. Padgett
"God and Time: Toward a New Doctrine of Divine Timeless Eternity." *Religious Studies* 25 (1989): 209-15.

"Can History Measure Eternity? A Reply to William Craig." *Religious Studies* 27 (1991): 333-35.

God, Eternity and the Nature of Time. London: Macmillan, 1992, reprint, Eugene, Ore.: Wipf & Stock, 2000.

"Eternity and the Special Theory of Relativity." *International Philosophical Quarterly* 33, no. 2 (1993): 219-29.

Nicholas Wolterstorff

"God Everlasting." In *God and the Good: Essays in Honor of Henry Stob,* edited by Clifton Orlebeke and Lewis B. Smedes. Grand Rapids, Mich.: Eerdmans, 1975. Reprinted in *Contemporary Philosophy of Religion,* edited by Steven M. Cahn and David Shatz, pp. 77-98. New York: Oxford University Press, 1982.

"Suffering Love." In *Philosophy and the Christian Faith,* edited by Thomas V. Morris, pp. 196-237. Notre Dame, Ind.: University of Notre Dame Press, 1988.

"Divine Simplicity." *Philosophical Perspectives* 5 (special issue *Philosophy of Religion,* edited by James Tomberlin, 1991): 531-52.

Other Important Books and Articles

Alston, William P. *Divine Nature and Human Language: Essays in Philosophical Theology.* Ithaca, N.Y.: Cornell University Press, 1989.

Hasker, William. *God, Time and Knowledge.* Ithaca, N.Y.: Cornell University Press, 1989.

Kretzmann, Norman. "Omniscience and Immutability." *The Journal of Philosophy* 63 (1966): 409-21.

Leftow, Brian. *Time and Eternity.* Ithaca, N.Y.: Cornell University Press, 1991.

Le Poidevin, Robin, and Murray MacBeath, ed. *Philosophy of Time.* Oxford: Oxford University Press, 1993.

Pike, Nelson. *God and Timelessness.* New York: Schocken, 1970.

Pinnock, Clark, Richard Rice, John Sanders, William Hasker and David Basinger. *The Openness of God: A Biblical Challenge to the Traditional Understanding of God.* Downers Grove, Ill.: InterVarsity Press, 1994.

Stump, Eleonore, and Norman Kretzmann. "Eternity." *Journal of Philosophy* 78 (1981): 429-58. Reprinted in *The Concept of God,* edited by Thomas V. Morris, pp. 219-52. New York: Oxford University Press, 1987.

Swinburne, Richard. *The Christian God.* Oxford: Clarendon, 1994.

———. *The Coherence of Theism.* Oxford: Clarendon, 1977.

———. "God and Time." In *Reasoned Faith,* edited by Eleonore Stump, Ithaca, N.Y.: Cornell University Press, 1993, pp. 204-22.

Wierenga, Edward R. *The Nature of God.* Ithaca, N.Y.: Cornell University Press, 1989.

Contributors

William Lane Craig is research professor of philosophy at Talbot School of Theology. Craig has published many articles and books about time and God's relation to time, including *Theism, Atheism and Big Bang Cosmology,* coauthored with Quentin Smith (Oxford University Press, 1993), *The Tensed Theory of Time: A Critical Examination* and *The Tenseless Theory of Time: A Critical Examination* (both Kluwer Academic Publishers, 2000). Other books he has published include *The Cosmological Argument from Plato to Leibniz* (Macmillan, 1980) and *Naturalism: A Critique,* edited with J. P. Moreland (Routledge, 2000).

Greg Ganssle serves with the Rivendell Institute for Christian Thought and Learning, which is a special project of the campus ministry of Campus Crusade for Christ at Yale. He has taught philosophy at Syracuse and has worked as a teaching fellow and part-time lecturer in the philosophy department at Yale University. He has published academic papers on God's relation to time, free will, and St. Augustine. He has coedited an anthology of philosophical essays for Oxford University Press called *God and Time: Essays on the Divine Nature.*

Paul Helm is the J. I. Packer Professor of Theology and Philosophy at Regent College in Vancouver, B. C. Previously he taught as professor of the history and philosophy of religion at King's College, University of London, from 1993 to 2000 and has published numerous books and articles, including *Eternal God: A Study of God Without Time* (Oxford University Press, 1988), *The Providence of God* (InterVarsity Press, 1994), *Belief Policies* (Cambridge University Press, 1994) and *Faith and Understanding* (Eerdmans, 1997).

Alan G. Padgett is professor of systematic theology at Luther Seminary (St. Paul). He has written *God, Eternity and the Nature of Time* (Wipf & Stock, 2000) and has coauthored *Christianity and Western Thought,* vol. 2, *Faith and Reason in the Nineteenth Century* (InterVarsity Press, 2000). Padgett has edited *Reason and the Christian Religion: Essays in Honour of Richard Swinburne* (Oxford University Press, 1994) and has published several papers on God's relation to time as well as in other areas of philosophy and theology.

Nicholas Wolterstorff is Noah Porter Professor of Philosophy at the Yale Divinity School. He has published many books and articles, including *When Justice and Peace Embrace* (Eerdmans, 1983), *Divine Discourse: Philosophical Reflections on the Claim That God Speaks* (Cambridge University Press, 1995) and *Locke and the Ethics of Belief* (Cambridge University Press, 1996) as well as the seminal paper "God Everlasting" (first published in 1975). Professor Wolterstorff's latest book is *Thomas Reid and the Story of Epistemology* (Cambridge University Press, 2001).

Name Index

IVP Academic
Evangelically Rooted. Critically Engaged.